the Kingdom of the Horse

the Kingdom of the Horse

A COMPREHENSIVE GUIDE TO THE HORSE

AND THE MAJOR BREEDS

CAROLINE DAVIS CONSULTING EDITOR

contributors: **CAROLINE DAVIS, CAROLYN HENDERSON,
BETSY SIKORA-SIINO, DYLAN WINTER, PETER UPTON, AND JANE KIDD**

FIREFLY BOOKS

A FIREFLY BOOK

Published in Canada in 1998 by
Firefly Books Ltd.
3680 Victoria Park Avenue
Willowdale, Ontario, Canada
M2H 3K1

Canadian Cataloguing in Publication Data
The kingdom of the horse
Includes index.
ISBN 1-55209-285-2
1. Horses. 2. Horse breeds. I. Davis, Caroline, 1961- .
SF285.K551998   636.1   C98-931152-X

This book was produced by
Quintet Publishing Ltd
The Old Brewery
6 Blundell Street
London N7 9BH

creative director: **RICHARD DEWING**
art director: **SILKE BRAUN**
design: **BALLEY DESIGN ASSOCIATES**
designers: **SIMON BALLEY** *and* **JOANNA HILL**
project editor: **DOREEN PALAMARTSCHUK**
editors: **LINDA HAGER** *and* **MARTIN DIGGLE**
picture research: **VICTORIA HALL**
illustrator: **EUGENE FLEURY**

The publishers acknowledge the financial support of the
Government of Canada through the Book Publishing Industry
Development Program for our publishing activities.

Typeset in Great Britain by Central Southern Typesetters,
Eastbourne
Manufactured in China by Regent Publishing Pte Ltd
Printed in China by Leefung Asco Pte Ltd

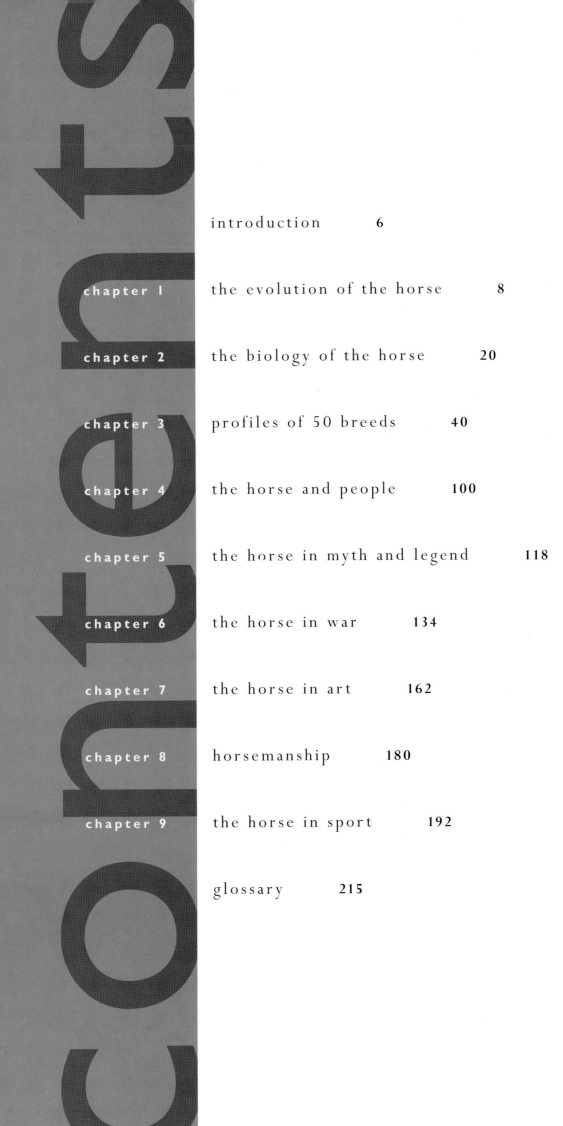

lthough the horse has existed on earth for millions of years, domestication only occured fairly recently, about five thousand years ago, and ever since the horse has been an invaluable servant to mankind. New lands and trading links in early times would probably not have been discovered so quickly, and lacking these material essentials, the human race would not have grown and prospered so rapidly into the most advanced form of animal life that exists today.

Horses provide humans with clothing and food, transport, and entertainment. Not surprisingly, we hold this versatile and invaluable creature in high esteem; immortalizing its character and beauty in art and literature and treasuring it as a companion and friend. In peacetime and war, the horse has played its part in history—magnificently and magnanimously.

From the most humble pony to the most regal Thoroughbred, within each unique equine burns a glow of dignity that can never be extinguished—its free spirit evident under all circumstances. For those that love horses, their companionship is something truly special. This book is dedicated to the horse; an animal without vanity, envy, malice, and greed, and indeed an unsurpassed creature of beauty and grace, with gentle strength, innocence, patience, and kindness.

Invariably one remembers the horse for its feats of glory or bravery, not the rider, as Aldaniti proved in 1981 when it won the world's greatest steeplechase, the Grand National, with its jockey Bob Champion. Many considered both horse and jockey write-offs because of Aldaniti's leg problems, while Bob had barely recovered from the cancer that had almost killed him. Aldaniti made a hero of Bob, and a hero of itself.

National (and twice a runner-up) between 1973 and 1977, was consigned to the sales ring due to ongoing foot problems. Some thought he'd never really be sound enough to make a top-class steeplechaser. Yet the horse's own determination and immense courage, along with devoted care from his trainer, Donald "Ginger" McCain and the healing properties of Southport's sea, saw one of the greatest racehorses of this century go on to create a record that will probably never be beaten. He became a hero and a household name. Red Rum stayed in people's hearts until his death, aged 30 on October 18, 1995. Fittingly, his final resting place abides by the winning post at Aintree, Liverpool's famous racecourse.

Faithful servants, horses endure so much and are endlessly generous in their desire to fulfil their owners needs for work and play. And for those that love and tend their horses carefully, the rewards remain simple but fulfilling—seeing a fit, healthy animal, and, ideally, one that will be a true partner whatever demands are made upon their horse. It would be a hard-hearted person indeed that could not find within himself or herself admiration for such a versatile, selfless animal; and a good rider strives to understand their horse, learn, and work with their equine partner.

Each author contributing to this book is an expert in various aspects of the equestrian world and they all have one thing in common—an unconditional love for all horses. They aspire that you, the reader, will enjoy and learn from *The Kingdom of the Horse*, and find as much pleasure in reading it as the authors had from writing the book.

uction

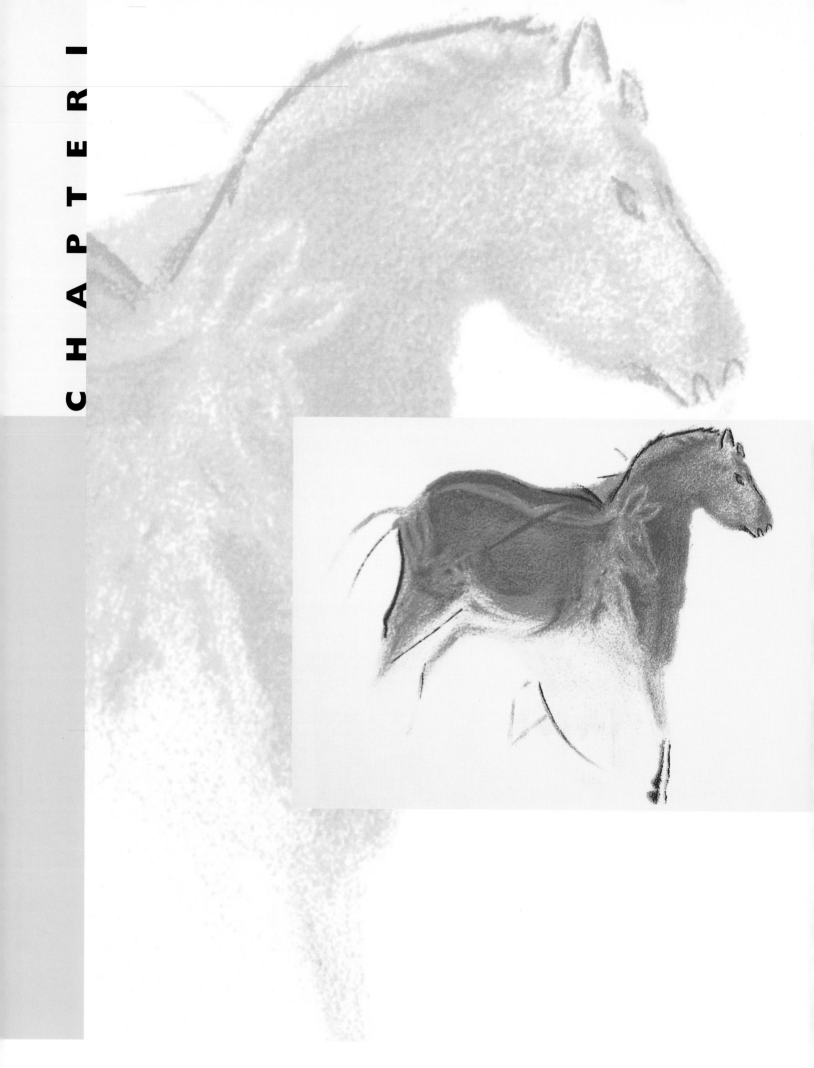

CHAPTER I

above: **Drawing of a Paleolithic cave painting of a horse from the cave roof in Altamira, Spain.**

Taken from Lord Avebury (1913) *Prehistoric Times* **after a drawing by H. Breuil.**

the
evolution
of the
horse

Stand a huge Shire horse, a Thoroughbred racehorse and a diminutive Shetland pony side by side, and it is hard to accept that they have a common ancestry. Yet all modern breeds of horses and ponies trace their ancestry back 55 million years—making humans relative newcomers. Most scholars regard our own earliest direct descendant as Ramapithecus, an advanced primate who lived about 14 million years ago.

Although we can chart the development of horses, they evolved in fits and starts rather than through steady progress; and advances in one part of the world were coupled with retreats in others. Theirs is a story of adaptation, luck, and even drama: at the end of the Ice Age, about 10,000 to 15,000 years ago, they became extinct in North America and were declining rapidly in Europe and Asia.

Trying to define starting points in evolution can seem like peeling an onion; for every layer you remove, there are more underneath. All mammals are descended from reptiles that survived an 85-million-year period of climatic and geological change called the Permo-Triassic Catastrophe, which dates from about 225 million years ago.

To appreciate the process of evolution, you have to think in huge timescales. Geological timescales divide into epochs, and it was in the Eocene epoch, approximately 55 million years ago, that horses as we know them first appeared.

About 70 to 75 million years ago, a group of prehistoric animals called Condylarths were on their way to extinction. These herbivores were the ancestors of all modern hooved animals; each foot had five toes with horny nails. However, the first definitive ancestor of the horse was Hyracotherium, a doglike creature approximately 14 inches tall at the withers, who had four toes on the front feet and three on the hind ones, all of thick horn.

The dawn horse onward

The name Hyracotherium comes from Hyrax, a genus of rabbitlike mammals. In one way the name was a mistake; it was given in 1839 by anatomist Sir Richard Owen to fossils found in clay beds in Kent, England. These were mistaken for those of a hyrax, and it was only in 1932 that they were discovered to have genetic links to a complete horse skeleton found a year earlier in the Big Horn Basin in Wyoming.

American paleontologists reconstructed the skeleton and called their horse Eohippus, which means the dawn horse. Although Hyracotherium is the scientific name, many people frequently use the vernacular American version, which is easier to pronounce and has a more romantic ring! O. C. Marsh, professor of paleontology at Yale University in New Haven, Connecticut, USA, named Eohippus in 1876, a new genus of fossil horse.

There were few similarities between Eohippus, who stood about 14 inches tall, and our modern horse. The eyes were in the middle of the head, like a dog's, rather than at the side, and the teeth were those of a browsing rather than a grazing animal—which is not surprising since there was no grass at this period of time.

Eohippus roamed throughout North America and Europe, feeding on plant shoots that were readily available in what was then a tropical climate. But as the climate cooled, plant growth became limited, and the dawn horse had to change to survive. There was no neat changeover from one member of the horse family to another. Instead, there were families within families,

EPOCH	APPROXIMATE NUMBER OF YEARS BEFORE PRESENT
Recent	10,000
Pleistocene	1.5 million
Pliocene	7 million
Miocene	24 million
Oligocene	38 million
Eocene	55 million
Paleocene	65 million
Cretaceous	135 million
Jurassic	190 million
Triassic	230 million

FAMILY TREE

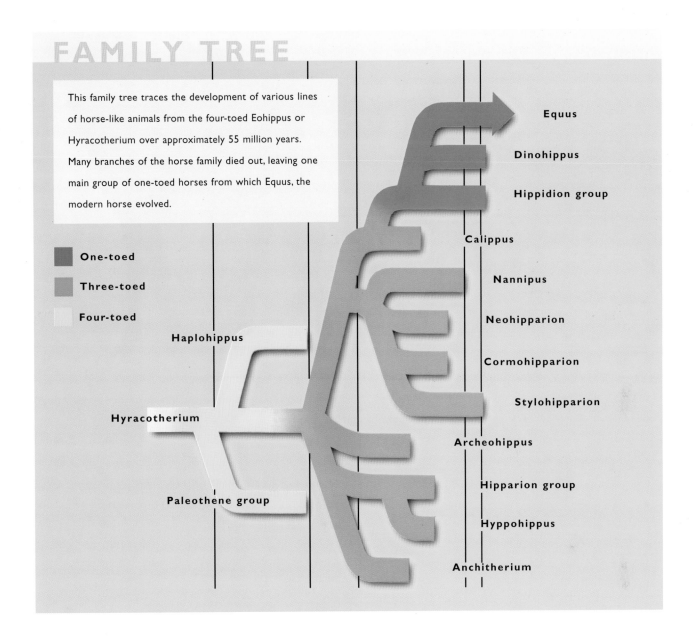

This family tree traces the development of various lines of horse-like animals from the four-toed Eohippus or Hyracotherium over approximately 55 million years. Many branches of the horse family died out, leaving one main group of one-toed horses from which Equus, the modern horse evolved.

One-toed

Three-toed

Four-toed

Equus

Dinohippus

Hippidion group

Calippus

Nannipus

Neohipparion

Cormohipparion

Stylohipparion

Haplohippus

Archeohippus

Hyracotherium

Hipparion group

Hyppohippus

Paleothene group

Anchitherium

and those with the characteristics for survival became dominant while others disappeared. It was a constantly changing process as the earth itself changed in climate and structure.

Mesohippus, a three-toed browser, evolved by the Oligocene epoch, about 35 to 40 million years ago. This animal stood about 18 inches tall and fed on fibrous plants rather than tender shoots. The increased height meant increased body weight and the loss of one toe—Mesohippus had a padded foot, like his predecessor, but most of the weight was supported on the middle toe; this was a more effective weight-bearing mechanism.

The next influential ancestor was Merychippus, from the Miocene epoch, some 20 to 25 million years ago. Merychippus also had three toes but increasingly used only the middle one and had grown

below: **The Condylarths were the ancestors of all hooved animals, they had five toes on each foot with smaller, thick horny nails.**

above: **The development from Eohippus to Equus. The evolution of Eohippus, a three-toed browsing animal to Equus took approximately 55 million years. Merychippus, evolving in the middle and upper Miocene period, was horse-like in appearance and the predecessor to Pliohippus, the subgeneric ancestor to single-hooved animals.**

12

HOOVES

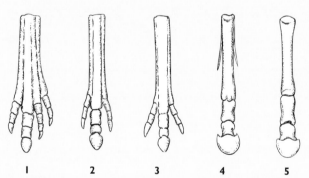

The development of the fore and hind feet, showing how the Equus hoof evolved.

1 Hyracotherium or Eohippus: Weight-bearing pad and three hooved toes.

2 Mesohippus: Weight-bearing central hoof and two hooved toes.

3 Merychippus: Weight-bearing central hooved toe with two reduced side toes.

4 Pliohippus: Weight-bearing central hooved toe. No discernible side toes.

5 Equus caballus: The ancestor of the modern horse. The cannon bone is at its longest and no side-bone is apparent.

to about 30 to 36 inches. Pliohippus, who appeared during the Miocene epoch into the Pliocene, was the first ancestor of the horse to run on one toe. It measured approximately 48 inches, and was also the subgeneric ancestor of zebras and wild asses.

Equus caballus, the first truly recognizable horse, appeared about one and a half million years ago. It was about 48 inches high and its eyes were at the side of its head rather than in the front. This afforded nearly all-round vision and thus offered a better chance of spotting and escaping from the increasing number of carnivores who were also developing.

The horse is a prey animal rather than a hunter, and *Equus* had longer limbs than its ancestors, giving it greater speed; its best defense was to run away. It had recognizable hooves with frogs, triangular indentations that act as shock absorbers. The teeth had also adapted and were now designed to cut and chew grass into small pieces rather than tear off soft leaves. Its neck had also become longer to enable it to graze from the ground.

A changing world

Today's horse is a grazing animal whose diet should be based on forage if it is to stay healthy. But it was a browser of tropical vegetation before it became a grazer and has changed as the earth itself has changed. In 55 million years, it has moved across the globe—a course forced upon it partly by the

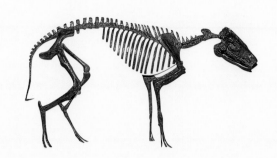

changes in our planet's structure and climate and partly by humans, as they domesticated the horse.

When Eohippus thrived during the Eocene epoch; its habitat was North America and Europe, when most of the northern hemisphere was covered by tropical and semi-tropical forests. From about 65 million years ago until seven million years ago, South America was an island. Veterinary surgeon and naturalist John Clabby, writing in 1976, believed that during this period, animals similar to, but distinct from, Eohippus evolved. In the Pliocene epoch, South America and North America were joined and horse ancestors from both continents merged. By the Pleistocene epoch, believed Brigadier Clabby, "true" horses from the north took over, and those from the south became extinct.

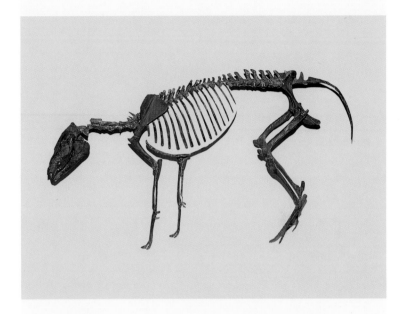

Throughout the Tertiary period—which covers epochs from the Paleocene to the Pliocene epochs—the earth took on a new look. At first there were no sharp temperature differences, and even Alaska had tropical forests. Then temperatures started to drop, new coastlines were exposed, and mountain ranges such as the Himalayas, the Alps, and the Rockies built up on previously flat land.

At this time, North America was the main home of our horse's ancestors. At the end of the Pleistocene epoch, about one and a half million years ago, they had developed into *Equus caballus* and were to be found in North America, South America, Europe, Asia, and Africa.

Cooler weather meant fewer trees and the emergence of grassland. The horse's ancestors of seven million years ago had sweeping plains and prairies to live on and seemed to have the ideal existence.

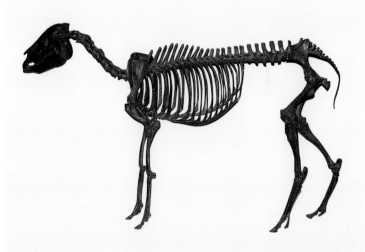

Equus flourished for up to a quarter of a million years, until the Ice Age began. Waves of ice masses from the polar region engulfed the earth, destroying grasslands and breaking down the land masses joining the American continent to Europe and Asia. The horse was forced move to south.

Back from the brink

North America was one of the birthplaces of the horse. It also became its grave from about 10,000 years ago until Spanish conquistadores arrived in the New World in the sixteenth century with a herd of mares and stallions.

top to bottom: **Fossils of Eohippus, Mesohippus, Merychippus, and Pliohippus from the Kentucky Horse Park, USA.**

As science writer Stephen Budiansky puts it, the horse had become a victim of its own success. It had adapted so well to the vast expanses of grassland that it simply could not cope when the climate started to warm up again and forests once more took over the open spaces. In North America, it disappeared altogether for thousands of years.

Most scientists now subscribe to the theory that the horse became extinct in North America simply because there were no resources to support it, and it was unable to revert back to being a browser. Another suggestion is that disease carried by insects may have played a role.

In Europe and Asia, the increase in temperatures had a similar effect. Neanderthal man, who dominated Europe and western Asia between 100,000 and 40,000 years ago, created cave paintings in what is now Lascaux in southern France, showing the wild horses he hunted. Some scientists believe that (until about 10,000 years ago) horses had fled to the only places where they could survive—the open grasslands of central Asia and the Ukraine.

So what saved the Eurasian horse from the fate of its North American relatives? The answer is probably domestication, or, the ability of the horse to exist alongside humans. Climate and conditions led to the development of many types, from heavier horses in lush regions to smaller horses with the speed and agility to travel in dry areas where food supplies were more sparse.

below: **At the Lascaux caves in Southern France, there are drawings of prehistoric horses that appear to resemble both the Asiatic Wild Horse and the Exmoor pony.**

Historians point to three types of horses who are all thought to have contributed to our modern horses and ponies. The Asiatic Wild Horse, *Equus Przewalski*—named after Nikolai Mikhailovitch Przewalski, a Polish-born explorer born on April 12th, 1839, who discovered a wild herd living in Mongolia in 1879—is dun colored, with black legs, mane, and tail. It stands about 13 hands (a hand is four inches) and its mane grows upright rather than falling to the side of the neck as does that of the modern horse. (For more information on "hands" see page 34.)

The Tarpan, *Equus caballus gmelini*, developed in parts of eastern Europe and on the Ukranian steppes and was approximately the same height, but more finely built. Some authorities believe that the pure Tarpan was hunted to extinction. Luigi Gianoli, author of *The Horse and Man* (George Allen and Unwin, 1968) recounts that the last Tarpan mare was tracked down and caught at the end of the nineteenth century, but broke her leg in the struggle and had to be destroyed whilst in captivity.

The term "Tarpan" covers not the biological description of a breed, but the characteristics of wild horses that lived in the region of the Pontic-Caspian Steppes. They could be recognized by their distinctive mouse-dun (grullo) coloring—a kind of slate-gray with black points and a darker or black head. However around 1932, the German zoologist and director of the Berlin Zoo Professor Lutz Heck began to cross Przewalski stallions with mouse-colored Polish Konik mares in the hopes of recreating the Tarpan. He was eventually successful, and some 30 years later the Tarpan was again breeding true to type.

The final member of the trio, the heavy Diluvial horse from northern Europe, is now extinct.

One other puzzle remains: Did a fourth type of wild horse, the Tundra horse exist, and do his ancestors still roam in Siberia? Horse remains were found alongside those of mammoths, in north-east Siberia, and sightings of mystery groups of white horses were recorded in the 1960s.

Przewalski's horse is the last remaining true wild horse and careful breeding programs are being undertaken to eventually return horses to the wild in Mongolia. This horse is the cause of much controversy, because it has 66 chromosomes compared to the 64 of the domestic horse. Scientists are split into two camps: One says that it cannot be an ancestor of today's horse, while the other believes that the domestic horse has "fused chromosomes."

14

The final step

So how did we arrive at the 150-plus recognized breeds of horses and ponies throughout the world? The favorite explanation is that just before the horse was domesticated, there were four types, categorized as Pony Types 1 and 2 and Horse Types 3 and 4.

Pony Type 1 was remarkably similar to the modern Exmoor pony—or perhaps it is more accurate to say that the Exmoor pony has stayed remarkably similar to its ancestor. This pony, who was found in north-west Europe, was about 12 hands high and had an "ice tail" and a "toad eye." These features are both seen in the modern Exmoor and are designed to protect it from severe weather conditions: The eyes are hooded, and the tail has a thick fan of hair at the top.

Pony Type 2 was about two hands bigger, heavily built, and based in northern Europe and Asia. Today's Highland pony is the nearest equivalent.

Horse Type 3, from central Asia, was about 15 hands and much narrower than either of the pony types. His nearest modern equivalent is the Akhal-Teké.

above: **Przewalski's horse is the last truly wild horse.**

Horse Type 4, from western Asia, is thought by many to be the basis for the Arab horse—and the Arab is said to have had more influence than any other breed on modern animals. The Caspian comes closest in appearance.

The Dureivka horses

Scientists now agree on a broad picture of the horse's early development, even if they disagree on the detail. In the early 1990s, American research has prompted a theory that may or may not gain general acceptance.

American science writer Stephen Budiansky believes that the modern horse was saved from extinction by what he calls "a single act of human daring and inspiration in a remote corner of a barely civilized world." That remote corner was the Ukraine, and he suggests that all today's domesticated horses may be descended from horses that were domesticated there by herdsmen 6,000 years ago.

At first, the horse was a source of food. Work by American

16

anthropologist David Anthony suggests that horses were perhaps ridden before they were used to pull carts or chariots —an idea that has always caused controversy amongst historians. They were first of all a source of food; cave paintings from the Neanderthal period suggest that horses were hunted, but not kept in herds for the benefit of humans.

Between 7,100 and 6,600 years ago, says Budianski, the people of the Dereivka region, on the edge of the Black Sea, hunted wild boar, deer, and aurochs. But as the human population increased, the animal population declined, and an alternative source of food had to be found. Cattle were already being raised, but archeological sites from about 6,600 to 6,100 years ago included large numbers of horse bones—and at sites dated at the end of that period, bone numbers show that horses provided nearly half the meat supply.

Dogs were domesticated as early as 12,000 years ago, with cattle, sheep, goats and other farm animals being taken into the system some 3,000 years later. The horse was therefore domesticated relatively late, but this meant that the people

top left: **The Exmoor pony closely represents Pony Type 1.**
top right: **The strong-limbed Highland Pony is a close relative of Pony Type 2.**
above left: **The Akhal-Teké is a descendant of Horse Type 3.**
above right: **The finely-built modern Caspian is a descendant of Horse Type 4.**

who made the first attempts already had some experience in controlling animals.

Budiansky points to archeological evidence that horses were hunted for food in Dereivka, but kept for riding. The most extraordinary finding at the Dereivka site was the skull of a stallion that had been buried with great ritual. With the skull were dog skeletons, clay figures, and—most interesting of all—pieces of antlers with bored holes. These are believed to be the first example of a bit, as they are similar to antlers from later archeological sites that are known to be cheek pieces that would have had a hide mouthpiece.

The teeth in the stallion's skull showed it to be about eight years old. By analyzing wear patterns, David Anthony showed that it had worn a bit for at least 300 hours. As this discovery pre-dated the first known wheel by 500 years, the assumption is that horses were ridden before they were driven.

Legacies of the past

So what does the modern horse owe to its ancestors? The answer is more than most people may think. The way it eats, sleeps, and adapts—or not—to the way we keep it all trace back to the little dawn horse, Eohippus.

Eohippus had jaws and teeth designed for compressing rather than grinding food. As time went by, climates and landscapes changed and as its successors became grazers, its teeth also had to change. They became taller and larger, and the incisors became less curved, giving a better cutting surface. This meant that it could take in more food, which was obviously an advantage. Nutritionist Dr. Derek Cuddeford, from Edinburgh University in Scotland, reports that Exmoor ponies in Britain whose natural habitat is harsh, especially in winter, have a much more rapid biting rate than many other breeds.

To accommodate the greater size and height of its teeth and for more efficient eating, the horse's skull also changed shape: Backward and forward movement of the jaw became limited and instead, the horse developed a side-to-side chewing movement. As the horse developed, its muzzle lengthened, allowing it to eat and watch for predators at the same time. It also developed a more pronounced diastema, a gap between the front incisors and rear premolars, which is lucky for us and perhaps not so lucky for the horse because it provides the perfect space for a bit.

In the wild, horses would travel about 15 miles per day searching for food, most of which would be rough, sparse grazing. They would also take in amounts of sand and dirt, which would wear down their teeth naturally. Today, we keep them in small paddocks and give them extra food, so they do not have to work for it. The result is that the domesticated horse has to have its teeth rasped to keep them in good food-processing condition.

Dr. Cuddeford says that teeth from fossil remains show that ancestors of today's horse deliberately ate plant stems and leaves rather than berries or fruits. This high-fiber diet meant that its digestive system also had to adapt—the caecum, which is part of the digestive tract, and colon became bigger so that fiber could be broken down and fermented.

A frightened horse reacts by running; as the horse developed into a single-toed animal, it was able to run faster. The vestiges of extra toes can still be seen on the modern horse in .the shape of the splint bones in the legs and the ergots, the horny growths at the back of the fetlocks.

The "stay mechanism," which allows the horse to rest without putting strain on its limbs, is another legacy of the times when it had to be ready to run for its life at a moment's notice. A horse who lies down is a vulnerable horse; the herd instinct that makes at least one horse remain on duty as

LOCKING JOINTS

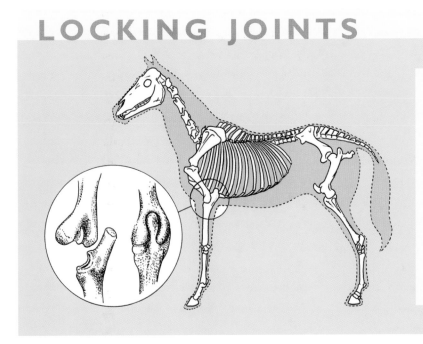

Horses have a special arrangement of "locking" joints and ligaments in their elbows and stifles. When the horse sleeps standing up, these joints lock, propping up the horse on its forehand. It can even relax one hind leg and still not fall over. To be able to sleep standing up was a great advantage to the horse in the wild because it could be off at a gallop within seconds.

above: **Large Connemaras are popular, but many breeders are anxious that traditional characteristics as shown by these ponies should still be preserved.**

"sentry" while others in its band lie down remains even today. Watch a group of horses in a field, and you will rarely see all of them lying down at the same time—one of them stays on watch for potential predators.

The stay mechanism is located in the patella; instead of sliding into a groove in the femur, as normally happens, it can be pushed over a bump in the groove, which locks the stifle joint open. The horse's weight can thus be supported without effort; since a 16.2-hands-high heavyweight can weigh more than 1,400 pounds, the advantage is obvious.

Where do we go from here?

As soon as humans started using the horse for working the land, as a means of transport, and in war, they started breeding selectively for qualities that were most useful to them. This was inevitable but has brought about changes in breed characteristics—some more dangerous than others.

Dr. Matthew Binns, an expert in genetics from the Animal Health Trust in England, says that inherited diseases are less common in horses than in dogs, because dogs have been bred for show, and horses are fortunately still selected primarily as athletes. But that has not prevented conditions such as Hyperkalemic Periodic Paralysis (HPP), which involves sporadic episodes of muscle tremors and paralysis.

Five years ago, HPP was becoming increasingly prevalent in Quarter Horses and breeds to which the Quarter Horse has made a genetic contribution. Dr. Binns says that there is evidence that the genetic defect may have been positively selected for, because affected animals are often heavily muscled—something regarded as a plus point in this breed. The good news is that genetic screening tests can now detect which horses have the defect, and they can be removed from the breeding program.

In a far less harmful way, but still with an echo of a brave new world, advances in genetics mean that in the next five years, breeders will be able to predict and therefore select coat colors resulting from particular matings.

Breed societies tread a narrow path between retaining traditional characteristics and satisfying the demands of today's buyers. This is particularly seen in Britain's native pony breeds, which are exported and bred all over the world, especially Europe and the United States.

The modern demand for a comfortable, athletic riding animal means that breeders naturally select for qualities such as a sloping shoulder and good length of rein. The Exmoor Pony Society has guarded traditional characteristics such as hardiness with the result that the Exmoor has lost popularity as a riding pony and is now officially a rare breed.

The Connemara pony is probably the most popular of all the large native breeds and is traditionally a deep-bodied animal with short legs. Demand for a taller animal has seen a rise in the number of ponies over 14.2hh (hands high)—who are therefore now horses—and in America, some breeders are deliberately aiming to produce Connemaras up to 16hh, moving farther and farther away from their native roots.

The opposite side of the coin can be seen with "toy" breeds. The Falabella, a miniature horse who can stand no more than 29.6 inches (76cms) at the wither, was developed by the Falabella family in Buenos Aires, but is based on the Shetland pony. Inbreeding has resulted in weaknesses such as poor limbs and feet and, of course, the Falabella is too small to be anything but a pet.

The last new breed was the Pony of the Americas. The first was born in 1954 and was a cross between a Shetland and an Appaloosa, now there are breed standards and a stud book.

There are still breeds that are referred to as "wild horses,"

top: **The Falabella, bred selectively for small size, is too tiny to be anything but a pet.**

below: **A group of Mustangs running free in Nevada.**

but apart from Przewalski's horse, the term is used in a romantic rather than scientifically accurate sense. The Mustangs of the American West, Australian Brumbies, and the horses of Canada's Sable Island are feral animals whose ancestors were once domesticated, but later escaped into the wild.

Horses first arrived in Australia on trading ships in the late 1700s. One story says that Brumbies owe their name to horse breeder James Brumby, who in 1804 left Sydney and at the same time left all his horses to fend for themselves. Others followed suit, and in the gold rush of the mid-1850s many horses were set loose.

They have been culled ever since, but there are still about 160,000 roaming free in the central areas, particularly the Snowy Mountains in New South Wales.

Sable Island, about 150 miles east of Nova Scotia, Canada, is only about 20 miles wide by 1½ miles long. It is the home of a herd of about 250 wild horses who have been there for between 250 and 400 years, depending on which of two theories you favor. One suggests that their ancestors swam ashore from a French ship wrecked in the 1600s, while another says that Thomas Hancock, a Boston merchant, imported a herd in the 1750s to provide food for the human survivors of shipwrecks!

above: **Diablo, a modern Friesian horse—part of an equestrian entertainment troupe.**

the
biology
of the
horse

the
biology
the of the
biology horse
of the
horse

The horse, *Equus caballus*, did not evolve to carry humans or jump obstacles, but it does an excellent job of just that. By the same token, its natural state is roaming freely in its country of origin, grazing herbage of its choosing as and when available, breeding by natural selection in which only the fittest and strongest survive, and living sociably in herds both for company and protection.

To a certain extent some feral equines are able to live like this: Britain's native mountain and moorland ponies such as Shetland, Welsh, New Forest, Dartmoor and Exmoor, Australian Brumbies, American Mustangs, French Camargue ponies, "Island" horses such as Chincoteague ponies (found off the coast of Maryland), Nova Scotia's Sable Island horses and, the only truly wild horse left in the world, Asia's Przewalski's horse. However, the majority of all earth's equine breeds today are domesticated and live as humans' dictate and desire.

below: **Free-roaming wild ponies are able to keep themselves fit and healthy in the main, unlike their domesticated counterparts.**

To live in captivity and perform as we would wish, the modern horse has to be fed a suitable diet to supplement what grazing it has access to, be housed in large airy stables, be groomed daily, have adequate exercise to keep it fit, strong, and supple enough for its work, and be shod so its feet can withstand the rigors of traveling paved roads.

Ideal conformation

A horse of good conformation—as near perfect structure as possible for each particular breed—is better placed than a counterpart of poor conformation to carry out the work expected of it. Those with the ideal physique are usually stronger, often faster, and less prone to illness. For example

THE POINTS OF THE HORSE

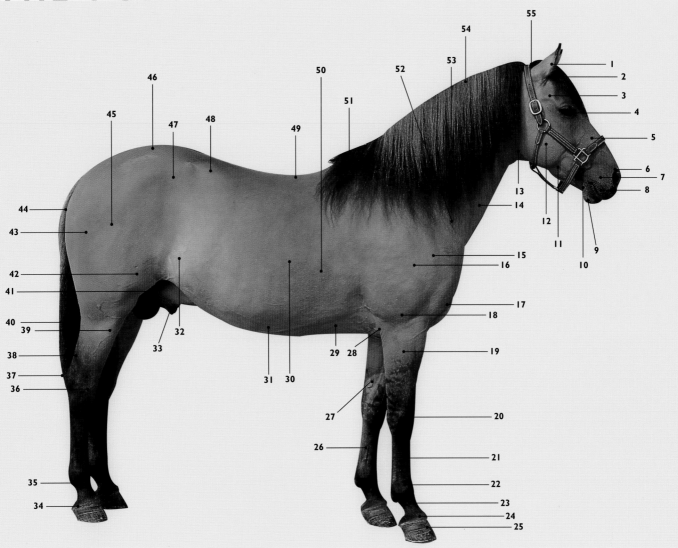

1. Ear	**14.** Jugular groove	**28.** Elbow	**42.** Thigh
2. Forelock	**15.** Point of shoulder	**29.** Brisket	**43.** Buttock
3. Temple	**16.** Shoulder	**30.** Ribs	**44.** Point of buttock
4. Eye	**17.** Breast	**31.** Belly	**45.** Hip joint
5. Nose	**18.** Upper arm	**32.** Flanks	**46.** Croup
6. Nostril	**19.** Forearm	**33.** Sheath	**47.** Point of hip
7. Muzzle	**20.** Knee	**34.** Heel	**48.** Loins
8. Lips	**21.** Cannon or shin	**35.** Ergot	**49.** Back
9. Chin	**22.** Fetlock joint	**36.** Hock	**50.** Chest
10. Chin groove	**23.** Pastern	**37.** Point of hock	**51.** Withers
11. Branches of jaw/ cheek bone	**24.** Coronet	**38.** Achilles tendon	**52.** Neck
12. Cheek	**25.** Hoof	**39.** Gaskin or second thigh	**53.** Mane
13. Throat	**26.** Splint bone	**40.** Tail	**54.** Crest
	27. Chestnut	**41.** Stifle	**55.** Poll

(and this is a bone of much contention for breed enthusiasts), many British native ponies stud-bred for showing—where good looks seem to overshadow practicality—would be unlikely to be able to stand up to the rigors of actually living in their natural habitat. Stud-bred New Forest and Welsh ponies tend to be bigger than their naturally bred counterparts. However, it is unlikely they would survive in the forest or on Welsh mountain terrain when food is at a premium, having larger frames to nourish.

Likewise the Arabian horse bred for showing in recent years, mainly due to American influence, is deplored by many breed purists in comparison to the true Arabian horse bred by lovers of this ancient and royal breed. Examples in the international showring display exaggerated dished heads, practically banana-shaped, with "bug-eyes," along with an artificially elongated stance that requires the hindquarters and legs to be thrust out behind—leading in turn to a dipped back. Breeding for ultra-elegance has led, in cases, to the "tough ballerina" of the horse world becoming a showpiece freak unable to perform the work for which it was bred.

And then there's the American Quarter horse—initially bred to be a compact work horse for cattle cutting and herding—willing, easy to train, muscular, tough, and able to survive on minimal rations, and fast over short distances. It is considered by many that these attributes are being diluted with Thoroughbred blood in favor of more elegant animals for the show ring. This leads to reduced hardiness, sensibility, and stamina for the job they were initially bred and designed to do.

Living in the wild, only the fittest horses and ponies survive—nature weeds out the weaklings and those that do not conform to what the climate and conditions dictate.

It is quite sad to see, in some cases, certain breeds being shaped by breeders to conform to what they call progressive ideals, or to fit in with fashion trends. Depending on the breed of equine and where its natural habitat is, conformation differs, with each breed having its own ideal shape. Arabians have 19 ribs as opposed to the usual 18, five lumbar bones instead of six, and have a straight croup giving them their characteristic high tail position. Draft horses are of a stocky, muscular build to cope with pulling heavy loads, generally with large plate-like feet to provide greater stability and ease in working on agricultural land. Racehorses are finely built with a slender, yet strong, bone structure designed for speed.

A question of balance

If you study equine physique, you will see that the very shape of the animal, even with perfect conformation, is simply not built to carry loads. Horses today have to learn to cope with and balance their rider's weight in addition to carrying themselves. The majority of a horse's weight is on its forehand—its head alone (based on an average Thoroughbred racehorse) weighs around 40 pounds. The spine's length itself

HORSE CONFORMATION

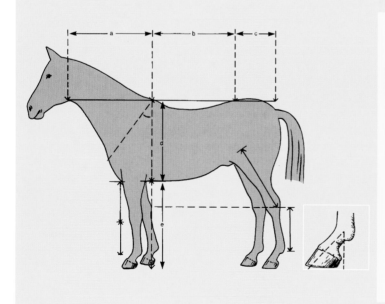

One system to gauge the horse's conformation is to look at the relative lengths of sections of the body: a=b=d=e   c=½ a
The distance should be more than from knee to ground. The distance from hock to stifle is more than from hock to ground. The hocks should be on a level with the front chestnuts. The angle of the shoulder should be 45 degrees to the upright. The pastern/fetlock angle should be 45 degrees. A good way to develop an image of a well-conformed horse is to visit top level shows and study the best horses in each class, looking carefully at the general proportions and points of the horses.

left: **The ability of a horse to perform well at a particular job depends upon its conformation.**

reduced. As well as strength in the back, the type of horse determines what amount of weight it can comfortably carry—assuming that the animal is fit and healthy. Allowances must be made for older and younger animals.

An animal's weight-carrying capacity is substantially determined by the amount of bone it has. The term "bone" describes the circumference of the fore cannon bone taken just under the knee. As an approximate guide, a horse having eight inches should, in theory, be able to carry up to 168 pounds, a horse with nine inches should be able to carry up to 196 pounds, and a horse possessing 10 inches of bone would be a real weight-carrier at up to 210 pounds.

These approximations, however, rest on the animal's bone density and its conformation. If it is, for example, "back at the knee" or "cow-hocked," then its weight-carrying ability will be lessened because of its imperfect conformation. The term "quality counts" definitely has a ring of truth because horses that have predominantly Arabian or Thoroughbred blood have greater bone density and are therefore better able to carry weight. Having said that though, Shetlands are renowned for

cannot support weight from above without considerable discomfort and damage (even the pressure from an ill-fitting rug, let alone an unsuitable saddle, can lead to a sore back); it is the muscles alongside the spine that do all the weight-carrying work. If these muscles lack mass and tone, the weight-carrying capacity of the horse will be substantially

THE FOOT AND HOOF

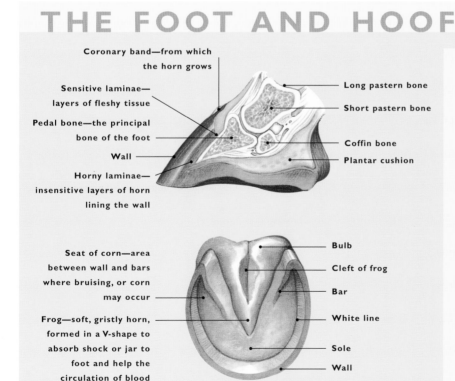

Coronary band—from which the horn grows

Sensitive laminae—layers of fleshy tissue

Pedal bone—the principal bone of the foot

Wall

Horny laminae—insensitive layers of horn lining the wall

Long pastern bone

Short pastern bone

Coffin bone

Plantar cushion

Seat of corn—area between wall and bars where bruising, or corn may occur

Frog—soft, gristly horn, formed in a V-shape to absorb shock or jar to foot and help the circulation of blood

Bulb

Cleft of frog

Bar

White line

Sole

Wall

The foot is the most important part of the horse, and it is vital to keep it well trimmed and regularly shod if the horse is to remain healthy. By getting to know the parts of the foot both on the outside and the underside you should be able to notice any problems should they occur. The outside wall is made of very hard horn and cannot expand should there be any inside inflammation caused by an abscess. The veterinarian will cut a small hole in the sole to release the pressure in some cases.

FORELEG CONFORMATION

The most important points of the horse are its limbs and feet as it depends upon them for survival. Feet and legs should therefore be as correctly conformed as possible, if the horse is to stay healthy and mobile. Correct conformation is an extremely valuable asset.

FRONT VIEWS OF FORELIMBS

Normal	Base-narrow	Base-wide	Base-narrow, toe-out	Base-narrow, toe-in	Base-wide, toe-out	Offset knees

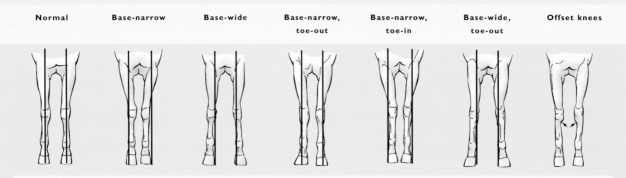

Normal conformation is when the point of the shoulder (middle of the shoulder joint) is in line with the knee and the hoof. Base-narrow conformation causes the lateral (outside) wall of the foot to land first bearing most of the weight and so it wears away faster. The medial (inside) wall should be trimmed to level out the foot. In base-wide conformation more weight falls on the medial side of the foot where it lands first, causing the medial hoof wall to wear faster. The lateral wall should be trimmed to level the foot.

Gaits sometimes caused by abnormal conformations:

• Winging: toe-out conformation often causes the forefoot to break over the medial side of the toe and arch to the inside.

• Paddling: toe-in conformation often results in the forefoot swinging to the outside as it leaves the ground.

• Plaiting, also known as lacing: in base-narrow, toe-out conformation one forefoot travels inward crossing in front of the other foot. Horses that do this are unlikely to be well-balanced and prone to tripping and damaging themselves, as well as having undue strain placed upon their joints.

LATERAL VIEWS OF FORELIMBS

Normal	Back at the knee	Bucked over at the knee	Standing under	Camped in front

• **Normal conformation:** the hoof is centred between the shoulder and elbow points.

• **Back at the knee:** this is indicated by a concave line running from the forearm to the fetlock joint so the leg looks rather banana-shaped. Being back at the knee is a serious conformation fault as excess strain is placed upon the back tendons of the leg.

• **Bucked knee,** also known as over at the knee: where the knee appears to bend forward. Usually seen in older horses due to wear on tendons and them becoming contracted. Although frowned upon in the show ring, being forward at the knee is not likely to affect the horse's way of going or soundness

• **Standing under:** the horse is under itself in front, this makes for less stability.

• **Camped in front:** a conformational fault that causes tendon strain.

HIND LEG CONFORMATION

REAR VIEW OF HIND LIMBS

Normal   Base-narrow behind   Cow-hocked

Normal conformation is when the point of the buttock is in line with the hock and hoof. Base-narrow behind conformation places heavy stress on the structures on the lateral side of the hind limb. Even if the forelimbs are normal, it often has an effect of causing bow-legged conformation that puts strain on hock bones and ligaments. Cow-hocked conformation, when the hind limbs are base-narrow to the hocks and base-wide from the hocks to the feet, is when excessive strain is placed upon the inside of the hock. It can often look more awkward than it is.

LATERAL VIEW OF HIND LIMBS

Normal   Standing under   Camped behind   Sickle hock   Too straight behind

- **Normal conformation:** the hoof is centred between stifle and buttock point.
- **Standing under:** the horse is under itself behind – a fault that can lead to forging.
- **Camped behind:** the leg is too far back and can cause sway-back.
- **Sickle hock:** the foot is aligned well forward of the normal position.
- **Too straight behind:** straight hocks may give speed, but also tends to limit movement.

their strength, and in years gone by were the only form of transport for farmers in the Shetland Isles, while Icelandic and Fell ponies carry large men with ease.

Considering that a horse has to balance both its own and its rider's weight on four relatively small feet, it is remarkable what the horse can achieve. While standing or moving normally, the horse's front legs and feet bear around 60 percent of its total weight. On landing after jumping an obstacle, one forefoot will bear all the horse's weight for a moment. The forelegs and feet are subjected to greater force

of impact as more kinetic energy is produced as the horse travels at faster speeds and when it lands after jumping an obstacle. You may be surprised to learn that a racehorse, traveling at 25 mph exerts a force of some nine tons on each foreleg and foot as it touches the ground. Half a ton of horse traveling at the same speed would exert a force of around 42 tons if it hit an obstacle.

It is important that riders, and those using horses for work, learn equine physiology and what the horse requires in terms of diet, care, and handling in order to get the best out

THE SKELETON

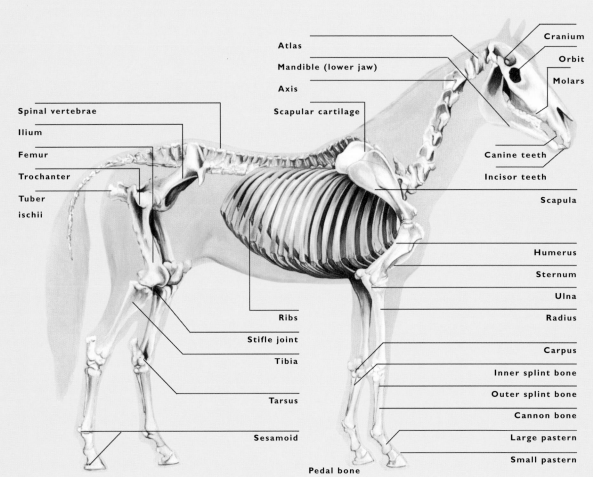

Atlas
Mandible (lower jaw)
Axis
Scapular cartilage
Cranium
Orbit
Molars
Spinal vertebrae
Ilium
Femur
Trochanter
Tuber ischii
Canine teeth
Incisor teeth
Scapula
Humerus
Sternum
Ulna
Radius
Ribs
Stifle joint
Tibia
Carpus
Inner splint bone
Outer splint bone
Cannon bone
Large pastern
Small pastern
Tarsus
Sesamoid
Pedal bone

The skeleton of the horse is a strong frame consisting of 205 bones and small amount of cartilage that support muscle and skin mass. The bones are articulated at the joints, spanned and held together by ligaments. The larger bones form a scaffolding to which the muscles are attached. The skeleton is constructed to protect vital organs, all of which are housed deep within its frame. As well as the supporting framework for the body, the skeletal bones are a storehouse for calcium and phosphorous; deficiencies in these minerals lead to weak bones. Certain bones also produce red and white blood corpuscles in the marrow.

INTERNAL ORGANS OF THE HORSE

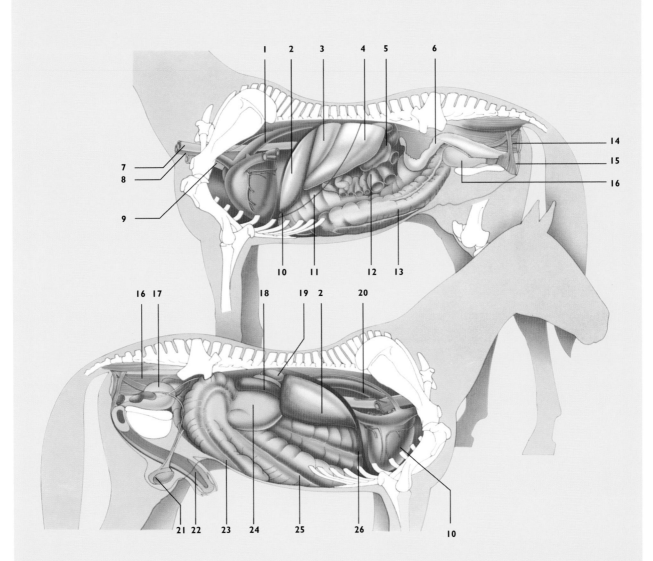

top: **LEFT SIDE OF A MARE:**

1. Aorta	**10.** Left ventricle of heart
2. Left lobe of liver	**11.** Left dorsal colon
3. Stomach	**12.** Small intestine
4. Spleen	**13.** Left ventral colon
5. Left kidney	**14.** External anal
6. Body of uterus	sphincter muscle
7. Oesophagus	**15.** Vulva
8. Trachea	**16.** Urinary bladder
9. Left vagus nerve	

above: **RIGHT SIDE OF A STALLION:**

2. Right lobe of liver	**21.** Right testicle
10. Right ventricle of heart	**22.** Body of penis
16. Rectum	**23.** Lateral caecal band
17. Urinary bladder	**24.** Dorsal sac of caecum
18. Descending duodenum	**25.** Right ventral colon
19. Right kidney	**26.** Caudal vena cava
20. Azygos vein	

above: **A half-ton horse traveling at 25 mph would exert around 42 tons of weight if it hit an obstacle. Racehorses can reach speeds in excess of 40 mph.**

of the animal and to ensure that it remains happy, healthy, and capable of carrying out its duties well and comfortably.

Physiology

In order to perform whatever work is expected of it today, the horse must be fit enough to carry it out comfortably. Just as human athletes need to get their bodies fit for their exertions, so must humans prepare their horses for the expected tasks ahead in order for their animals to remain happy, healthy, and comfortable. A biological system designed for grazing in order to ingest enough nutrients to stay alive and healthy cannot be expected to perform tasks required by humans without a correct feeding, care, and fittening regime.

The circulatory system

The equine circulatory system is powered by the heart. This is a powerful muscular organ in the chest cavity and is basically a four-chamber pump—sending oxygenated blood from the lungs around the body and bringing back de-oxygenated (used) blood to be re-oxygenated (recharged). An average-size horse of 1,100 pounds has a heart weighing around nine pounds. Normal heartbeat (pulse) rate in the horse is 35 to 45 beats per minute depending on size (the smaller the animal, the faster the heart beats).

Oxygenated blood is carried, at high pressure, by arteries, which carry blood away from the heart, while de-oxygenated blood is transported, by low pressure, through veins back to the heart. The exceptions are the pulmonary vein, which carries oxygenated blood from the lungs back to the heart, and the pulmonary artery, which carries de-oxygenated blood from the heart to the lungs.

The four chambers of the heart are the right ventricle, left ventricle, right atrium, and left atrium. Oxygenated blood from the lungs enters the left atrium, then the left ventricle, travels around the body before entering the right atrium, then the right ventricle and back to the lungs for re-oxygenation.

The heart is inexorably connected to the respiratory system; neither could function without the other. Other major organs, such as the brain, liver, and kidneys, and therefore the rest of the body, would fail if either the respiratory or circulatory systems suffered complete failure.

The respiratory system

The equine respiratory system comprises the upper respiratory tract (airways), including the nostrils, nasal cavities, pharynx, larynx, and trachea, and the lower respiratory tract, including the lungs, bronchi, and bronchioles.

Normal respiration in a healthy horse at rest is eight to 16 breaths per minute. The smaller the animal, the quicker it breathes. During strenuous exercise the respiration rate can increase to 120 breaths per minute in order to supply extra oxygen to the body.

The digestive system

Amazingly, the horse's digestive tract, from the stomach to the rectum would measure around 95 feet if unraveled. With all this length of intestine coiled and folded to fit into the horse's abdomen, it is small wonder that digestive upsets such as colic and problems such as a twist in the gut arise.

Food travels from the mouth, where it is chewed into small swallowable pieces, down the oesophagus into the stomach—which holds a low capacity of around two gallons—before passing first into the small, then into the large intestines and finally, once all the nutrients have been extracted from it, out through the rectum. The small intestine comprises the duodenum, jejunum, and ileum, while the large intestine comprises the caecum, large colon, small colon, and rectum.

FEMALE REPRODUCTIVE ORGANS

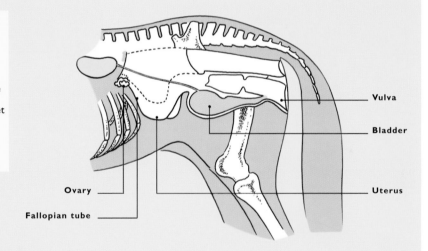

The mare's sexual organs consist of ovaries, Fallopian tubes, uterus, cervix, vagina, and vulva. During the mare's sexual cycle eggs are released from the ovaries into the Fallopian tubes to meet up with the stallion's sperm and allow fertilization to take place.

Vulva
Bladder
Uterus
Ovary
Fallopian tube

MALE REPRODUCTIVE ORGANS

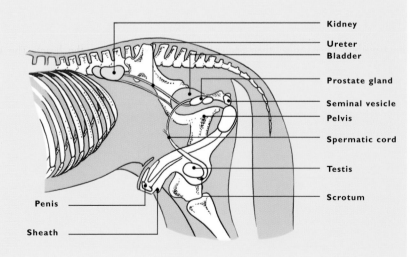

The stallion's sexual organs consist of the penis, two testes in the scrotum which are linked by the spermatic cord to the prostate and bulbourethral glands, and the seminal vesicle. Sperm is produced in the testes and passes down the penis to meet up with the mare's egg. If mating is successful, a sperm will pierce an egg and fertilize it.

Kidney
Ureter
Bladder
Prostate gland
Seminal vesicle
Pelvis
Spermatic cord
Testis
Scrotum
Penis
Sheath

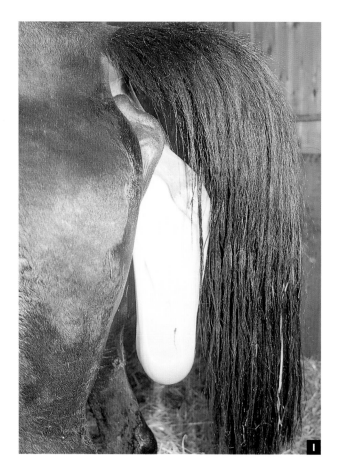

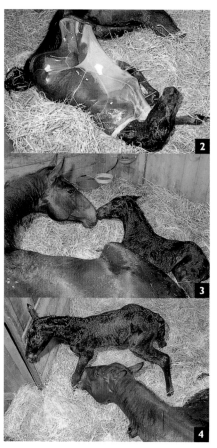

Reproduction

The gestation period for equines is approximately 11 months. Once labor begins, the whole process is over quickly, with the foal being born in 15 to 30 minutes providing all is well. Foals should be on their feet and suckling within an hour. This first feed from the mare is extremely important as the milk is rich in colostrum that contains essential nutrients, natural antibodies, and cholestron (a natural laxative to make the foal's bowels work). In the wild, it is important that the foal is up and moving about quickly so that it can flee from danger with its mother if necessary.

The majority of young horses are generally not ridden and worked fully until they are at least four years old. At this age, they are usually considered strong enough, both mentally and physically, to cope with a rider's demands. Heavy breeds and large horses take a little longer to mature because they have such big frames, even though they appear to be mature and strong to the unknowledgeable.

Today the process of artificial insemination (using frozen semen to impregnate mares) is well advanced, which enables horse owners to have their mares impregnated by stallions many miles away or even in other countries. This helps to

above: **Horses rarely have any difficulty giving birth which often takes place at night and is over very quickly. In most cases the foal is presented and delivered forelegs first, closely followed by the head. The foal pictured here is being born normally within its sac of amniotic fluids (1). These rupture during the final expulsive effort by the mare (2). The foal's first movements after birth are usually to shake and to shiver (3), and a normal foal should be up on its feet between half an hour to two hours (4) and the mare licks her foal clean and dry.**

improve the quality of horses bred economically and may even help to prevent bloodlines and breeds from dying out. Another innovative idea is having fertilized eggs taken from a valuable competition mare, or one that cannot carry foals to full term, and implanted into a surrogate mare.

Gaits

Most equines have four natural gaits—walk, trot, canter, and gallop. Icelandic ponies possess a fifth gait—tolt—that is a fast "running" walk. A tolt is smoother than a trot and is a two-time action—both legs on the same side move together, with all

EQUINE MOVEMENT

WALK – a pace in four-time

TROT – a pace in two-time

CANTER – a pace in three-time

GALLOP – a pace in four-time

WALK: All four feet come into contact with the ground separately. Placed laterally, the sequence, if the horse started to walk leading with the left hind leg, is left hind, left fore, right hind, and right fore.

TROT: In a two-time gait the horse moves diagonal pairs of legs in succession, such as, right fore, left hind, and left fore, and right hind. Trot is the only gait where the horse's head should be steady, if it nods, then the horse is lame.

CANTER: A three-time gait, if the horse was to lead into canter with the right foreleg, the sequence of leg movement would be left hind, right hind and left fore simultaneously, right fore, a moment of suspension (when all four feet are off the ground), and then the left hind, etc, again.

GALLOP: A four-time gait, gallop is a fast canter. The sequence of leg movement with the left fore leading would be right hind, left hind, right fore, left fore, moment of suspension, right hind, and so on.

four feet being off the ground at one point. Horses specially bred and trained for harness racing have a fifth gait too—pacing. This is similar to a tolt, but much faster. Horses are trained to do this by using special leg harnesses.

Height

A horse or pony is traditionally measured in "hands" and inches—each hand being four inches. For example, an animal measuring 58 inches from the ground to its wither would be 14.2 hh (14 hands and two inches high). This measurement derived from olden days when people measured their animals by placing their hands (four inches being the approximate width across a man's knuckles) sideways and going up from the ground to the highest point of the wither.

These days, metric measurements are beginning to replace the traditional hand measuring—for example a pony measuring 13.2 hh (54 inches) is approximately 137 centimeters high. An equine is considered a pony if it measures 14.2 hh and under, whereas a horse measures over 14.2 hh. Some breeds, such as Shetlands and Miniature horses are only measured in inches. A Shetland of 40 inches would be 10 hh. When measuring a horse, it is essential that the animal is stood up square on level ground to ensure its correct height is measured. If it is shod, allow half an inch for shoes. A measuring stick gives the most accurate reading.

In pure breeds one can be fairly certain, to an inch or so, what height a foal is likely to mature to, because they are consistent in height. However with cross-breeds, like the Welsh Cob cross Thoroughbred, it is often difficult to ascertain what height the animal will grow to unless a mating between a particular mare and stallion has been done before, and the resulting offspring's height was recorded at maturity.

There are no definite guidelines on the final height of cross-breeds, however, useful information comes from the growth charts plotted by Russia's Budennyi Stud as well as Sue Featherstone, an English instructor. Measuring an assortment of differently bred foals every two weeks from day one until maturity, the Featherstone charts show a consistently fast growth rate for all animals up to the age of four to six months.

below: **A correctly calibrated measuring stick with a spirit level on the arm gives the most accurate height reading.**

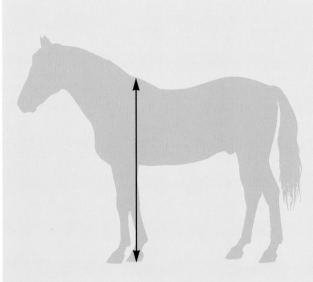

MEASURING

Measuring a horse: One hand is equal to the width of an average hand of four inches (10.2 cm). The horse is measured with a stick from the bottom of the forelegs to the highest point at the withers.

above: **Horses, are herd animals and, in most cases, enjoy each others' company for play, mutual grooming sessions, and protection. As is nature's way, the stronger, fitter horses are top of the group hierarchy with the younger, weaker horses at the bottom. In domesticated groups it is important to segregate the "bullies" from "underlings" to prevent the former attacking the latter.**

After this period, the growth rate began a curve with smaller-breed animals' growth rate slower than their larger-breed counterparts. The chart shows that the earlier the growth rate slows, the greater the chance that the animal will be small in height. Using her chart Featherstone has so far been accurate when predicting a foal's height at maturity.

The senses

The nervous and sensory systems of the horse are essential to its health and well-being. Perceptions and reactions to its environment are dependent on its senses, while its movement is controlled by the central nervous system (brain and spinal cord). The endocrine system (hormone-producing glands) control the horse's behavior patterns.

Sight Because of the position of the eyes—high up on the head and set to the side—horses have excellent all-round vision, which is essential for seeing potential danger creeping up on them. Their only blind spots are directly in front and directly behind them. They can see very well in dim light and, although they cannot distinguish colors, they see shades of light and dark gray.

Hearing Possessing a highly developed sense of hearing, horses can detect a wide range of sounds from very low to extremely high-pitched—well beyond human detection. Horses can rotate their ears independently through 360 degrees to hone in on specific sounds—a useful radar system for detecting danger.

Smell Smell is an essential sense for detecting suitable food and water, enemies, friends, and their offspring. Stallions can smell a receptive in-season mare up to half a mile away. Horses can also smell fear in their rider or handler by a particular scent the person exudes.

Taste Horses can taste the same four basic things as humans: sweet, sour, bitter, and salt. Taste is strongly associated with smell and through the two, horses can distinguish good food and drink from bad.

Touch The skin harbors a highly sophisticated sensory system that detects pain, heat, cold, and itching. Whiskers around the muzzle, and long eyelashes help the horse to assess

FIELDS OF SOUND AND VISION

The position of the horse's ears on the sides of its head enables it to hear almost all around it. Each ear can pick up sounds to the front and side, leaving a gap immediately behind it which it can cover with a turn of the head.

A horse's field of vision. The shaded area in front represents the area of binocular vision, which is extremely limited. The horse's eye is one of the largest in the animal world, weighing around three ounces, the eyeball is about the size of an egg.

THE LANGUAGE OF EXPRESSION

Alert and interested

Sleepy, unwell, or submissive

Relaxed, bored, or unwell

A horse does not instantly panic at an unfamiliar sound; it will pay attention to it and remember it. If something happens at the same time as the sound, it will, in future, associate the happening with that sound, and this is an important part of training and learning. Screaming and screeching often frighten horses, whereas soft monotones calm them. Horses are as agitated by constant, raucous sounds as humans can be, and some horses prefer a busy atmosphere, whilst others prefer peace and quiet. It is important to watch your horse and try to tell by its behavior and expression which category it falls into. If it seems slightly (or very) tense, its ears flicking around a lot, not resting much during the day, it could be that there is too much noise going on for its liking.

Angry and aggressive

TEETH

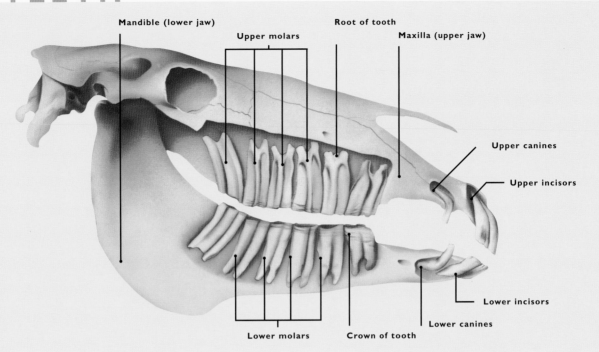

Mandible (lower jaw)

Upper molars

Root of tooth

Maxilla (upper jaw)

Upper canines

Upper incisors

Lower incisors

Lower canines

Crown of tooth

Lower molars

above: A lengthways section through a horse's skull. The incisor teeth at the front crop off the grass. The molars are very large, strong, grinding teeth. They need to be powerful to break down grass, which is tough and fibrous. The canines or tushes serve no useful purpose today, but are a throwback to a primitive ancestor.

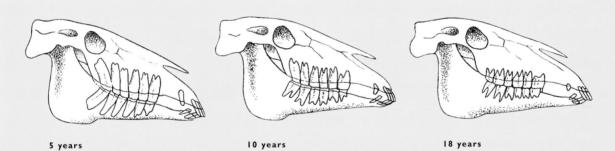

5 years   10 years   18 years

above: The teeth continue to erupt from their sockets throughout the horse's life. The length of the crown in the gum shortens and the roots develop with age, and only a small amount of tooth is left by the time a horse becomes elderly.

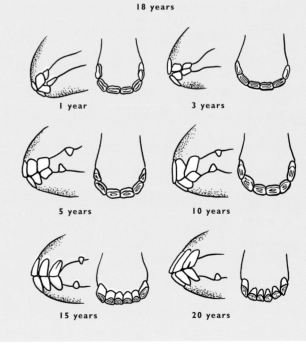

1 year   3 years

5 years   10 years

15 years   20 years

right: As the teeth wear down throughout a horse's life, the pattern that can be seen on the surface of the incisors gradually changes, giving a fairly accurate idea of the horse's age. The teeth also become more triangular as a horse gets older, giving another clue to its age.

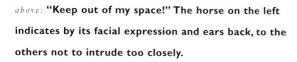

above: **"Keep out of my space!" The horse on the left indicates by its facial expression and ears back, to the others not to intrude too closely.**

its location in dim light and prevent it from bumping into things. In cold weather, coat hairs act as an insulator by standing up to trap air between them, and if the horse is extremely cold, it will shiver, which produces heat. If it is excessively hot, the horse sweats, helping it to cool down as the sweat evaporates off the skin. Touching things, such as plants and live creatures, helps the horse recognize his environment.

Dentition

An adult male horse usually has 40 teeth—12 incisors (the biting teeth situated at the front of the mouth and referred to as centrals, laterals, and corners according to their position), 24 molars (grinding teeth at the back of the mouth), and four canine teeth (tushes or tusks), one on each side of the top jaw and one on each side of the bottom jaw, which are situated behind the incisors. Canines are rarely seen in mares.

Sometimes a horse may have small "wolf" teeth (one on each side of the top jaw just in front of the molars). These have no mastication value and are generally best removed by a vet (a relatively quick and easy procedure) if they interfere with bit action and cause discomfort.

In addition to chewing food up small enough to swallow and be digested, a horse's teeth (incisors) give a good indication of the animal's age up to eight years. After this time, it becomes harder to ascertain accurately the animal's age because of wear and tear.

The "sixth sense"

Like many other mammals, the horse is renowned for having a "sixth sense"—an intuitive response or reaction to a situation that is not apparent to others. Examples of this are horses that stop and refuse to go on despite their riders seeing no obvious reason for this fear or stubbornness. Later, investigation would show there was danger ahead, even to the extent of a tree crashing to the ground seconds later, which would have crushed the horse and its rider had they been progressing as normal. Other seemingly inexplicable reactions included a horse that was uneasy with and refused to go near a certain tree in a field. Investigation revealed that a plane had crashed there, killing the pilot, many years previously.

Communication

By nature horses are gregarious animals, evolved to live in herds with a social pecking order. Herd hierarchy consists of the stallion or lead, mare (usually an older, and wiser, matron), other mares and youngsters. Colts are normally thrown out of the herd by their dominant father by the time they reach sexual maturity, so they don't become a threat to his superiority. These colts wander off, usually in small groups until, individually, they can accumulate a herd of their own. This often means fighting another stallion for control (see page 35). In this way only the strongest win, stamping their own dominant genes on future generations.

In the modern world of captive horses, it is up to owners to decide which stallions represent the best of their particular breed, or are particularly good at producing excellent stock, and therefore suitable to breed from—and mistakes are often made! Sometimes a horse can excel at its particular profession yet throw insignificant progeny, or even be sterile.

below: **Mutual scratching is a benefit enjoyed by those horses kept in groups; alone, a horse would need to find a tree or fence to alleviate an itch in inaccessible places.**

Just like humans and other animals, horses have their likes and dislikes where other equines are concerned—some form a strong bond with another horse in their field, while others are actively aggressive toward a particular field partner. While many domesticated horses benefit from being in company, it is vitally important that the group get on together. A horse that is continually bullied will become anxious and depressed, and it will need to be put with horses that do not display aggression toward it.

Horses communicate through body language, voice, touch, and smell. An aggressive stance, such as having the ears back and looking threatening, warns off intruders and those who stray into the horse's personal space.

Acceptable social behavior and learning how to survive in the wild are taught from generation to generation. Foals will learn how to behave, recognize what represents danger, and discover what's good and safe to eat from their mothers and the other horses in their herd.

It is a proven fact that groups of young horses kept together until they are old enough to be worked are more mentally complete and easygoing than youngsters brought up on their own.

above: **Camargue horses drinking from the marshy Rhône River Delta, southern France**

the
breeds

50 horse breeds
from around the world

Since the dawn of recorded history humankind has lived in one way or another with horses. Whether coexisting as wild creatures on the steppes of what is now Europe, or sharing the legendary equine/human partnership that ensued in the wake of the horse's domestication, what emerged from this relationship was an illustrious family of breeds that continue to fascinate to this day. For centuries, human beings, with a little help from Mother Nature here and there, have skillfully sculpted the members of the equine species into a vast array of animals of all sizes, shapes, and even colors to satisfy just about every whim our species could conjure up. What follows are profiles of 50 of these breeds from around the world. As unique as they are genetically, physically, and functionally from one another, together they stand as a living history of the equine species.

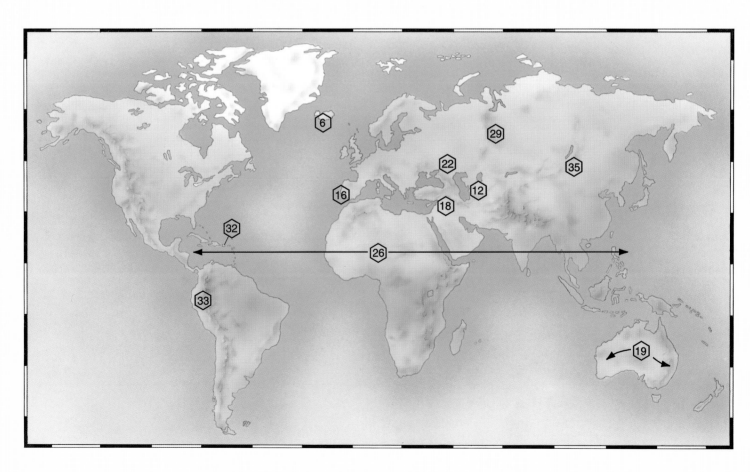

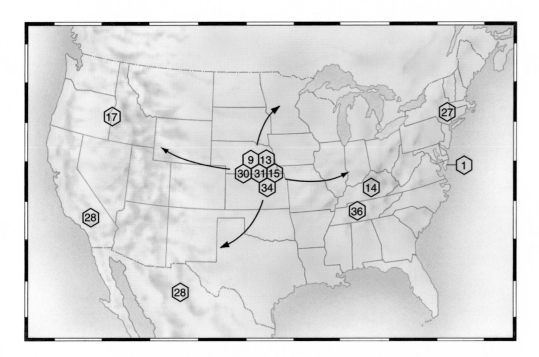

PONIES

1. Chincoteague – Assateague Island, USA
2. Connemara – Ireland, Connemara
3. Dales and Fell Pony – England, Pennine Hills
4. Dartmoor Pony – England, Dartmoor
5. Haflinger – Austria, South Tyrol
6. Icelandic – Iceland
7. New Forest – England, New Forest
8. Norwegian Fjord – Norway
9. Pony of the Americas – USA
10. Shetland – Great Britain, Shetland
11. Welsh Pony and Cob – Wales

LIGHT HORSE BREEDS

12. Akhal-Teké – Turkmenistan
13. Quarter Horse – USA
14. Saddlebred – USA, Kentucky
15. Standardbred – USA
16. Andalusian – Spain, Andalucia
17. Appaloosa – USA
18. Arabian – Middle East
19. Australian Stock Horse – Australia
20. Camargue – France, Rhône River Delta
21. Cleveland Bay – England, Cleveland Bay
22. Don – Russia, Don River Steppes
23. French Trotter – France, Normandy
24. Hackney Horse and Hackney Pony – England
25. Lippizaner – Austria/Slovenia
26. Miniature Horse – Worldwide
27. Morgan – USA, Vermont
28. Mustang – USA, California and Mexico
29. Orlov Trotter – Russia
30. Paint – USA
31. Palomino – USA
32. Paso Fino – Puerto Rico
33. Peruvian Paso – Peru
34. Pinto – USA
35. Przewalski's Horse – Mongolia
36. Tennessee Walking Horse – USA, Tennessee
37. Thoroughbred – England

WARMBLOODS

38. Dutch Warmblood – The Netherlands
39. Friesian – The Netherlands, Friesian
40. Hanoverian – Germany, Lower Saxony
41. Holsteiner – Germany, Schleswig-Holstein
42. Oldenburger – Germany
43. Selle Français – France, Normandy
44. Trakehner – Germany, East Prussia

HEAVY HORSE BREEDS

45. Belgian – Belgium
46. Clydesdale – Scotland
47. Irish Draught – Ireland
48. Percheron – France, La Perche, Normandy
49. Shire – England
50. Suffolk Punch – England, Suffolk

43

the chincoteague pony

n 1947, author Marguerite Henry published a book entitled *Misty of Chincoteague*, the chronicle of the small, wild ponies that occupy Assateague Island off the eastern coast of the United States.

44

The book, which continues to delight children today, drew international attention to a herd of wild ponies that are presumed to have come to the island either as strays released by early settlers on the mainland, or, according to a more romantic theory, as refugees from a Spanish ship that sunk off the coast of the ponies' contemporary island home. Regardless of their origin, the ponies have long been considered unique American treasures.

Given their island existence, the Chincoteague ponies have had to survive on the poorest of feed and the most rugged of terrain, the combination of which has created a hardy animal with a wise, gentle soul and a tough constitution. Because it is the progeny of originally domestic stock, the Chincoteague that returns to a domestic lifestyle, which many do, is typically a willing student and subsequently a suitable mount for children.

Some controversy has followed the management of this unique pony through the years. Each year in July, the ponies are rounded up and swum across the water to the neighboring island of Chincoteague, where, under the guidance of the Chincoteague Volunteer Fire Department, a selected bunch of their kind are adopted out to the public. In previous years, animal welfare groups have objected to this practice, which too often resulted in the premature separation of foals from their dams and in the negligent care of the ponies by inexperienced adopters. Cooperation between these groups and the Fire Department has now resulted, however, in improvements in the care and handling of these unique creatures. Veterinarians, animal welfare representatives, and equine educators now all work together to ensure that the ponies are delivered into proper hands.

characteristics

ancestry

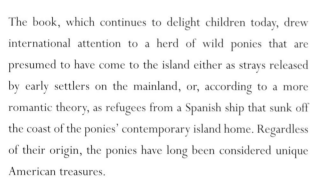

ORIGIN: United States, Assateague Island **HEIGHT:** 12–13 hh **COLORS:** Most solid colors and pinto patterns **PHYSIQUE:** Rather horselike with a straight head; some weakness in the legs and hindquarters **FEATURES:** Hardy; personable if handled properly **USES:** Child's pony if properly trained, also roams wild

• **VARIOUS ENGLISH AND SPANISH BLOODLINES**

the connemara

Though Ireland is renowned for its horses, the Connemara pony is the Emerald Isle's only true indigenous breed. Sculpted through the years by the rugged mountainous terrain and scant food supplies of its homeland— the Connemara region of western Ireland from which this pony takes its name—the contemporary Connemara embodies the best and brightest equine bloodlines Europe has to offer.

An ancient breed of mysterious origin, the Connemara began as a native resident of Ireland that was subsequently influenced by the influx of visitors, conquerors, and even Irish citizens themselves who came in contact with this talented pony through the centuries. Through the ages its own inherent gifts have been enhanced by infusions of a variety of bloodlines: Arabian, Barb, various Spanish horses, Welsh Cob, and Thoroughbred, to name the most prominent.

The result is the modern Connemara pony. From its roots within its treacherously rocky homeland, it has honed a profound jumping ability coveted by both children and adults seeking proficient hunter and jumper prospects. As an added bonus, the Connemara is one of the most refined of the ponies of the British Isles, having benefited genetically from the beautiful horses that have influenced its development through the ages. What began as a shaggy, typically dun-colored pony eking out a precarious survival on the rocky cliffs of western Ireland has evolved into one of Europe's most elegant riding ponies.

characteristics

ORIGIN: Ireland, Connemara **HEIGHT:** 13–14 hh **COLORS:** Gray, black, bay, brown, and primitive dun **PHYSIQUE:** Athletic full neck; straight back; thick mane and tail; attractive head with straight profile; deep chest; clean, well-muscled legs **FEATURES:** Elegant; great stamina; good jumper **USES:** Riding, light draft

ancestry

- CELTIC PONY
- IRISH HOBBYE
- BARB
- ARABIAN
- ROADSTER/HACKNEY
- WELSH COB
- CLYDESDALE
- THOROUGHBRED
- ANDALUSIAN

the dales and fell ponies

I t is logical to discuss these two pony breeds together, as they share a common ancestry and a common homeland in the Pennine Hills of northern England.

Yet they are not identical, for though they existed in their home territory since Roman times, and perhaps before, and though they both benefited from similar genetic contributions, they evolved in separate regions that subsequently resulted in two distinct British pony breeds.

The most prominent influence seen in the Dales and Fell ponies is the beautiful and ancient black Friesian of the Netherlands, one of Europe's oldest breeds. Though many equine bloodlines are presumed to have enhanced the Dales and Fell through the years, the Friesian's influence is evident in the ponies' color, which, though the ponies may be bay,

brown, or gray, is considered most classic in black with few, if any, white markings. The ponies also share the Friesian's feathering on the feet and the high-action trot, characteristics that have long endeared them to people seeking attractive teams of black ponies to pull their carriages.

The Fell ponies, bred in northern parts of the Pennines primarily for riding and driving, are typically smaller and lighter than the Dales from the eastern Pennines, which were bred for hard work as pack, farm, and draft animals. Today both are coveted by serious equestrians for their stamina, sure-footed grace and beauty in driving, light riding, and trekking.

46

right: **The Dales and Fell ponies are excellent examples of the fine quality inherent in Britain's family of native ponies. The ponies embody the results of a perfect combination of genetics and environment.**

characteristics

ORIGIN: England, Pennine Hills **HEIGHT:** Fell: up to 14 hh; Dales: up to 14.2 hh **COLORS:** Black with little or no white markings is most popular; also found in bay, brown, and gray **PHYSIQUE:** Both are well-muscled, powerful animals with hard feet and good bone; the Dales is larger and broader all-around than the Fell **FEATURES:** Strong, good stamina; sure-footed; good-natured disposition **USES:** Light riding, trekking, driving

ancestry

- DALES
- CELTIC PONY
- GALLOWAY
- FRIESIAN
- WELSH COB
- CLYDESDALE

the dartmoor pony

That the **Dartmoor** pony still exists is something of a miracle. That it today stands as one of the most admirable and coveted of **Britain's** family of native pony breeds is a credit to those individuals who have not only repeatedly snatched it back from the brink of extinction, but did so with foresight and wisdom.

The Dartmoor pony hails from the steep rugged moors of southwest England, a defining and very ancient ancestry that made this pony tough, sure-footed, easy to keep and a popular choice for a variety of historical callings. First documented officially in the 1012 will of a Saxon bishop by the name of Aelfwold of Crediton, the Dartmoor pony would for centuries be called to duty for everything from working the tin mines to farming to just plain carrying riders across a rugged trail. And through it all, once the demand for the pony had waned, it would be cast off to fend for itself, frequently almost lapsing into all-out extinction until some wise soul would intervene and decide that this small, talented pony deserved salvation yet again.

The pony's rescue through the years has entailed infusions of the blood of such breeds as Arabians and Welsh Mountain ponies, resulting in the Dartmoor of today that is renowned for its elegance and very smooth, very un-ponylike gait. Considered both an ideal first pony for children and a talented mount for more experienced adults, the sweet-tempered Dartmoor is also frequently used to produce larger saddle ponies, an endeavor that is especially successful when Dartmoors are crossed with Arabians or Thoroughbreds.

characteristics

ORIGIN: England **HEIGHT:** 12.2 hh (maximum) **COLORS:** Bay, brown, black, some gray; few white markings; no pinto **PHYSIQUE:** Good front; medium back; muscular hindquarters; small, distinctive head with small ears; wide forehead and soft, inquisitive expression **FEATURES:** Elegant; intelligent; smooth horse-like gait **USES:** Riding, occasionally driven

ancestry

- **CELTIC PONY**
- **BRITISH NATIVE PONY STOCK**
- **ROADSTERS/TROTTERS**
- **WELSH MOUNTAIN PONY**
- **ARABIAN**
- **SHETLAND PONY**
- **THOROUGHBRED**

the haflinger

From the beautiful southern Tyrol region of the Austrian Alps hails this "blond" pony that is as attractive as it is strong and capable.

The Haflinger's golden coat, highlighted by a thick flaxen mane and tail, defy the image of a dedicated working pony, but that is exactly the role the Haflinger willingly plays in its homeland and beyond.

The Haflinger is believed to have descended from horses of Arabian breeding that were brought into their somewhat isolated native territory and crossed with calm, cold-blooded, native draft mares. The Arabian influence is evident today in the breed's beauty and athletic conformation, while the cold-blooded matriarchal influence is seen in the breed's level-headed disposition. Their hybridized genetics in place, Haflingers bred relatively pure for generations within their mountain home, retaining their well-constructed physical attributes, golden color, and gentle temperament even after

they were no longer Austria's best-kept secret. Bred originally for farm work and as pack animals for mountain travel, the sure-footed Haflinger is today a popular choice for both riding and driving in Europe and the United States (those for driving and pack work tend to be stockier in build than those used under saddle).

Enthusiasts are invariably first attracted to the breed by its external golden beauty, but they stay with the breed because of its inner beauty—its quiet, docile temperament. Recognizing a national treasure with an international following, the Austrian government works to preserve the quality of the Haflinger within its homeland, involving itself avidly in the breeding of the fine animals to ensure that only the finest carry on the breed's genetic quality and traditions.

48

right: **The Haflinger's golden coat, and flaxen mane and tail defy the image of a hard-working mountain pony.**

characteristics

ORIGIN: Austria, South Tyrol **HEIGHT:** 13.3–14.2 hh **COLORS:** Golden chestnut with flaxen mane and tail **PHYSIQUE:** Deep chest and girth; good muscle and bone; strong feet; short legs; small, pretty Arabian-influenced head **FEATURES:** Great stamina; sure-footed; gentle disposition **USES:** Riding, driving, pack

ancestry

- **HEAVY INDIGENOUS MOUNTAIN PONY STOCK**
- **ORIENTAL**
- **NORIBER**
- **ARABIAN**

the icelandic

Though its size has earned the Icelandic a reputation as a pony, to refer to it as such to its extremely devoted fans is to invite argument.

The Icelandic, a breed that, given its isolated island homeland at the top of the world, was for a millennium afforded the luxury of breeding pure, is one of the world's oldest breeds and one of its most fiercely guarded. No horses are permitted to be imported into Iceland which still keeps this breed pure.

Known for its five-gait repertoire, the Icelandic garners most attention for the tolt, a unique running walk reserved for only the most experienced rider. Though the Icelandic, the descendant of presumably Scandinavian horses imported to the island by its first settlers a thousand years ago, is a sweet-tempered animal whose diminutive size implies suitability for all riders, it can be a firecracker under saddle. Hailing as it does from a decidedly rugged, not to mention freezing corner

of the world, the Icelandic had to be smart as well as athletic to survive. It has thus developed, as the only equine inhabitant of its homeland, a wisdom that can handily outsmart most humans, a stamina that requires daily activity, and a deep affection for most people.

Icelandic ponies were bred originally for all manner of work required of a harsh island life. Popular for everyday transportation, driving, farming, packing, and light riding, the breed garners deep respect from the Icelandic people, as well as from horse lovers worldwide. In fact, many individuals now make the pilgrimage to Iceland to trek through its environs on the back of this fine sturdy breed every year.

characteristics

ORIGIN: Iceland **HEIGHT:** 12.3–13.2 hh **COLORS:** Most equine colors; classic is dun or chestnut with a flaxen mane and tail **PHYSIQUE:** Sturdy, compact, almost rectangular build with short well-boned legs; good feet; thick mane and tail **FEATURES:** Great stamina; affectionate; spirited **USES:** Riding, trekking, packing

ancestry

- **NORWEGIAN FJORD**
- **CELTIC PONY**
- **NATIVE BRITISH STOCK**

the new forest pony

One of Britain's renowned pony breeds, the New Forest pony originated from and continues to occupy the approximately 65,000-acre New Forest in southern England.

Here herds of semiwild ponies are known to have roamed since the eleventh century—and probably a thousand years prior to that—often receiving infusions of blood from larger, more domestically oriented, horses that happened to be passing through during various periods of British history. Centuries of crossbreeding, coupled with an often tough and variegated career, have created an equally tough pony that, when taken from its forest home, has worked farms and mines and carried riders along rugged, obstacle-laden roads with ease.

New Forests continue to embrace a semiwild lifestyle, much to the delight of visitors to the region. Today, as in days past, the wild, though privately owned ponies roam their ancient homeland unencumbered, their notched tails indicating that their owners have paid the appropriate fees for grazing rights. Then, come fall, the ponies are rounded up in the annual "drift," in which they are evaluated for breeding by representatives of the New Forest Pony and Cattle Society. This organization, enforcing registration policies set in motion in the late nineteenth century, oversees the management and breeding of the ponies, thus ensuring that they continue to grace their homeland with their ancient and dignified presence.

New Forest ponies have become a valued export from their home turf as well, their sound disposition and conformation attracting the attentions of those seeking talented riding ponies. This small, though sturdy animal is considered an ideal choice for families seeking a mount appropriate for both children and adults alike, skilled at adapting to the various skill levels of various riders.

characteristics

ORIGIN: England, southwest Hampshire **HEIGHT:** 12.2–maximum 14 hh

COLORS: Any equine color (no pinto patterns); most are bay and brown

PHYSIQUE: Classic pony-type conformation with strong, slender legs; hard feet; good joints; sloping shoulders; well-muscled hindquarters **FEATURES:** Good jumper; gentle disposition; smooth gaits; sure-footed **USES:** Riding, light driving

ancestry

- **NATIVE BRITISH STOCK**
- **THOROUGHBRED**
- **ARABIAN**

the norwegian fjord

Though the Vikings of old are considered giants of history, the short stature of one of their favored mounts, the Norwegian Fjord, suggests that those famed warriors may not have been all that tall. But regardless of height, they were wise to emulate the toughness of the animals that carried them fearlessly through both battle and conquest.

51

Considered by some a pony, by others a horse, the Norwegian Fjord, resembling as it does Stone-Age cave paintings of its species, is a primitive animal that evokes the image of the wild horses that once roamed prehistoric Europe in abundance. Its dun-colored coat, highlighted by a dark dorsal stripe that runs from mane to tail, and stiff stand-up mane traditionally trimmed in a curved arch, make the very ancient Fjord a unique addition to the contemporary horse population.

Today, the callings of the Vikings having long been rendered obsolete, the sweet-tempered Norwegian Fjord remains a valued breed within its Scandinavian homeland, where it is a willing and athletic saddle horse and a hardworking farm, pack, and driving animal. It is also gaining a following throughout the rest of Europe and in the United States. An easy keeper with a quiet, gentle disposition, the powerful, versatile Fjord can be the ideal equine addition to the horse-loving family, suitable for the needs of both children and adults alike.

characteristics

ancestry

ORIGIN: Norway **HEIGHT:** 13–14 hh **COLORS:** Dun with dark dorsal stripe, and zebra striping on the legs **PHYSIQUE:** Stocky build with short legs; thick neck; broad chest; well-muscled hindquarters **FEATURES:** Hardy, even-tempered; great stamina; sure-footed **USES:** Riding, driving, farming, pack

- **PRZEWALSKI'S HORSE**
- **CELTIC PONY**
- **ANCIENT ICE AGE STEPPE HORSE**

pony of the americas

Most ponies that today call the United States home are imports from other nations, but the US does have one pony to call its own.

That pony is the Pony of the Americas, or POA.

This attractive animal, whose conformation is more horselike than that of a pony, sports what has long been considered a very American equine characteristic: the spotted patterns of the Appaloosa.

Not surprisingly, the POA's roots are with the Appaloosa, small representatives of which were crossed in the 1950s with Arabians and various small horses of Appaloosa coloring to create a well-built, brightly patterned American pony ideal for young people. Today the POA's breed registry, the Pony of the Americas Club, is extremely active in its promotion of the pony and of POAC events for young members. The pony at the heart of these efforts has subsequently rocketed in popularity in a relatively short period of time, hardly surprising, considering the immense popularity of its larger spotted cousin. The POA is certainly deserving of the accolades it receives, displaying a skilled repertoire of athletic talents and a sweet-tempered disposition, as well as the much coveted spotted coat and unique classic characteristics of the Appaloosa breed.

Though the POA was bred originally for western events, which are considered ideal for the very American, very western spotted horse, its talents for dressage and jumping are now gaining it entrance to all manner of equine endeavor. The POA is thus proving to be a colorful, not to mention eye-catching, addition to show rings of both English and western disciplines, and an excellent companion for young riders.

characteristics

ORIGIN: United States **HEIGHT:** 11.2–14 hh **COLORS:** Appaloosa spots (blankets, leopard, etc.) and characteristics: white sclera, mottled skin, some striped hooves **PHYSIQUE:** Well-proportioned and athletic; strong Arabian influence, slightly dished face; short back; deep chest; sloped shoulders; good muscle overall **FEATURES:** Athletically versatile; interactive; great for young riders **USES:** Riding

ancestry

- SHETLAND PONY
- APPALOOSA
- QUARTER HORSE
- ARABIAN

the shetland pony

Even people who don't know horses know the Shetland pony, a breed that boasts not only a universal appeal, but also a universal presence. The Shetland is often the first representative of the equine species with which youngsters have contact. Following that initial meeting, few can forget that tiny rounded form, thick mane and tail, and playful expression.

The Shetland pony, the smallest of all the pony breeds, hails from the Shetland Islands off the coast of Scotland, where the terrain is rugged, the climate harsh, and the animals—ponies, cattle, and even dogs—are small in size but tough and smart. Presumed to be the progeny of horses brought to the islands by Vikings and other conquerors and explorers that sporadically visited hundreds of years ago, the ponies were subsequently sculpted by their homeland into hardy animals that would ultimately gain the world's attentions to their vast talents.

The Shetland's career, like its native lifestyle, has not always been pretty. Recognized for its sure-footedness and hardy constitution, it has been put to work in all manner of often cruel and exploitive activity. It has worked the dark pits of mining operations until it dropped; it has carried overloaded packs upon its back and pulled heavily laden carts along mountain roads; it has performed tirelessly in circuses that often employed inhumane training methods and housing conditions; and it has carried countless children around and around in circles as part of commercial pony rides.

Yet despite a long history in which humans too often failed to offer the Shetland the respect it was due, this diminutive animal has prevailed. Ever forgiving of human demands, the Shetland has enjoyed a somewhat easier time of it in the twentieth century, where it has basked in the affections of both children and adults who seek to celebrate rather than exploit the Shetland's substantial gifts (those who consider Shetlands nasty have obviously met those ponies that have been mistreated by their owners). Today Shetland ponies have found niches worldwide as both pets and show ponies, some exhibiting the stocky conformation and shaggy coat of the classic "old-style" Shetland, others presenting a flashier, more refined appearance often coveted by American driving enthusiasts. Regardless of type, the Shetland is a truly charming pony.

53

characteristics

ORIGIN: Scotland, Shetland Islands **HEIGHT:** 42 inches 10.2 hh maximum
COLORS: Black is classic, but found in all equine colors and pinto patterns
PHYSIQUE: Short, stocky, and compact; round, well-muscled hindquarters; powerful shoulders; hard feet; lush mane and tail **FEATURES:** Sure-footed; wise; extraordinarily strong **USES:** Riding, light driving

ancestry

• **CELTIC PONY**
• **NATIVE BRITISH AND SCANDINAVIAN PONY STOCK**

the welsh pony and cob

The simple words "Welsh pony" require some definition, for the Welsh pony and cob breed, as it is called, actually refers to four distinct animals, all divided by size and type within the breed's registry. Sift through this confusion, and you will find a family of ancient Welsh equines with an international popularity rooted in their athletic versatility—ponies that are considered by many to be the most talented, most beautiful ponies that the British Isles have to offer.

right: **Welsh Mountain pony; Section A: Many Section As often look like small, stocky miniature Arabs due to the Arab blood in their ancestry, yet still have Celtic Pony characteristics.**

The Welsh Mountain pony (Section A) is the smallest, oldest, and perhaps best-known member of the legendary Welsh family. Presumed to have existed in its Welsh homeland since before the arrival of the Romans, it blossomed into a rugged, agile creature that exhibits an undeniable Arabian influence in its appearance. This is rooted in suspected historical crossings with visiting horses of Oriental breeding through the centuries, evident today in the contemporary Mountain pony's attractive head and well-proportioned physique. Indeed this is a trustworthy, intelligent pony that is equally adept at jumping and driving and is frequently considered an ideal choice for young equestrians.

In addition to pursuing its own athletic callings, the Mountain pony has provided the foundation for the other

characteristics

ORIGIN: Wales **HEIGHT:** Section A: maximum 12.2 hh; Section B: maximum 13.2 hh; Section C: maximum 13.2 hh; Section D: over 13.2 hh **COLORS:** Any solid color; no pinto patterns **PHYSIQUE:** All are inspired by the Welsh Mountain pony; strong, athletic build; handsome head; muscular neck and hindquarters; strong legs and feet **FEATURES:** Versatile, gentle temperament; sure-footed; trustworthy; natural jumpers **USES:** Riding, driving, light draft

ancestry

- CELTIC PONY
- ANDALUSIAN
- HACKNEY
- NORFOLK ROADSTER/TROTTER
- YORKSHIRE COACH HORSE
- VARIOUS ORIENTAL BLOODLINES

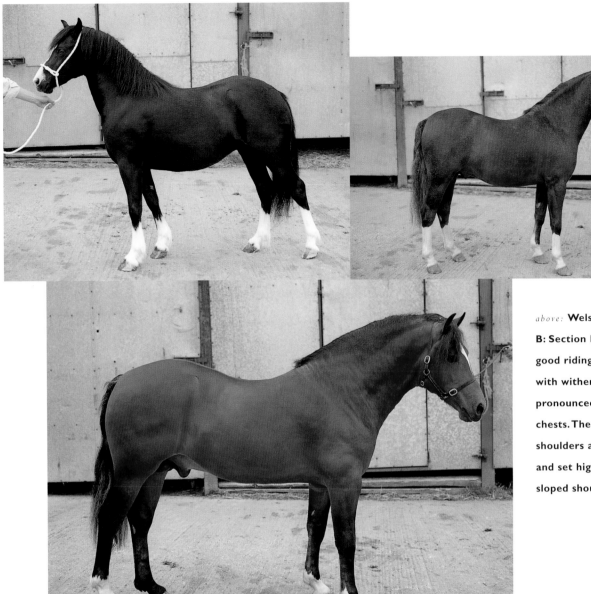

above: **Welsh pony; Section B: Section Bs often have good riding conformation with withers moderately pronounced and deep chests. The neck and shoulders are quite long and set high onto well-sloped shoulders.**

top: **Welsh pony of Cob type; Section C: The Section C is almost a scaled down version of a Section D, however, it is fairly difficult to breed. It is a strong and agile breed and makes good riding for teenagers and shorter adults.**

above: **Welsh Cob; Section D: Section Ds are compact, well balanced and strong. They capable of light farm work, have speed and stamina for harness transportation, and the willingness for riding.**

members of its family: the Section B Welsh pony (a larger counterpart to the Mountain pony, which is prized for its skills as a riding pony), the Section C Welsh pony of cob type (a smaller version of the Section D cob skilled both under saddle and in harness, which should not exceed 13.2 hands in height), and the Section D Welsh Cob (a strong, versatile animal valued

for centuries for farm, general transportation, pack and military work that must stand taller than 13.2 hands). In addition to the Welsh Mountain pony foundation, various breeds have been used in the development of the Section B, C, and D ponies and cobs: primarily Hackney and Thoroughbred blood for the very athletic Section B pony, and Andalusians for the Section C and D cobs.

For centuries, Wales has served as a source of fine horses, a fact that became immediately evident to early visitors of all nationalities who discovered during their travels the equine treasures waiting there. Animals of Welsh pony and cob breeding have since gone on to provide foundations to other breeds throughout the world, including America's Morgan, Britain's Hackney and Fell and Dales ponies, and various polo ponies. The demand for such genetic contributions is always a tribute to a breed's quality.

the akhal-teké

Obsessed as mankind has always been with the quest for gold, a few select individuals have discovered that gold exists in equine form in a horse native to Turkmenistan in what was formerly the Soviet Union. A brief glance at a classic representative of this breed, the Akhal-Teké, might lead one to believe that this is not a flesh-and-blood animal, but rather a 24-karat equine sculpture.

Akhal-Tekés are rare, predominantly golden-colored horses, some of which literally shimmer with a golden almost metallic sheen upon their coats. An ancient breed, the Akhal-Teké hails from a region of the world historically considered the font of central Asia's finest horses and perhaps even one of the birth-places of equine domestication. The Akhal-Teké, for instance, gave rise to the Iomud, a valued saddle horse also native to Turkmenistan. It also had a profound influence on other breeds beyond Turkmenistan's borders, including the rare but athletically gifted Karabair from Uzbekistan, another region historically renowned for spectacular horses; the solidly constructed Kabarda of Caucasus; and the shortest of Central Asia's horses, the Lokai of Tadzhikistan.

While the true beginnings of the Akhal-Teké are murky, its origins are presumed to have dovetailed with those of fellow ancient desert dwellers, the Arabian and the Barb. A talented athlete of endurance, speed, and courage, the Akhal-Teké is unique not only in color, but in its extraordinary long-backed, high-withered conformation and muscular, though somewhat bony, structure. Yet modern times and politics have repeatedly placed the Akhal-Teké in precarious positions, struggling continuously against extinction. Recognizing this threat, a handful of breeders in the United States are attempting to bolster its numbers there, and in the process, perhaps give the

Arabian, the reigning monarch of endurance riding, a run for its money. So far, their efforts, as well as similar efforts in Europe and Russia, are boding well for this ancient and very gifted desert war horse.

characteristics

ancestry

ORIGIN: Turkmenistan **HEIGHT:** 14.2–16 hh **COLORS:** Honey gold or dun, bay, chestnut; some blacks and grays; most with a metallic sheen **PHYSIQUE:** Muscular and slender with high withers, sloping shoulders; long back; thin skin; somewhat shallow rib cage; sparse mane and tail **FEATURES:** Elegant; extraordinary endurance and stamina, can tolerate extreme heat **USES:** Riding, endurance, racing

• TURKOMAN

the quarter horse

One of America's most successful worldwide exports is the Quarter Horse. Indeed this quintessentially American breed, the symbol of the American cowboy and a legend in the American West, has made its name and its presence known throughout the world since the launching of its breed registry, the American Quarter Horse Association (AQHA), in 1940.

However, the Quarter Horse's establishment had been set into motion long before the formation of its breed association. In fact, its story mirrors that of the United States itself, beginning with the Spanish horses brought to North America by Spanish explorers in the sixteenth century, some of which made their way into the care of Native Americans, who proved quite competent in the raising and training of the equine species. These horses were later crossed with horses of English lines brought to America by early settlers along the east coast, the resulting progeny valued for their ability to run quarter-mile races in the blink of an eye. As the early Americans' racing passions became dominated by the longer-distance Thoroughbreds, the Quarter Horse followed westward-bound pioneers to a new territory where it would claim its destiny as premier cow horse.

Today the Quarter Horse continues to expend its talents in whatever endeavor is asked of it. Still a working cow horse with phenomenal cow sense, it now excels in the show ring as well, continually striving to prove that it is the world's most versatile horse. Though western events, such as reining, cutting, and barrel racing, and those traditional quarter-mile races are its forte, the Quarter Horse, with its powerful hindquarters and willing disposition, is today competing in everything from dressage to showjumping to driving. In doing so, it is attracting the attention of the international horse community, evident in the fact that the AQHA now boasts members and registered Quarter Horses all over the world.

But there is more to this horse than athletic versatility and a signature conformation of clean muscle, rounded lines, and a kind, intelligent head recognizable immediately to anyone with an interest in horses. What holds the devotion of its admirers to the breed is the Quarter Horse's legendary disposition. Celebrated for its calm, cool demeanor on the trail, in the show ring, on the track or on the range, the Quarter Horse is quintessential companion, family horse, and friend—a horse people just like to have around.

57

characteristics

ORIGIN: United States **HEIGHT:** 14.3–16 hh **COLORS:** Thirteen solid colors are recognized; sorrel and chestnut are classic **PHYSIQUE:** Balanced structure; substantial muscle; sloping shoulders; immense hindquarters; deep, broad chest; medium, slightly arched neck; short head **FEATURES:** Extremely versatile, strong, gentle disposition; family horse **USES:** Riding, driving, working cattle, racing

ancestry

- **VARIOUS BRITISH AND SPANISH BLOODLINES**
- **CHICKASAW INDIAN HORSES**

the saddlebred

An American original, the Saddlebred is a specially gaited breed that was developed to serve the plantation owners of the southern United States.

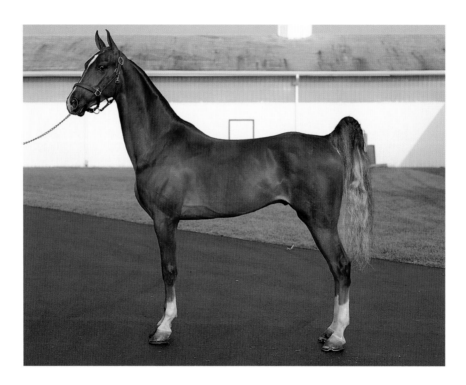

Plantation owners and farmers there in the early days sought to produce a horse that could be ridden comfortably and quickly along the primitive trails and roads of the newly developed rural area and that would look stylish in harness when transporting the family to church on Sunday morning. To make this dream a reality, these early southern breeders enlisted the horses available to them: Morgans, Thoroughbreds, various Spanish horses, and the now-extinct Narragansett Pacers. The combination proved magical, resulting in a beautiful horse of comfortable gaits that went on to gain national fame beyond Kentucky's borders—and beyond the realm of plantation work. For instance, the American Saddlebred served proudly in the American Civil War, seeing both Ulysses S. Grant and Robert E. Lee through the conflict with courage and stamina.

Today, with its war duties a thing of the past, the American Saddlebred is a premier show horse, strutting elegantly in saddleseat and driving classes designed to showcase its special gaits under saddle and in harness. Saddlebreds are also often cast to play the token horse in movies.

In addition, Saddlebreds are now expanding their talents into the more traditional show ring, many an enthusiast recognizing that this talented gaited breed might also be a natural at dressage. The hunch is paying off, and dressage is now considered the next frontier to be conquered by the American Saddlebred.

characteristics

ORIGIN: United States, Kentucky **HEIGHT:** 15–16 hh **COLORS:** Most solid colors, as well as pinto patterns **PHYSIQUE:** Refined yet athletic; long neck; long legs; short back; prominent withers; lovely head with expressive eyes
FEATURES: Elegant; graceful; energetic; proud **USES:** Riding, light driving

ancestry

- ENGLISH/EUROPEAN TROTTERS AND PACERS
- NARRAGANSETT PACER
- CANADIAN PACER
- MORGAN
- THOROUGHBRED

the standardbred

While England is home to the Thoroughbred, the United States boasts an illustrious racer of its own; a harness-racing horse known as the Standardbred.

Despite its name, breed standardization had nothing to do with the founding of the Standardbred, which was developed in the early nineteenth century to satisfy early American passions for the sport of harness racing. The name refers to the practice later in the century of registering only those horses that could pace or trot a mile within a standard time.

Several breeds contributed to the development of this, the fastest harness racer in the world. These included Narragansett Pacers, Morgans, Cleveland Bays, Canadian Pacers, Thoroughbreds and Norfolk Trotters, but the granddaddy of the breed is considered to be a Thoroughbred imported from England in the late eighteenth century by the name of Messenger.

Messenger in turn begat the line that produced the legendary Hambletonian several generations later, and the rest was harness-racing history.

Today harness racing continues to attract the passions of racing enthusiasts, the Standardbred now an institution within the sport. While not a beautiful horse in the classic sense, it is considered downright breathtaking in temperament. Organizations have cropped up to take in retired trotters and adopt them out to people seeking saddle horses. After some training, Standardbreds acclimatize well to civilian life and receive nothing but praise from their new owners, who are invariably stunned at how courtly and genteel these horses tend to be.

characteristics

ORIGIN: United States **HEIGHT:** 14–16 hh **COLORS:** Most solid colors; bay is most prevalent **PHYSIQUE:** Powerfully muscled with a deep girth; strong legs; hard feet; hindquarters that slope down toward the withers; a straight or convex profile; longish ears, and kind eyes **FEATURES:** Athletic; quiet disposition; graceful **USES:** Harness racing, riding, driving

ancestry

- THOROUGHBRED
- CANADIAN TROTTER
- HACKNEY
- NARRAGANSETT PACER
- MORGAN

the andalusian

Spain has long been heralded as a homeland of some of the finest horses the world has to offer. While horses of various types and breeding have called Spain home for thousands of years, perhaps the most beautiful of these—and one that continues to dazzle the public today as dramatically as it did hundreds of years ago—is the Andalusian.

Positioned as it is at a crossroads between Europe, Africa, and the Middle East, Spain was historically populated by a variety of peoples who would routinely cross their respective regions' borders for trade and conquest. Needless to say, accompanying these visitors were horses, who naturally crossed with the horses indigenous to the Iberian Peninsula. This resulted over time in what we know today as the Andalusian, an amalgamation of both hot and cold blood combined to create a stunning animal of presence with a flowing and very lush mane and tail, and a high knee action that together are the epitome of equine elegance.

A horse of such quality could not be kept a secret, and for centuries the Andalusian was a favorite of European aristocracy, in demand as a war horse and High School horse throughout the continent. It performed in all disciplines with style, elegance, and beauty that made it unforgettable to all who encountered it. Few breeds have escaped the Andalusian's genetic influence, the most dramatic case being the foundation it provided for the illustrious Lipizzaner stallions of the Spanish Riding School of Vienna. The magic of the Andalusian has transcended the centuries; even today in a society jaded by technology, a well turned out Andalusian in the dressage ring or on the trail can still stop onlookers in their tracks.

left: **An ancient breed with intelligent eyes, the classic Andalusian is universal in appeal.**

characteristics

ORIGIN: Spain, Andalusia **HEIGHT:** 15.1–15.3 hh **COLORS:** Gray predominates, but also found in black, bay and chestnut **PHYSIQUE:** Strong sloping back; muscular hindquarters; prominent withers; sloping shoulders; strong legs; low tail-set; arched neck; and lush mane and tail; convex profile **FEATURES:** Commanding yet gentle; high leg action **USES:** Riding, driving

ancestry

- NATIVE SPANISH STOCK
- BARB
- ARABIAN
- BERBER

the appaloosa

While spotted horses have resided on the planet for millennia, in the contemporary horse world, the most popular of the spotted horses—the Appaloosa—is considered quintessentially American.

The breed actually began as the guarded treasure of the Nez Percé Indian tribe in the northwestern United States, whose devotion to the mystical spotted horses they cultivated was unwavering. The defining moment in their relationship occurred when the tribe was targeted for relocation by the US Cavalry in the late 1800s. Under the leadership of their beloved Chief Joseph, the Nez Percé made a legendary trek in excess of 1,000 miles into Canada. Though they failed in their escape, they never could have made it as far as they did without their beloved Appaloosas.

Though the Appaloosa, too, was targeted for destruction for its powerful links to the Native Americans, the breed, thanks to the efforts of several western enthusiasts, prevailed, and today it is one of the most popular breeds in the United States. Few can resist the appeal of the Appaloosa with spots sprinkled upon a blanket of white across its rump, or the ever-popular leopard pattern with spots spanning from head to tail.

But there is more to an Appaloosa than just its spots, the patterns for which can occur in a variety of configurations and in most every color of the equine rainbow. A true Appaloosa must also exhibit other classic characteristics, including a prominent white sclera in the eye that imparts a wise, almost human, expression; mottled skin on the muzzle, lips and genitals; and striped hooves. Also inherent to the breed, a product of its rich life with the Nez Percé, are courage and stamina and the athletic ability to participate in a variety of equine activities.

Given its heritage, the Appaloosa is typically labeled a western horse, but in recent years it has proven that it is equally at home in such English-style pursuits as dressage and jumping disciplines, as well. Though its flashy appearance may at times meet with some prejudice from judges in these rather conservative disciplines, the breed's fiercely devoted enthusiasts remain undaunted. More disturbing to these purists is the trend in which solid-colored progeny of Appaloosa breeding are granted breed recognition by the Appaloosa's breed registry, but even that will not bring this breed down. It will carry on as it always has as a unique and steadfast treasure upon the equine landscape.

characteristics

ORIGIN: United States **HEIGHT:** 14.2–16 hh **COLORS:** All colors in a variety of spotted patterns **PHYSIQUE:** Well-muscled with short back; strong legs; hard hooves; slightly sloping croup; long neck; prominent withers; sloping shoulders; sparse mane and tail **FEATURES:** Intelligent; hardy; versatile; good endurance **USES:** Riding

ancestry

- **VARIOUS SPANISH BLOODLINES**
- **ARABIAN**
- **TURKOMAN**

the arabian

Sprung from the deserts of the Middle East many thousands of years ago was the Arabian.

The circumstances surrounding its true origins will always remain a mystery—though folklore suggests Biblical, Islamic, and even supernatural involvement—but what is clear is the spell this beautiful desert breed has always cast upon the human species. From Islamic prophet Mohammed's mythical devotion to the breed that inspired him to employ its talents to spread the word of Islam, to various and sundry Bedouin chieftains who would sacrifice all for a prized Arabian mare's well-being and comfort, to Napoleon Bonaparte whose beloved Marengo was an Arabian, to modern-day enthusiasts who spend millions for a prized stallion, the Arabian's magic has never waned.

Though today it is one of the best-known breeds in the world, and to many the most beautiful and athletically gifted, for centuries the Arabian remained the world's best kept secret, living among the nomadic Arabs who cultivated and cherished the breed as their most valued possession. Legends abound of the esteem in which the Bedouin nomad held his most treasured mare, allowing her to sleep within his desert tent, offering her ample water and only the finest quality food,

characteristics

ORIGIN: The Middle East **HEIGHT:** 14.1–15 hh **COLORS:** Most solid colors with dark skin; gray and black are popular **PHYSIQUE:** Long neck; short back; sloped shoulders; deep chest; muscular legs; prominent withers; good bone; dished face, wide forehead, large nostrils and eyes **FEATURES:** Beautiful; versatile; hot-blooded; affectionate **USES:** Riding, endurance, light driving, racing

ancestry

- **POSSIBLY ASIATIC AND EASTERN EUROPEAN STOCK OF HOT-BLOODED TYPE**

and traveling days across the desert to ensure the mare was bred with only the finest stallion. In exchange, the mare offered her keeper her speed and endurance, wisdom, beauty, and companionship. In fact, few horses harbor so great an affection for the human species as the Arabian, no doubt another element that has so long attracted humans to this breed.

In time, word of the Arabian spread out beyond the borders of its homeland. Meeting this horse for the first time —often on the battlefield—newcomers recognized instantly its profound gifts. In time, the Arabian became a valued export from its home territory, extending its genetic influence throughout Europe, and ultimately throughout the world. Indeed, the pedigree of almost every horse on our planet today has been influenced in one way or another by the Arabian, including, among countless others, the Thoroughbred, the Welsh Mountain Pony, the Trakehner, and even the large Percheron draft horse.

What startles many who first encounter the Arabian is that in addition to possessing great beauty, this is also the quintessential equine athlete. Centuries of selective breeding in the desert have resulted in a versatile horse known for its talents in all equine activities, including dressage, showjumping, driving, western events, trail and, the event to which the breed is a natural, endurance. Throughout the world, the Arabian is considered a national treasure in nations as diverse as England, the United States, Egypt, Hungary, Poland, and Russia. Breeding programs have been designed in these countries to ensure that the quality of the Arabian never diminishes.

left: **The Arab is often described as "dish-faced," a concave outline to the front is desirable. Eyes are often large and expressive and set wide on the forehead.**

australian stock horse

Horses were not indigenous to Australia; they were brought in by settlers and others who traveled to the continent in the eighteenth century. But once those first horses arrived—primarily horses of Arabian and Thoroughbred extraction—they established Australia's own unique equine community.

The most prominent of Australia's horses today is the Australian Stock horse, an animal developed for working the vast herds of livestock managed upon the country's rugged terrain. But the Stock horse's story actually begins with that of another breed: the Waler. Long before the name Australian Stock horse was coined, Australian breeders developed a horse of profound endurance, strength, jumping ability, and intelligence that could withstand extreme heat. While this horse, the Waler, was bred originally to work the outback sheep stations, it soon gained a reputation as a military horse, as well. It served in many conflicts away from its home territory; more than 100,000 were used in World War I alone. By the end of World War II, its population greatly declined and without benefit of a studbook, the Waler virtually faded away.

Many horses, in Australia, if not most, descended from original Waler stock. Some horses became feral, escaping into the outback or were released purposely by their owners. These horses of all shapes and sizes became the very hardy Brumbies. Viewed by many as vermin and a threat to livestock, competing for water and grazing land, Brumbies have thus been targeted for years for destruction.

While the Brumby has offered little inspiration to contemporary Australian horse enthusiasts, the Waler's legacy inspired a group of horsemen in the 1970s to establish the Australian Stock Horse Society, through which a fine line of Australian horses would be bred and preserved. Despite its name, the horse at the heart of that effort, a horse primarily of

Waler, Thoroughbred, and Quarter Horse blood, is used for ranch work, as well as more pleasurable pursuits. These include trail riding, showing, and a unique Australian version of American cattle cutting called campdrafting that highlights the horse's innate ability to work and control livestock. It appears that the Australian Stock horse is here to stay.

characteristics

ORIGIN: Australia **HEIGHT:** Approximately 14.2–16 hh **COLORS:** All colors **PHYSIQUE:** Should have good muscle overall; sloped shoulders; slightly sloped croup; strong back; good legs; powerful hindquarters **FEATURES:** Tough, good cow sense; fine athlete; good stamina **USES:** Riding, ranch work

ancestry

- VARIOUS SPANISH BLOODLINES
- INDONESIAN TIMOR PONIES
- NATIVE BRITISH PONY STOCK

- ARABIAN
- BARB
- QUARTER HORSE
- THOROUGHBRED

the camargue

Long before the Romans entered the Rhône River delta in the south of France, horses had made the region their home. Today those horses, the feral horses of the Camargue, continue to maintain their herds in the marshy area, where a lovely white equine apparition is the last thing one might expect to see.

Molded since prehistoric times by the rugged terrain, sparse vegetation, and extreme temperatures of their homeland—and by infusions of outside blood from army horses of Arabian, Spanish, and other fine bloodlines that have traveled through the region during various times in history—Camargues are survivors. As they have done for millennia, the horses exist in natural equine herds of mares and small dark foals that will gradually lighten in color with maturity, each herd headed by a dominant stallion.

While many a Camargue horse has through the years been taken out of the herd and trained for a domestic life working cattle, or carrying packs or tourists through its home territory,

most Camargues exist as wild as is possible nowadays. They are, however, subjected to some outside management, designed to keep the herds under control in size and quality. Personnel with the Biological Research Station of *la Tour du Valat* monitor the herds closely and regularly, gelding colts they deem to be unfit for breeding, all the while studying the relationships displayed within this unique, confined, and somewhat isolated population that allow humans to witness the social interactions and lifestyles of wild horses. The Camargue has made priceless contributions to human understanding of equine behavior that could never have otherwise been discovered and researched.

characteristics

ORIGIN: France, Rhône River Delta **HEIGHT:** 13–14 hh **COLORS:** Born dark, lighten to white between four to seven years of age **PHYSIQUE:** Well-muscled with short back and neck; prominent withers; deep chest; straight shoulders; strong legs; hard feet **FEATURES:** Rugged, independent, easy keeper; robust **USES:** Riding, packing, also run wild

ancestry

- **NATIVE FRENCH STOCK**
- **ARABIAN**
- **BARB**
- **THOROUGHBRED**

the cleveland bay

When the imagination travels back in time to eighteenth century England and conjures up images of carriage horses pulling black carriages along uneven cobble-stoned streets, the horse providing the necessary muscle is very likely a **Cleveland Bay.**

Long renowned for its unmatched skill as a plow, carriage, coach, pack, and all-around driving horse, the Cleveland Bay, England's oldest established breed, was historically celebrated throughout its native England for hundreds of years. Originally named the Chapman for its partnership with early traveling salesmen by that same name, the breed's name was officially changed to Cleveland Bay in 1884 in honor of its easily matched bay color and its home region by the newly formed Cleveland Bay Society.

The launching of this society, which was dedicated to preserving the pure bloodlines of the breed, was crucial to the Cleveland Bay, for this very old breed has been faced consistently throughout its history with extinction. Perhaps cursed with the misfortune of crossing beautifully with

Thoroughbreds for the production of stunning carriage and saddle horses, its own identity as a purebred has frequently been threatened from such practices that could lead to a fatal dilution of the gene pool.

Luckily, the breed's salvation has been the generations of dedicated enthusiasts who have followed the Cleveland Bay through its history and have done all they can to protect it from vanishing into the genes of other breeds. Although this breed's numbers are not as great today as they were when society relied upon horses for transportation, the purebred population now seems secure in England, especially with Queen Elizabeth II as a patron, and numbers are beginning to increase in the United States, as well, where it also once enjoyed a strong following.

characteristics

ancestry

ORIGIN: England, Cleveland **HEIGHT:** 16–16.2 hh **COLORS:** Bay; a small white star; some gray in the black mane and tail is permissible **PHYSIQUE:** Well-muscled; deep, wide girth; medium back; deep, sloping shoulders; strong loins; level hindquarters; good joints; excellent feet; slender neck **FEATURES:** Powerful; elegant; level-headed **USES:** Riding, driving, light draft

- **NATIVE CHAPMAN HORSE**
- **THOROUGHBRED**

the don

The story of the Don, a horse hailing from the Don and Volga Rivers steppe region of Russia, would read like an epic novel. This horse, a mix of hardy native steppe horses and those of the nomadic Turks and Mongols, and such fine hot-blooded Oriental horses as the Karabakh and the Turkoman, was the horse of the Cossacks since the sixteenth century and probably earlier.

Of course, these warriors demanded a horse of great courage, stamina, and athletic ability, and they certainly found it in the Don. The highlight of the breed's phenomenal cavalry career occurred when Napoleon's army was driven from Russia in the winter of 1812. While French horses perished, dying of starvation and exhaustion in the frigid Russian winter by the thousands, the Cossacks' Dons withstood the conditions with ease. And, still they had the energy to make the long journey back to Moscow.

While the Dons of the Cossacks were praised for their collective stamina and courage, it was not until after the Napoleon campaign that serious selective breeding of Dons began. Though it was upgraded with infusions of Thoroughbred, Arabian, Karabakh, and Russian Saddle horse from the late eighteenth century on, standardization in conformation of the breed and even its soundness have remained somewhat elusive. What has remained constant in the Don is the horse's tough constitution, its ability to work and survive on meager rations, and its typically light chestnut coat that often shimmers with a metallic sheen inherited from its Karabakh and Turkoman ancestors.

With its original purpose now obsolete, the Don is free to ply its talents in less violent pursuits. Though its conformation is criticized by purists for its deviation from the classic equine form, its endurance and stamina are unmatched, and its numbers remain healthy—as does the demand for its genetic contributions to other breeds seeking upgrades in stamina. The Don still suffers from some conformation problems. The structure of its hip joint and angle of the pelvis often hinder free movement, and its action can be short and quite jarring.

characteristics

ORIGIN: Russia, Don River steppes **HEIGHT:** 15.2–16.2 hh **COLORS:** Light chestnut or bay, perhaps with a golden, almost metallic sheen **PHYSIQUE:** Straight shoulders; low withers; straight, broad back; long legs with a tendency toward problems in the knees, hocks, and pasterns; medium neck and head **FEATURES:** Tireless, easy keeper; courageous **USES:** Riding, light driving

ancestry

- INDIGENOUS RUSSIAN STEPPE HORSE
- TURKOMAN
- KARABAKH
- ARABIAN
- ORLOV TROTTER
- THOROUGHBRED

the french trotter

Given the great love of the French people for harness racing, it is no wonder that nation boasts a much-treasured jewel of a trotting breed to satisfy their racing pleasures. That horse is the French Trotter, or Norman Trotter, a horse whose development was set into motion in 1836 after the first French harness races were run in the breed's home territory of Normandy.

Native to one of Europe's premier horse-breeding regions, within decades of its founding, the French Trotter, though not so named as yet, had become a presence throughout France. Its breeders did this by enlisting Thoroughbreds and Norfolk Trotters from England and Standardbreds from the United States to place their collective stamp of skill and speed on the new French version of a harness racer.

The first stage in this process was the development of a horse referred to as the Anglo-Norman, a horse that would beget both the Selle Français and the French Trotter. Though it raced throughout the nineteenth century, the French Trotter was not officially granted its own studbook until 1922.

Though the French Trotter, renowned for its smooth, diagonal trot, is the product of fine bloodlines originating outside its native borders, it is a unique entity within the worldwide harness racing community. It is larger and more powerful than its typical counterpart, and for good reason. French harness racing involves both the traditional wheeled version as well as a unique under-saddle variation, the latter requiring rather more strength and endurance than might be needed of a horse participating solely in the traditional style of racing.

characteristics

ORIGIN: France, Normandy **HEIGHT:** Average 16.1 hh **COLORS:** Bay and chestnut are most common **PHYSIQUE:** Strong overall with prominent withers; sloped shoulders; powerful hindquarters; sloping croup; hard feet; straight profile

FEATURES: Races both in harness and under saddle; powerful, spirited

USES: Harness racing, riding

ancestry

- ANGLO-NORMAN
- NORFOLK ROADSTER
- STANDARDBRED

68

the hackney
and hackney pony

England is often considered the Mecca of harness horses. Some of the world's finest driving horses hail from the island nation, where they have been selectively and carefully bred for centuries. Two of these animals, and perhaps the most dazzling of the bunch, are the Hackney and its smaller cousin the Hackney pony.

An entire herd of breeds, most hailing from trotting backgrounds, were involved in the development of the Hackney, which preceded the development of the Hackney pony. On the time line, the process occurred simultaneously with the efforts being made to establish the Thoroughbred during the seventeenth and eighteenth centuries; in the long run, both would emerge as national treasures.

The Hackney was the result of a blending of Norfolk Trotters and Yorkshire coach horses, the newly established, quite flashy, high-stepping breed first enlisted as a horse for hire—the engine for nineteenth-century taxi-cabs. In 1883, the Hackney Horse Society was founded to govern the breeding of Hackneys, which quickly became coveted coach and carriage horses, as well as highly celebrated show horses, the latter role being its forte in the twentieth century, when the demand for horse-drawn taxis was replaced by the combustion engine.

The Hackney pony, too, is a popular and even flashier show animal—and a much coveted export to other countries. An offshoot of the Hackney horse, the Hackney pony shares the genetic heritage of its larger cousin, in addition to infusions of Fell and Welsh Pony blood. Whether horse or pony, the Hackney never ceases to delight spectators with its unique way of going, a natural gift it inherited from generations of some of England's finest harness horses, and its ability to transport its admirers back to a simpler time when horses ruled the roads.

characteristics

ORIGIN: England **HEIGHT:** Horse: 14–15.3 hh; Pony: 14 hh **COLORS:** Black, bay, dark brown, chestnut **PHYSIQUE:** Compact and elegantly muscled with long neck; small head; broad chest; sloping shoulders; straight back; high tail-set; excellent feet and legs **FEATURES:** Flashy, innate trotter; excellent show animal **USES:** Light driving, particularly for show

ancestry

PONY:
- ENGLISH TROTTING STRAINS
- FELL PONY • WELSH MOUNTAIN PONY

HORSE:
- EARLY ENGLISH TROTTING STRAINS
- ARABIAN
- YORKSHIRE AND NORFOLK TROTTERS
- THOROUGHBRED

the lipizzaner

That General George S. Patton was fond of horses is no secret. That he possibly saved Austria's illustrious Spanish Riding School and its legendary white Lipizzaner horses from destruction may not be so widely known.

But that is precisely what happened in the spring of 1945. Germany had lost World War II. Miraculously, Hitler had chosen early on to spare the Riding School, but it had been scattered, and moved out of its Viennese home. As the war came to an end, the school's director feared for the fate of his beloved horses. In a dramatic move, he presented the school and its horses to General Patton and asked that they be placed

under American protection until the war's end. Needless to say, General Patton complied.

Lipizzaners are the product of some of the most successful breeding efforts in history. It all began when magnificent horses of Spanish blood, considered the best in the world at the time, were brought into Austria by members of the monarchy in 1562. A breeding program ensued in Lipizza (formerly a part of Italy, now in Yugoslavia) that would ultimately lead to the development of the Lipizzaner horse, a vision of white that seems to sprout wings whenever it performs. It led to the establishment of Vienna's Spanish Riding School, which has for more than 250 years offered those horses a home both for training and for demonstrating their incredible "airs above the ground," a vocation known as High School, which is classic horsemanship taken to the extreme.

The Lipizzaners of the Spanish Riding School are now bred at the stud in Piber. Here dark-colored foals that will lighten in color with age prance and play with their dams. Training will begin gradually. In fact, these athletically gifted horses will not feel the weight of riders on their backs until they reach four or five years of age.

But Lipizzaners reside outside of Austria too. A well-known if not abundantly populous breed worldwide, they enjoy a dedicated following of so-called civilian horse owners. These fortunate individuals value their horses' intelligence and docile nature as well as their talents, applying all in their pursuit of excellence in such activities as dressage, driving, combined training, and even plain old trail riding.

characteristics

ORIGIN: Austria **HEIGHT:** 15–16 hh **COLORS:** Born dark, lighten to gray or white with maturity **PHYSIQUE:** Muscular overall; long head of straight or convex profile; arched neck; sloping shoulders and croup; long back; deep chest; clean joints; good feet and legs **FEATURES:** Intelligent, natural show horse; proud **USES:** Riding, light driving

ancestry

- **NATIVE SPANISH/ IBERIAN STOCK**
- **ARABIAN**
- **KLADRUBER**
- **FREDERICKSBORG**

the miniature horse

While at first glance one might assume that the Miniature horse is naturally a pony, such an assumption would be incorrect. A close look at this diminutive animal reveals why.

Though this is a tiny animal, the foals of which are no larger than large puppies, it is a horse in every sense of the word, having been bred down from larger horses to create, as its name implies, an animal with all the classic characteristics of a full-sized horse in a miniature package.

This is no new trend. The miniaturization of horses began centuries ago when royal families and other wealthy aristocrats decided that their children—children who had everything, no doubt—simply must have miniature horses. While ponies are naturally small, having evolved that way for survival within what are typically harsh and rugged native pony environments, Miniature horses have been bred down artificially from small representatives of larger horse breeds. As a result, various types of Minis exist, some exhibiting decidedly Arabian characteristics, for example, while others may possess a chunkier stock-horse conformation.

Though Miniature horses are not strong enough to be ridden, they are popular show horses, participating in breed shows and classes designed to showcase their unique attributes. Enthusiasts can purchase specially adapted miniaturized tack and even carts, allowing the small horses to demonstrate their ability in, among others, halter and driving classes. But the Miniature horse's true calling is that of pet and companion, making this breed the ideal choice for anyone who has ever dreamed of owning a horse that could join the family in the living room from time to time.

characteristics

ancestry

ORIGIN: Worldwide **HEIGHT:** For American registration, 34 inches or less from the last hair of the mane **COLORS:** All colors and patterns **PHYSIQUE:** Varies, but should be horse-type conformation, not that of a pony **FEATURES:** Best suited as pet; easily spoiled; good show horse **USES:** Companionship, light driving, halter

• VARIOUS HORSE BREEDS, DEPENDING ON TYPE

the morgan

Once upon a time in colonial America, there lived a small bay stallion named Figure. Though his horse was dismissed universally for his small size, Figure's owner, Justin Morgan, was able to rent him out to a Vermont farmer, who soon discovered that this diminutive animal was nothing short of a wonder horse.

Blessed with almost supernatural strength, speed, and stamina —and a sweet disposition, to boot—Figure, who was later renamed Justin Morgan following his owner's death, became a legend in Vermont and beyond and has remained so for more than 200 years. In fact, he would ultimately be immortalized in Marguerite Henry's book *Justin Morgan Had A Horse*.

Though this horse was more than up to the challenge, life was no picnic for Figure. He worked tirelessly all day, hauling logs and pulling plows across the rocky Vermont soil and was then expected to entertain the masses with his unmatched brawn during his off hours. A fearless animal that no other horse could beat in pulling contests or races, this small hard-working horse went on to found the dynasty that is the Morgan breed. After proving his physical mettle, he then proved to be quite prepotent, and the demand for his stud services spread throughout New England.

No one knows for sure just where those dynamic genes originated, and indeed many breeds have jumped to claim ownership, but it is presumed that little Figure was probably a combination of Welsh Cob and Friesian, perhaps a bit of Thoroughbred for good measure, and maybe even a splash of Norwegian Fjord. The world will never know. What is known is that the Morgan, perhaps the only breed to have truly been founded by a single extraordinary sire, has since gone on to influence the development of countless other breeds as well.

characteristics

ORIGIN: United States, Vermont **HEIGHT:** 14.1–15.2 hh **COLORS:** Preferably dark with little or no white markings; bay is classic **PHYSIQUE:** Compact and solid with sturdy legs; somewhat arched neck; short back; sloping shoulders; prominent withers; deep chest **FEATURES:** Intelligent, alert; fast; versatile **USES:** Riding, driving, light draft, police work

ancestry

• FRIESIAN
• WELSH COB
• NATIVE AMERICAN STOCK

Regardless of the magical alchemy that produced its founding sire, the Morgan breed is today immensely popular. Obviously inspired by the small horse that started it all more than two centuries ago, it continues to excel in virtually all equine activities, yet always retaining its sprightly disposition and gentle manner. Much beloved by children for its compact structure and gentle nature, admired as a successful show horse both under saddle and in harness (despite some contemporary conflict between enthusiasts who are devoted to the old-style Morgan and those who are promoting a flashier, more refined type of Morgan), and the first choice of recruiters seeking robust, level-headed police mounts, the Morgan's place in history is secure.

all: **The head of the Morgan indicates quality with a straight or slightly concave profile, widely flaring nostrils when the horse is in action or excited, and expressive eyes and ears, creating an interested friendly impression.**

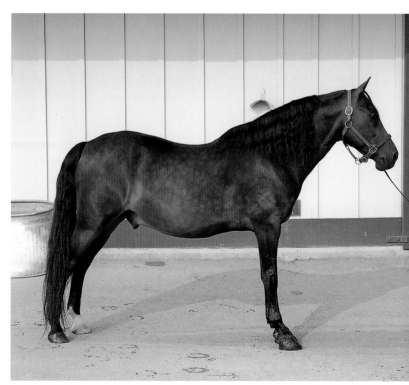

the mustang

Though millions of horses have been raised in the United States through the centuries, those horses, like many of the human residents of the nation themselves, are the descendants of immigrants. America was horseless when the first Spanish conquistadores arrived in the sixteenth century, so it was up to them and the countless others who followed from all over the world, to populate the land with the equine species.

The word Mustang comes from the Spanish *mestengo* or *mesteño*, meaning "stranger" or "outsider." Mustangs are descendants of the horses brought over by Columbus and the Spanish conquistadores and they thrived in the western region of the United States as favorites of cowboys and Native Americans until the nineteenth century, when settlers and the coming of the railways threatened the Native American's nomadic way of life. The buffalo herds were exhausted, the Mustangs retreated to higher ground, and their numbers greatly depleted.

As they have done for centuries, Mustangs continue to run wild in the western United States, but their overall fate remains uncertain. While their story is romantic, their circumstances have not always been so. Since their arrival, Mustangs have had to wrestle with opposition, destroyed by ranchers and settlers who deemed them threats to agriculture and unnecessary competition for grazing lands and water earmarked for domestic livestock. But in the early 1970s, federal action was taken to end the mistreatment and mass extermination of America's Mustangs, which are now protected under the law. They are rounded up periodically, and

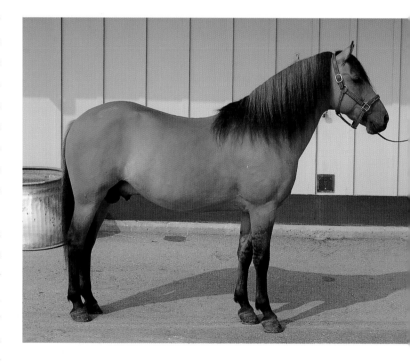

some are adopted out to the public—and controversy always follows the management of the program—but the Mustangs are protected and the majority of the American public wants to see them stay that way.

characteristics

ORIGIN: United States **HEIGHT:** 14–15 hh **COLORS:** All colors, as well as pinto and Appaloosa patterns **PHYSIQUE:** Varies by type **FEATURES:** Romantic past; feral; athletic **USES:** Riding when properly trained, also run wild

ancestry

- NATIVE SPANISH STOCK
- ARABIAN
- BARB
- TURKOMAN
- QUARTER HORSE

the orlov trotter

In eighteenth-century Russia, Count Alexei Grigorievich Orlov decided that Russia needed a harness-racing horse. He then set about making that idea into a reality. Until the end of the century, he crossed some of the finest breeds known to man: Arabian, Friesian, Thoroughbred, and Don, to name but a few.

The lineage began with an Arab stallion, Smetanka, who sired a moderate colt, named Polkan, who was then mated with a Danish mare and produced a great trotting stallion called Bars I, often regarded as the founding father of the Orlov Trotter. Throughout the nineteenth century, the Orlov Trotter enjoyed a demanding racing career (even though it could not approach the American Standardbred in speed or talent), and it also found a niche as a carriage horse among the elite, who admired this large, powerful horse of fine pedigree, elegant stature, and sprightly gait. At the beginning of the twentieth century, as a tribute to their talent, Orlovs were recruited for a new breeding venture, in which they were crossed with Standardbreds to produce what would become the Russian Trotter.

This new kid on the block, however, did not render the Orlov obsolete. Its predecessor had thrived in its driving career off the track and was still coveted for that purpose. The twentieth century thus spelled the end to the Orlov's serious harness-racing career, even though efforts continue to be made to upgrade the breed's competitive edge in this area. But the breed has essentially moved on, plying its skills in the riding ring, in the breeding barn, on the road, and yes, on Russian tracks reserved solely for the display of this old and very distinctive breed's harness-racing talents.

characteristics

ORIGIN: Russia **HEIGHT:** Approximately 16–17 hh **COLORS:** Gray is most common; also black, chestnut, bay **PHYSIQUE:** Muscular overall with distinctive head; long neck; wide chest; long, straight back; substantial legs, sometimes with feathering; good joints **FEATURES:** Elegant; versatile; sound **USES:** Riding, harness racing, light driving

ancestry

- **ARABIAN**
- **NATIVE DANISH AND DUTCH STOCK**
- **NATIVE RUSSIAN STOCK**
- **THOROUGHBRED**

the paint horse

Though the pinto spotted pattern is a natural equine pattern that is readily recognizable throughout the world, and though the Paint is a horse that sports that design, a horse of pinto patterns is not necessarily a Paint. In fact, some registered Paints are solid-colored horses without even a suggestion of painted designs.

While this may sound confusing, the American Paint Horse Association (APHA) clarifies the quandary by explaining that unlike Pinto registration, Paint registration is based on bloodlines—namely, Quarter Horse, Thoroughbred, and Paint bloodlines. A horse that cannot demonstrate the proper registration attachments cannot be registered as a Paint. So though the APHA, one of the largest breed registries in the United States, is essentially a color registry, it actually falls somewhere in the middle of a traditional registry and one reserved solely for horses and color.

Registration politics aside, pinto patterns that today exist in the United States, patterns that may be either Tobiano or Overo, are thought to derive from horses so marked which

Spanish explorers bought with them to the New World. Because pinto patterns exist in horses all over the world, it is logical that some of those horses would have carried the genetic blueprints for those patterns. Given the popularity of the Paint in the US as an eye-catching performance horse in both English and western events, a horse that embodies both pinto patterns and the immense popularity of the Thoroughbred and the Quarter Horse, it would appear those blueprints have found quite a devoted and permanent following in America. Though the Paint's flashy appearance can meet with some prejudice in such English-style disciplines as dressage and hunt, the future of this versatile animal is secure in all realms of equine endeavor.

characteristics

ancestry

ORIGIN: United States **HEIGHT:** 15–16 hh **COLORS:** Tobiano or Overo pinto patterns (see Pinto, page 80) **PHYSIQUE:** Depends on breed, but overall should be balanced; well-muscled and constructed for athletic endeavor
FEATURES: Eye-catching, versatile **USES:** Riding

- **NATIVE BRITISH AND SPANISH STOCK**
- **QUARTER HORSE**

the palomino

The Palomino, a horse of gold with a white mane and tail, has found a niche within activities that aren't naturally included on a list of traditional equine callings.

The Palomino has been around for a long, long time, having existed all over the world as a natural genetic coat-color expression in all types of horses. But through the years, Palominos have come to be associated most closely with the American West; western show events were considered natural venues for Palomino competitors. Deeming the Palomino a color breed, American Palomino registries welcome horses of all backgrounds as long as they satisfy the color requirement of being three shades darker or lighter than the color of a newly minted gold coin. White is permitted on the head and lower legs only.

The name is presumed to have come about when Queen Isabella of Spain gave some of these golden-colored horses to Cortés to take to the Americas, who on arrival presented one to Juan de Palomino.

The American Palomino has enjoyed quite an illustrious show business career. Palominos have not only delighted audiences with their golden glory on the big and small screens, but also inspired the formation of surprisingly enthusiastic fan clubs during the peak of their popularity. Hardly a parade passes by, either, without at least one Palomino, within its ranks, dazzling spectators with its golden beauty.

77

characteristics

ORIGIN: The color is worldwide; color registration in the United States
HEIGHT: Varies with breed **COLORS:** Golden coat with white or flaxen mane and tail **PHYSIQUE:** Varies with breed **FEATURES:** Striking appearance
USES: Riding, parades

ancestry

- **NATIVE SPANISH STOCK**
- **MUSTANG**
- **QUARTER HORSE**

the paso fino

Often neglected in accounts of Christopher Columbus' "discovery" of the New World are the equine passengers aboard his ships.

Of course, a European seafaring explorer at the turn of the fifteenth and sixteenth centuries would not dream of venturing forth without horses, and Columbus was no exception. The equine cargo of his second voyage was of special significance to contemporary fans of the Paso Fino horse, for from those horses, horses of primarily Andalusian and Spanish Jennet blood, the Paso Fino would emerge.

The horses from that second voyage were delivered to the Caribbean island now known as the Dominican Republic, where they would provide the foundation for Caribbean breeding farms designed to supply subsequent explorers and settlements with horses. The Paso Fino is one of the three main types of South American gaited horse which came from the same genetic stock.

Eventually, Puerto Rico would become home to the Paso Fino line, a family of horses that exhibited a special fiery spirit called *brio*, a dramatic appearance, and a unique and very comfortable lateral four-beat gait called the *paso fino*.

While a partnership with people seeking to explore and conquer is no longer part of the Paso Fino's agenda, it continues to display its unique gait, which is passed on naturally from generation to generation, much to the delight of its many fans in the United States. Today's Paso Finos are fine candidates for both pleasure and show, performing their famed gait on the trail and in the show ring at varying speeds, ranging from the walk-speed *paso fino*, to the trot-speed *paso corto*, to the rapid *paso largo*.

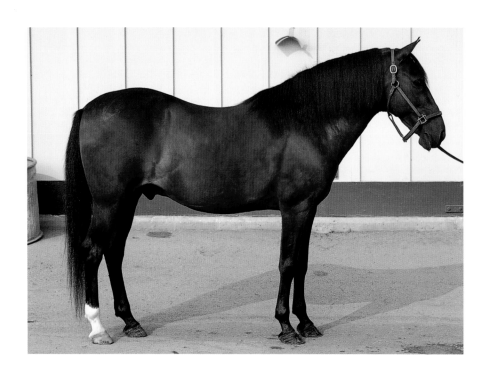

characteristics

ORIGIN: Puerto Rico **HEIGHT:** 14–15 hh **COLORS:** Most colors
PHYSIQUE: Refined yet strong, with small head; deep shoulders; typically short back; straight, delicate, though densely boned legs **FEATURES:** Affectionate and personable; quiet and calm in hand, spirited under saddle **USES:** Riding

ancestry

- BARB
- SPANISH JENNET
- ANDALUSIAN

the peruvian paso

The Peruvian Paso is a distant blood brother to the Paso Fino, both bred from the same stock imported into the Americas by the Spanish *conquistadores* in the sixteenth century.

The Peruvian Paso has gradually evolved with different functional characteristics, such as, the ability to work in high altitudes. It can also carry a rider comfortably over long distances and mountainous terrain. These qualities have been selectively and carefully developed within the breed from the horses originally brought to Peru in 1531 by Francisco Pizarro. The result was a beautiful horse of predominantly Andalusian and Barb blood famed for a unique four-beat lateral gait—a horse that continues to represent the golden era of Spanish equine culture.

What stands out in the Peruvian Paso is not only its great beauty and gentle temperament, but the comfort its unique gait provides to the rider. Historically, the Peruvians embraced this horse for its ability to carry them comfortably and reliably over what could be hostile, unpredictable ground. It possesses mountain sense and is independent, calm, and sure-footed. Today, in this same spirit, enthusiasts both in Peru and the United States display the breed's gifts in Peruvian Paso breed shows with riders often dressed in traditional Peruvian costume, and praise the breed as the ultimate pleasure and trail horse.

characteristics

ORIGIN: Peru **HEIGHT:** 14–15.1 hh **COLORS:** Most colors
PHYSIQUE: Compact and muscular; small head; prominent withers; sloped shoulders and croup; good legs **FEATURES:** Gentle disposition; spirited; comfortable ride **USES:** Riding

ancestry

- SPANISH JENNET
- ANDALUSIAN
- BARB
- NATIVE SPANISH PACK HORSE

the pinto

As Stone Age cave paintings have indicated, it would appear that horses of vibrant pinto patterns have existed worldwide for thousands of years.

Few breeds are immune from the genetic code that paints a horse with color, and for enthusiasts, there is no greater thrill than spotting that color on the coat of a newborn foal.

Though pinto patterns are an international equine phenomenon, they have long taken on a special significance within the United States. Originally transported to North America via the horses of the Spanish explorers, pinto patterns were considered a gift from the spirits to the Native Americans, who held painted horses in the utmost esteem. Such horses, they believed, were infused with great power

above: **Pinto: Dark Warrior, Grandeur Arabians, Florida, USA.**

embodied in their natural war paint. American cowboys, too, often coveted horses of painted patterns, perhaps secretly sharing the Native Americans' view of the special magic within those bold splashes of color.

So enamored has the United States been of Pinto horses,

characteristics

ancestry

ORIGIN: Worldwide, but registration originated in the United States
HEIGHT: Depends on breed **COLORS:** All colors (skewbald and piebald) in Tobiano and Overo patterns **PHYSIQUE:** Depends on breed **FEATURES:**
Eye-catching; unique **USES:** Depends on breed, popular in shows

- **VARIOUS BREEDS OF AMERICAN AND EUROPEAN ORIGIN**

left: **Texano, a pinto show horse used in equestrian entertainment.**

below: **A pinto horse with a one-wall eye.**

that the Pinto Horse Association of America (PtHA) was established in 1947 to celebrate horses and ponies of all breeds that are blessed with pinto patterns. Having struck a universal cord, the PtHA now boasts members and registered horses and ponies throughout the world, the animals required to display one of two recognized patterns.

The *Tobiano* exhibits smooth-edged, uniformly shaped splashes of color that typically extend across the back, flanks, and head. The *Overo*, on the other hand, typically sports white across its back and its face, imparting an appearance that is quite distinct from that of the Tobiano. Adding to that unique appearance are the design of the Overo's color splashes, which are typically lacier around the edges than the

straight, clean lines of the Tobiano. Pintos are further described by color, as is typically done in Britain. A *piebald* is a pinto of black and white, while a *skewbald* is a pinto of white and any other color.

Pintos never cease to attract attention, whether on the trail, in a parade, at pasture, or in the show ring. This latter situation can benefit the horse in a western event where pinto patterns, traditional symbols as they are of the American West, are considered a bonus, but in more conservative English events, judges may not appreciate the flashy display of color. Yet times are changing, and even the very formal discipline of dressage now boasts its share of pinto color in the ranks of its equine competitors. Increased acceptance will surely follow.

przewalski's horse

While several breeds of horses run wild in various regions of the world, there is only one true wild horse: Przewalski's Horse. Named by Polish Colonel Nikolai Przewalski, who spotted a small herd of the animals in Mongolia in 1881 (though they had previously been seen by other individuals), Przewalski's Horse boasts its own species name and a wild, untrainable heart.

Przewalski's Horse is classically primitive in appearance, its dun color with dark dorsal stripe, striped legs, short neck, muscular physique, and coarse erect mane reminiscent of Stone Age cave paintings discovered in Europe and Asia. This unique animal, which probably once roamed throughout Europe and Asia, has not changed through the millennia, and given its resistance to what efforts have been made to tame it, it does not look like it has any intention of doing so.

Up until a few years ago, no more Przewalski's Horses remained in the wild in China and Mongolia, having been all but exterminated by habitat destruction and hunting. Those that remained were protected in zoos. Thanks to the Foundation for the Preservation and Protection of the Przewalski Horse, efforts are now underway to increase its numbers through captive breeding and release programs. Sixteen horses were released into the wild at Mustain Nuruu, near Waanbaatar on July 5, 1992, and programs continue for further horses to be returned to other designated areas in Asia.

right: **There are currently around 1,200 Przewalski Horses in captivity. Following captive breeding and release programs there are now three herds that have successfully been released into the wild.**

characteristics

ORIGIN: Mongolia **HEIGHT:** 12–14 hh **COLORS:** Primitive dun with dark dorsal stripe and zebra stripes on the legs **PHYSIQUE:** Short, stocky, and primitive with large head; straight profile; deep chest; long back; heavily muscled **FEATURES:** Wild; untamable; strong herd instincts **USES:** None

ancestry

• **PRIMITIVE ASIAN/MONGOLIAN WILD HORSES**

tennessee walking horse

One of the sweetest-tempered horses to emerge from America's equine history is the Tennessee Walking Horse.

With humble beginnings as a basic transportation horse in nineteenth-century America—in Tennessee, to be exact—the Walker was bred from, among others, Narragansett Pacer, Canadian Pacer, Thoroughbred, American Saddlebred, Standardbred and Morgan bloodlines, as a sure-footed horse of great stamina that could carry a rider for hours over rough terrain with astounding comfort.

In addition to being comfortable to ride, and of sound constitution, the breed also proved pleasant to look at. The plantation owner surveying his domain, the country doctor making house calls, and the traveling preacher all found their equine wishes granted by the Tennessee Walker.

The twentieth century brought a new calling to this horse.

As modern-day equine enthusiasts direct their attentions toward more pleasurable pursuits, they find the Walker again granting their wishes with its comfortable ride and gentle disposition. But recent history has also spelled controversy for this breed, a popular show horse throughout the United States. The conflict arose several years ago over the illicit practice of soring, in which painful chemicals and equipment are applied to the show horse's feet to cause it to lift them higher when performing the gait known as the running walk. This led to the passage of the US Horse Protection Act and many related lawsuits since. Unfortunately, the battle still rages, unfairly tainting the name of a sweet-tempered animal whose true calling is that of quintessential family horse.

characteristics

ORIGIN: United States, Tennessee **HEIGHT:** 15–16 hh **COLORS:** Most solid colors and pinto patterns; black is considered classic **PHYSIQUE:** Short neck and back with strong hindquarters and sloping croup; well-boned legs; large, plain head **FEATURES:** Kind disposition; family horse; comfortable ride **USES:** Riding

ancestry

- NATIVE SPANISH STOCK
- NARRAGANSETT PACER
- MORGAN
- THOROUGHBRED
- STANDARDBRED
- SADDLEBRED

the thoroughbred

Aristocratic athlete – that is the Thoroughbred. The moment the Thoroughbred foal arrives, the hot blood it shares with all the Thoroughbreds who came before makes itself known. As soon as it can walk, it feels the urge to run, and soon it will do just that. Granted freedom to roam the pasture alongside its dam, the foal's legs will take on a life of their own, and the youngster will take flight with the energy inherent to all members of this fine breed.

Though many horses contributed to the development and establishment of the Thoroughbred, also referred to fondly as the Blood Horse, three founding sires are credited with ensuring the Thoroughbred's place in history. It began in 1660, when Charles II, a great racing enthusiast, was crowned king of England. Although there had been attempts to breed faster and faster horses in Britain for centuries, Charles recognized the valuable contribution the swift horses of Oriental blood might make to English breeding programs. A great many of these horses were imported for this grand mission, from which the legendary three—the Byerley Turk, the Darley Arabian, and the Godolphin Arabian (or Barb)—emerged. The racing world—as well as the horse world at large—has never been the same.

What resulted from these efforts and these sires, was a family of horses that were not only fast, but breathtakingly beautiful as well. Established by selective breeding throughout the seventeenth and eighteenth centuries, the Thoroughbred continues to dominate as the racing breed supreme worldwide, the annals of Thoroughbred history being peppered with names that even those who are not members of the horsy set readily recognize. Big money has followed the breed through the generations, as well. Thoroughbreds typically command higher prices, sometimes from corporate syndicates, than any other breed on the planet.

But there is more to the Thoroughbred than racing. This aristocratic breed is also valued highly for its considerable skills in the Olympic disciplines—dressage, three-day eventing and showjumping—and international equestrian teams are frequently populated by a hefty complement of top-winning Thoroughbreds. So successful has it been in these endeavors, that the breed has also been enlisted to assist genetically in the development of Europe's fine athletic warmblood breeds, the Thoroughbred often being the only outside breed approved for that purpose. Needless to say, this talented and typically hot-blooded horse is best reserved for experienced riders, but obtaining the skills required is a grand goal to which the fledgling equestrian may enthusiastically aspire.

characteristics

ORIGIN: England **HEIGHT:** Approximately 15–17 hh **COLORS:** Most solid colors **PHYSIQUE:** Sloping shoulders; longish back; prominent withers; strong hindquarters; long legs; small hooves; long neck; refined head; typically straight profile; large nostrils **FEATURES:** Elegant; athletic; hot-blooded **USES:** Racing, hunting, and most equestrian sports

ancestry

- **ARABIAN**
- **TURKOMAN**
- **BARB**
- **NATIVE SPANISH AND ORIENTAL STOCK**

right: **Secretariat, a well-known US Thoroughbred stallion, had the head of a typical Thoroughbred—elegant, defined with good skin, chiselled features, large nostrils that can flare easily to permit maximum air flow, and a somewhat superior air.**

above: **Racing at Santa Anita, USA. The Thoroughbred was bred purely for racing, for the enjoyment of the British royalty and aristocracy. Horse racing is now one of the most popular, expensive but profitable sports in the world.**

left: **With an enviable reputation as both racehorse and Olympic-level athlete, the Thoroughbred has been called upon to refine and enhance many horse breeds throughout the world.**

the dutch warmblood

While Germany is typically the first nation that comes to mind when the subject is European warmbloods, Holland too, boasts its own contributions to these spectacular sport horses. One of these is the Dutch Warmblood. A big, bold horse originally of Friesian influence by way of the Gelderlander and the Groningen, it has enjoyed considerable success in dressage and jumping events on a world class level.

While in some countries the breeding of warmbloods is carried out under state control through state-run studs and stallion and mare inspections, the Dutch Warmblood is bred within a more personalized, non-governmental program. At the heart of this program are the small breeding operations of Dutch farmers, who as a community have for decades worked to sculpt this gem of a horse first into a valued farm and carriage horse with roots deep within Holland's rich agricultural traditions, and then, with the twentieth-century's emphasis on equine competition, into a top-flight athlete.

Breeding started in 1958 and the organization responsible for enforcing the strict breeding policies guiding the production of Dutch Warmbloods is the Warmbloed Paardenstamboek In Nederland. This group oversees the breeding of the distinct types of Dutch Warmbloods, all of which are targeted toward such specific uses as riding, dressage and jumping competitions, and driving. Each horse used for breeding is judged and graded by officials from the breed registry, who try to put as much emphasis on temperament as they do on physical structure when approving mares and stallions as breeding stock. Originally bred for showjumping,

the Dutch Warmblood has had great success in dressage with its stylish action, a cooperative temperament, and a reputation as easy to handle, the Dutch Warmblood has flowing gaits which makes it attractive to watch, and allows it to function well in competition.

characteristics

ORIGIN: The Netherlands **HEIGHT:** 15.3–16.3 hh **COLORS:** Typically chestnut, bay, black, and gray **PHYSIQUE:** Varies with type, but should be a big-boned athletic horse with refined features; well-muscled legs; well-ribbed body, excellent feet **FEATURES:** Easy to handle; athletically versatile **USES:** Riding, driving

ancestry

- **GRONINGEN**
- **GELDERLANDER**
- **THOROUGHBRED**
- **HANOVERIAN**

the friesian

Another jewel in Holland's equine crown is the Friesian; a big, black horse with feathered feet that has quietly been employed all over Europe and the United States for the establishment and improvement of other breeds for centuries. An old breed developed as a hard-working farm hand, dynamic saddle horse, and elegant carriage horse, the Friesian is also quite breathtaking, evoking images of knights on horseback.

Its old name, Harddraver, means "good trotter" in Dutch, and although its influence has been widely acknowledged, the Friesian is not typically thought of as a warmblood in the classic sense. It is not seen taking oxers in the show ring or tackling cross-country courses in the Olympics, nor is it seen in many regional shows performing dressage, but when it does appear, it dazzles. People cannot take their eyes off the beautiful black Friesian. Until the release of a film entitled *Ladyhawke* several years back, many people, especially people in the United States, had never heard of the Friesian. But this film featured a Friesian named Goliath, who utterly stole the show, and the horse lovers in the audience couldn't wait to meet a Friesian in person.

When they do meet a Friesian, people are inevitably captivated by the black coat, the feathered feet, the large head and gentle expression, the powerful build, and the noble carriage that suggests the horse is much larger than its 15 to 16 hands. Their impressions are further bolstered when they realize the horse is as gentle in temperament as it is stunning in appearance. Happily, Friesians are now cropping up more and more within the everyday equine population. Though it is not likely soon to take the world's Olympic teams by storm, the breed is proving its mettle at dressage and driving events, all the while embodying the horse of the human imagination.

87

characteristics

ORIGIN: The Netherlands, Friesland **HEIGHT:** 15–16 hh **COLORS:** Black
PHYSIQUE: Compact and muscular with prominent withers; short, thick, well-boned legs and hard feet; arched neck; powerful hindquarters; thick mane and tail
FEATURES: Friendly; gentle; regal **USES:** Driving, riding

ancestry

- **NATIVE DUTCH STOCK**
- **ANDALUSIAN**
- **ARABIAN**

the hanoverian

Throughout Germany, warmbloods are bred that proudly carry the names of their native regions. The Hanover region of Germany in Lower Saxony is home to the most numerous and well-known of these warmbloods: the Hanoverian.

While horses had been bred in the area for centuries for farming, general draft purposes, and military uses, the program became a national institution in 1735, when England's King George II, Elector of Hanover, established a stud in Celle, which would make fine breeding stallions available to local broodmare owners in an attempt to upgrade the local horse population. The goal was to produce fine homebred military horses (especially in light of France's growing power) through the infusion of Thoroughbred blood in local equine lines. From that time on, the Hanoverian would rely periodically on the Thoroughbred for improvement whenever some refinement or increased athleticism was required. So successful were these initial efforts, that by the end of the eighteenth century, Hanoverian horses were already making a name for themselves beyond their home turf, and being tracked with detailed pedigrees.

In the mid-nineteenth century, a policy began by which stallions were inspected and approved for breeding, an effort designed to ensure that only the finest stallions would pass their gifts on to future generations. This is a tradition that, like the activities of the Celle State Stud itself, continues to this day in Germany. The many other nations to which the Hanoverian

characteristics

ORIGIN: Germany, Lower Saxony **HEIGHT:** 16–17.2 hh **COLORS:** Primarily chestnut, bay, brown, black, gray **PHYSIQUE:** Big-boned, yet refined; large, sloping shoulders; muscular hindquarters; flattish croup; powerful hock action; definite Thoroughbred influence **FEATURES:** Calm; level-headed; athletically versatile **USES:** Serious riding

ancestry

- HOLSTEINER
- THOROUGHBRED
- NATIVE GERMAN STOCK
- MECKLENBURG
- TRAKEHNER

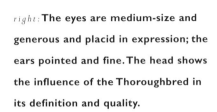

right: **The eyes are medium-size and generous and placid in expression; the ears pointed and fine. The head shows the influence of the Thoroughbred in its definition and quality.**

left: **Weyden, a Hanoverian, ridden by Sven Rothenberger at the 1996 Olympics in Atlanta. This breed is a frequent participant in the Olympic disciplines.**

has migrated have followed suit, inviting officials from the breed's homeland to conduct the necessary testing and stallion inspections each year.

Throughout its history, the Hanoverian's breeders have proven themselves skilled at making the necessary adjustments to their breed to meet the public's current demands. In addition to its influence in the development of such breeds as, among others, the Oldenburg, Westphalian, and Danish and Dutch Warmbloods, the Hanoverian has itself been nimble at changing with the times, as well. Thanks to the foresighted and skilled efforts of the breed's caretakers the large heavy draft

and coach horse became a more refined cavalry mount, which, now with the post-World-War-II, twentieth-century emergence of the sport horse disciplines, has become a World Class competitor with phenomenal jumping skills.

Modern national equestrian teams are rich with Hanoverian representatives, who in turn make their riders quite wealthy with medals. In a variety of disciplines, from dressage, to showjumping, to three-day eventing, the Hanoverian's success has proven to its homeland, as well as to the many nations that have embraced the breed and bolstered its import value, what a long-term vision can accomplish.

the holsteiner

Back in the fourteenth century, before any of the warmblood breeds were even a twinkle in their creators' eyes, a monastery in the marshy area of the Elmshorn district of Schleswig-Holstein in what is now a German state, began breeding horses.

The monastery established their stud with horses of Neapolitan, Oriental and Andalusian extraction, as well as native stock who roamed the rugged, marshy region. Soon they were producing premier farm and war horses that would ultimately be named the Holsteiner, the oldest of Germany's warmblood breeds.

Because of its regal appearance and action, the Holsteiner, in addition to its role as a hard-working plow horse, was recruited early on for what would be a long and illustrious military career, in demand in Spain, England, Italy, and Denmark for whatever conflict these countries were facing at any given moment. In the eighteenth century, its gifts were recognized for another, more peaceful purpose; that of saddle and carriage horse. More selective breeding ensued with the influence of Cleveland Bay and Thoroughbred bloodlines. Such activities were made official in the late nineteenth century, with the establishment of a breeder organization (now called the Society of Breeders of the Holstein Horse and headquartered in Elmshorn where it all began) to oversee breeding practices and breeding stock inspections.

Following World War II, which took a heavy toll on all the warmbloods, the Holsteiner emerged a contender on the international show scene. With Thoroughbred influence to add refinement, this calm, affectionate, rather distinct warmblood, has made a name for itself as a horse of stamina that excels in jumping, dressage and eventing.

characteristics

ORIGIN: Germany, Schleswig-Holstein **HEIGHT:** 16–17.1 hh **COLORS:** Most are bay, chestnut or gray **PHYSIQUE:** Solid and somewhat heavy with muscular neck; prominent withers; sloping shoulders; powerful hindquarters; short back; strong legs **FEATURES:** Friendly; good stamina; more handsome than classically beautiful **USES:** Serious riding, driving

ancestry

- **NATIVE SPANISH STOCK**
- **THOROUGHBRED**
- **NEAPOLITAN**
- **YORKSHIRE COACH HORSE**
- **CLEVELAND BAY**

the oldenburg

World War II marked a turning point for the European horse community, particularly within the rich horse-breeding regions of Germany that had long made horses an integral part of their culture.

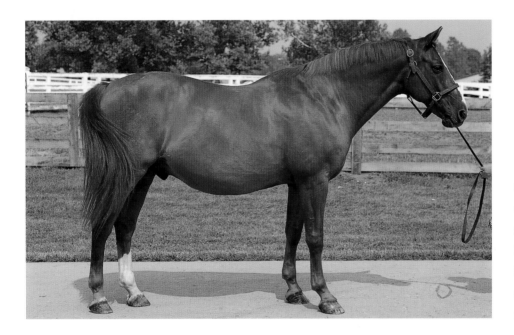

left: **The Oldenburg is one of the heavier warmbloods, an excellent carriage horse, and more increasingly seen in showjumping and dressage.**

Not only had Germany been devastated by the war, but a century and a half earlier, the Industrial Revolution had altered the role of horses in society throughout the world. World War II was significant to equine development because once Europe rebuilt, a new niche for fine saddle horses emerged; that of the top-level sport horse.

The Oldenburg from the Oldenburg region of northwest Germany, had been hit particularly hard by progress and war. Of all the German warmbloods, it was the one most in danger of extinction. Happily, that did not occur, however, for those enamored of this breed that had been produced in its homeland for close to 300 years set about modernizing their horse to meet the demands of the new equine community.

Some fine bloodlines have gone into the Oldenburg through its many incarnations as farm horse, coach and carriage horse, military mount, and now sport horse. The breed was based originally on Friesians that were brought into the Oldenburg's home region in the seventeenth century to cross with local native mares. From then on the blood of Spanish and Oriental horses were added to the mix, as well as Cleveland Bay, Hanoverian, Anglo-Norman, and the warmblood's greatest asset, Thoroughbred. Similar alchemy has been practiced in post-World War II efforts to rescue and re-establish the Oldenburg, successfully pulling this stunning athlete back from the brink of extinction and relocating it in the World-Class show arena where it belongs.

characteristics

ORIGIN: Germany **HEIGHT:** 16.2–17.2 hh **COLORS:** Bay, black, brown, and gray are most common **PHYSIQUE:** Strong shoulders and hindquarters; deep girth; strong back; good legs and bone **FEATURES:** Handsome; level-headed; good jumper **USES:** Serious riding

ancestry

- FRIESIAN
- NEAPOLITAN
- BARB
- NATIVE SPANISH STOCK
- THOROUGHBRED
- NORFOLK ROADSTER
- HANOVERIAN
- NORMAN HORSE
- CLEVELAND BAY

the selle français

France boasts a long and much-admired history of horse husbandry, and in fact it was France that originated the idea of state-run equine breeding programs now so prevalent in the warmblood world.

French breeders have also long understood the magic of hybrid vigor, enlisting some of the world's finest horses, particularly those of Spanish and English extraction, to breed to their colder-blooded native stock for their rigorous breeding programs. The result of one such program was a distinctive horse from the illustrious horse breeding region of Normandy that was called, because of its rich genetic mix, the Anglo-Norman.

This fine animal that was originally developed in the nineteenth century and would in the mid-twentieth century become known as the Selle Français, actually shared a common background with the French Trotter, the two finally choosing separate athletic paths in the fork in their collective road. The Trotter became one of the strongest and fastest harness racers in the world, while the Selle Français became what some have described as the world's greatest showjumper.

Producing top-flight jumpers has been an overriding goal of French breeders for several decades now, and the success of the Selle Français during that time has been phenomenal. In addition to racking up an impressive collection of medals for their own world-class performances, so have they also been called to the breeding barn to impart those gifts to future generations, again with astounding success in carrying on the extraordinary French equine dynasty.

characteristics

ORIGIN: France, Normandy **HEIGHT:** 15.3–17 hh **COLORS:** Chestnut and bay are most common **PHYSIQUE:** Long neck; large head; deep girth; short back; good joints; powerful hindquarters and shoulders; big boned **FEATURES:** Courageous; for expert riders; great jumper **USES:** Serious riding

ancestry

- **NORMAN HORSE**
- **ARABIAN**
- **NATIVE FRENCH DRAFT STOCK**
- **NORFOLK ROADSTER**
- **ANGLO-NORMAN**
- **ANGLO-ARAB**

the trakehner

World War II was no picnic for any of the German warmbloods, but for the Trakehner it was particularly harrowing. Hailing from the celebrated Trakehnen stud in East Prussia in a region that is now part of Lithuania, the breed was forced to evacuate its home many times since it was established in 1732 by Frederick William I of Prussia.

But the permanent evacuation of this excellent farm, military, carriage, and saddle horse of primarily Arabian, English, and Spanish lines, occurred at the end of World War II in an epic drama that has been called the Trek. With the Russians threatening to invade, the horses of Trakehnen were loaded with packs and harnessed to carts for a traumatic evacuation of 500 to 900 miles to Allied forces in what was then West Germany. Fewer than 1,000 Trakehners of the 50,000 that embarked survived the journey.

Those Trakehners that survived were highly praised for their heroism and endurance in seeing that they and the people with whom they traveled did not fall into Russian hands—at that point a more fearsome prospect than surrendering to the Allies. Though the equine refugees were at first scattered throughout Germany, in 1947, they were reunited, and the Trakehner Verband was established to rebuild the Trakehner breed through the traditional warmblood practices of stallion inspections, selective breeding, quality checking performance and temperament testing.

The combination of a tumultuous history and a dedicated army of breeders has resulted in a horse that has made a name for itself in eventing and dressage in the twentieth century.

Today, its numbers healthy, its sport-horse track record building momentum, the prettiest, most versatile of all the warmbloods may now enjoy a more peaceful existence. War and flight no longer a threat, now the world class show arena is the Trakehner's battlefield.

characteristics

ORIGIN: East Prussia, West Germany **HEIGHT:** 16–16.2 hh **COLORS:** Most common are bay, chestnut, black, brown, and some gray **PHYSIQUE:** Lighter than other warmbloods; dense bone; sloped shoulders; defined withers; good joints and feet; Arabian influences **FEATURES:** Elegant; friendly; alert; courageous **USES:** Serious riding

ancestry

- TURKOMAN
- SCHWEIKEN
- THOROUGHBRED
- ARABIAN

the belgian

When human beings made that monumental transition from a life of hunting and gathering to that of a more agrarian nature, they recognized fairly early on that perhaps they could use some help in this endeavor.

They looked around and obviously recognized that of all the creatures with whom they coexisted, the horse was the obvious candidate. The horse was thus domesticated and put to work. As selective breeding practices took hold, the best horses for farming were considered those of immense size and muscle and a variety of such breeds were developed, one of the most popular of these being the Belgian Draft horse, also known as the Brabant.

The Belgian hails from Belgium in the midst of a crossroads through which a number of ancient heavy war horses were known to pass. These animals are presumed to have contributed much to the Belgian, an ancient breed that has changed very little in appearance through the centuries, and which contributed much to the establishment of its fellow draft horses, including the Clydesdale and the Suffolk Punch.

At the breed's peak, almost all of Belgium's horses were Belgians. This changed with the dawn of the twentieth century, however, and the domination of farm machinery in the fields, which rendered the steadfast farm horse, despite its years of loyal service, virtually obsolete. Nevertheless, the Belgian remains a presence. Today, while it is viewed more as a meat animal than a farm hand in its homeland, the Belgian has found a rebirth in the United States where it has gained a devoted following for showing and even some farming.

94

characteristics

ORIGIN: Belgium **HEIGHT:** 15.3–17 hh **COLORS:** Most are chestnut or sorrel with flaxen manes and tails **PHYSIQUE:** Compact and massively muscled with short legs; short neck; broad back and chest **FEATURES:** Kind temperament; hard worker; extraordinarily strong **USES:** Heavy draft

ancestry

• FLANDERS OR FLEMISH HORSE

the clydesdale

One of the most dazzling and well-known of the heavy draft breeds is the Clydesdale. Though it shares a history that coincides with those of its heavy draft brethren, the Clydesdale was not hit as hard by the effects of the Industrial Revolution as its counterparts.

The Clydesdale was developed in the Clyde Valley of Scotland. In a region that could be somewhat inhospitable to farming efforts, draft horses had long played an integral role in working the land. But it was not until the eighteenth century that the production of such horses was formalized, when Flemish Great Horse, Belgian and Friesian stallions were enlisted to cover native draft mares in hopes of increasing the size and muscle of future generations. The plan was successful, and it marked the primitive beginnings of the modern Clydesdale.

The next step involved the infusion of Shire blood, which was carried out primarily in the next century and is probably responsible for the feathering that graces the great feet of the Clydesdale to this day. As the breeders worked their magic, they became increasingly pleased with the foals they were producing—and so apparently were people beyond the Clyde Valley area, and beyond the borders of Scotland, as well. By the late-1800s, the Clydesdale was becoming a favored feature in livestock shows. Such publicity spurred the demand for these horses, which were admired not only for their size and strength, but for their, as the British Clydesdale Horse Society describes it, "flamboyant" style and spirit.

With such positive notices propelling it forward, the Clydesdale entered the twentieth century and the perils of the Industrial Revolution with a rich support system that would see it survive this draft-horse transition period handsomely. Its current popularity that enables it still to command high prices,

to delight show and parade spectators, and to benefit from a continued demand for its export is credited in part to the image of the Clydesdale as symbol of the Anheuser-Busch brewery. Though this seems a novelty in modern times, the image of a team of lovely Clydes pulling a Budweiser beer wagon actually plays upon a very traditional use of draft horses employed for that very purpose throughout Europe. The breed's association with the brewery has brought the Clydesdale into the lives and homes of the public, presenting an image, particularly of these magnificent beasts naked (*sans* harness) and running free, that few can forget. Anyone who has witnessed this, knows it is a vision worth its weight in gold.

characteristics

ORIGIN: Scotland **HEIGHT:** 16.2–18 hh **COLORS:** Typically bay or brown with a white blaze and white legs up to the knees (stockings) **PHYSIQUE:** Large though refined with a deep girth; long neck; sloped shoulders; powerful hindquarters; excellent legs with flat hooves **FEATURES:** Flashy; calm disposition; graceful; eye-catching **USES:** Heavy draft

ancestry

- **NATIVE SCOTTISH STOCK**
- **BELGIAN HEAVY DRAUGHT**
- **FRIESIAN**
- **SHIRE**

the irish draft horse

When one thinks of draft horses, the image of big-boned, massively muscled horses in yoke and harness just naturally comes to mind. But that portrait would be inaccurate if the draft horse in question is the Irish Draft, a horse much lighter in build and agile in action than its draft counterparts.

The history of Ireland has long been entwined with that of the horse. Renowned for its rich equine culture, Ireland has long cultivated its horses to meet the unique needs of the island nation, the result being an equine population of international reputation and popularity.

Thousands of years in the making, the Irish Draft horse carries the blood of the small horses of the Celts, the fine horses of Spain (particularly the Andalusian), the heavy Great Horses of knights in armor, and, in later years, the lovely Thoroughbreds of England. With access to such bloodlines, Irish farmers concocted an all-purpose draft horse that could not only work the fields, but also pull a cart and carry a rider on its back, even over jumps if need be. In fact, the Irish Draft provided the foundation for the celebrated Irish Hunter.

Though the world knew of the Irish Draft for centuries, it was not until the twentieth century that its breeding became an institution with the founding of the Irish Draught Society in 1976 and the breed's first studbook. Today, though the breed has suffered some bumpy moments wrought by the rise of mechanization, the future of the Irish Draft as both popular show horse and the producer of extraordinary halfbred hunters and jumpers looks rosy.

characteristics

ORIGIN: Ireland **HEIGHT:** 16–17.1 hh **COLORS:** All colors except for Clydesdale pattern of bay with white legs **PHYSIQUE:** Lighter draft build with strong back and hindquarters; deep shoulders; powerful, clean legs; hard hooves; prominent withers **FEATURES:** Versatile; proud; good jumper; exceptionally efficient metabolism **USES:** Riding, draft

ancestry

- **NATIVE IRISH STOCK**
- **BELGIAN HEAVY DRAFT**
- **ANDALUSIAN**
- **CELTIC PONY**

the percheron

Yet another illustrious breed to emerge from the rich horse-producing region of Normandy, France, is the Percheron. This celebrated draft member of the Normandy family, a horse of classically round draft build and a signature dappled gray or black coat, has become one of the world's most recognized draft breeds.

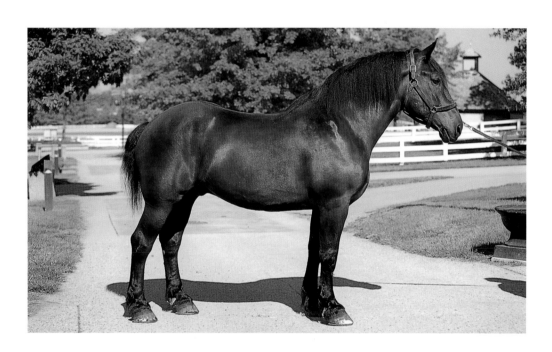

Despite its immense size and muscle, the Percheron is an elegant animal, developed not only for farming but also as an attractive urban draft animal, its roots presumed to span back thousands of years to the time of the Romans, and possibly earlier. The precise story of the Percheron is somewhat murky, as its home territory was a traditional stopping place of many different cultures and thus many different horses through the centuries. What is most evident in the contemporary Percheron, however, is the heavy Arabian influence that obviously contributed to its development. The Percheron's fine head, gray or black coat, bright eyes, balanced construction, and commensurate stylish action just naturally evoke the overall image of an Arabian in draft form.

Today that form is familiar to spectators all over the world, from European streets where the breed may still be seen from time to time pulling carriages or brewery wagons amid more contemporary motorized vehicles, to Disneyland where the Percheron is the breed of choice for the horse-drawn vehicles on Main Street, USA, to shows and parades where matched teams of Percherons invariably meet with enthusiastic applause. The Percheron is not only one of the world's best-known draft horses, but also one of its best-loved.

characteristics

ORIGIN: France, La Perche, Normandy **HEIGHT:** 15.2–16.2 hh
COLORS: Gray or black **PHYSIQUE:** Heavily muscled with handsome head; prominent withers; deep chest; broad overall structure; short legs; short back; heavy Arabian influence **FEATURES:** Elegant; agile; calm disposition
USES: Heavy draft

ancestry

• **NATIVE LA PERCHE STOCK**
• **ARABIAN**
• **NATIVE FRENCH STOCK**

the shire

Few get through childhood without an introduction to the image of the knight in shining armor aboard a magnificent charger.

The Shire horse deserves much credit, for it had to be courageous in its own right and it must have been extraordinarily strong to carry not only a man on its back, but a man wearing a suit of armor.

The Shire, the world's tallest horse, hails from a cluster of English counties, but from there the story of this magnificent animal is a subject of debate. Horses resembling the Shire occupied England since the days of the Romans, but it was almost 1,000 years later that many scholars believe the wheels were set in motion that would result in the creation of the modern Shire when Flanders Horses from Holland were imported to work the marshlands. From then on, such names as Friesian, Great horse, Old English Black horse, Old Black English Cart horse, and even Thoroughbred pepper accounts of the Shire's development, tracing its career as plow horse, carriage and cart horse, and steed of the medieval knight.

The Shire's story is clearer in the eighteenth and nineteenth centuries, where the size and strength of this massive, sweet-tempered horse with thick white feathering on its legs solidified the Shire's reputation as England's most coveted cart horse. Though mechanization took a heavy toll on the Shire, one event that helped see the breed through this transition was the establishment of the Shire Horse Society (initially the English Cart Horse Society) in 1876. The breed's numbers decreased dramatically in the twentieth century, and it now is considered a somewhat rare breed, especially in the once Shire-rich United States, yet there are those who refuse to see the Shire go the way of the armored knight. Given the awe a stunning black Shire inspires in an admiring crowd who spot it at England's annual Shire Horse Show or pulling a brewery wagon, one can only hope that it will continue to embody the soul of the knight and his steed for hundreds of years to come.

characteristics

ORIGIN: England **HEIGHT:** 17–18 hh **COLORS:** Black with white feet is most popular; also found in gray, bay, and brown **PHYSIQUE:** Massive and well-muscled with a long, arched neck; deep shoulders; sloped croup; broad chest; strong, feathered legs; distinctive head with convex profile **FEATURES:** Gentle disposition; tallest horse; willing worker **USES:** Heavy draft

ancestry

- OLD ENGLISH BLACK OR ENGLISH GREAT HORSE
- FRIESIAN
- FLEMISH OR FLANDERS HORSE
- NATIVE HEAVY BRITISH STOCK

the suffolk punch

The Suffolk Punch, or Suffolk horse, holds the distinction of being England's oldest pure draft breed. Though heavy horses have occupied England for thousands of years, the Suffolk, aided by the isolation of its East Anglian homeland, has existed since the sixteenth century, and bred consistently to type since the arrival in 1768 of its foundation sire, Mr. Thomas Crisp's horse of Ufford (Orford), near Woodbridge, Suffolk.

left: **Suffolks are heavily muscled, short-legged and tough. They are willing workers and need less food rations than other draft breeds.**

99

This single stallion is responsible for a dynasty of equine powerhouses that all share their founding sire's chestnut coat, gentle disposition, and rounded muscle structure, representatives of the breed continuing to display these characteristics, virtually unchanged, to this day.

Everything about the Suffolk is massive, from its crested neck to its powerful hindquarters to its short, clean legs that harbor the phenomenal pulling ability necessary to pull plows, carts, and wagons through the dense clay soil of the breed's homeland. So powerful was this relatively short-statured draft horse, that it became in the eighteenth-century England's most celebrated weight-pulling horse in contests. This notoriety

ultimately led, along with its performance in the field and its reputation as an easy keeper, to the founding of the Suffolk Horse Society in 1877.

Like all the heavy draft breeds, the Suffolk suffered the effects of twentieth-century mechanization with varying success. While its numbers declined dramatically in the United States, the breed has maintained a healthy position in its homeland and is now finding itself a popular export worldwide, most notably to Pakistan for the production of army horses. How rewarding to know that purity and quality of this magnitude and antiquity can still be so appreciated on an international level.

characteristics

ancestry

ORIGIN: England, Suffolk, East Anglia **HEIGHT:** 16–17 hh **COLORS:** Chestnut; seven recognized shades **PHYSIQUE:** Massive overall with short legs; deep chest and girth; crested neck; powerfully muscled hindquarters; handsome head with broad forehead **FEATURES:** Docile temperament; great strength and stamina; easy keeper **USES:** Heavy draft, crossbreeding

- **NATIVE HEAVY BRITISH (SUFFOLK) STOCK**
- **FLANDERS HORSE**

above: **A horse and rider rounding up cattle in Nevada.**

the
horse
and people

Brazilian folklore says that "God first made man. He thought better of it, and made woman. When he got time, he made the horse, which has the courage and spirit of man and the grace and beauty of woman."

Consider this: Servant, companion, friend, partner, clothing, food, drink, transport. The horse provides all of these things for Man—and more besides, including income, entertainment, glory, and achievement—yet asks for nothing in return, save clean, fresh water to drink and nourishing food to eat in order that he may carry out his service to the best of his ability. Can there be any other beast who can measure up against the equine service to the human race?

"Love horses, tend them well, for they are worthy of your tenderness. Treat them like your own children, nourish them like friends of the family, clothe them with care. For the love of Allah, do not neglect this, or you will repent of it in this house and the next."

Omar, companion of Prophet Mohammed.

In the beginning...

Although the horse evolved millions of years ago, researchers suggest that evidence points to it not being domesticated until after the Ice Age around 10,000 years ago by Mesolithic man (c.10,000–8,000 BC), between Paleolithic and Neolithic man. Yet the cave paintings and archeological artifacts found in Lascaux, France, (bone and stone ornaments depicting horses)

prove that the horse played a significant role in the lives of Ice Age people from around 35,000 to 10,000 BC. It is known that horses were hunted for their meat and skin for leather during this time, so is it not also possible that some were domesticated as well—if not used as a means of transport, then as herd animals? While young adult horses were considered food on the hoof, killed by spear (which took great courage and skill as wild horses, especially the stallions, were quite aggressive) and by driving herds of horses over precipices, it is possible that surviving foals were saved for "domesticated" herd animals, which in turn may have led to them being used for transport. This theory has yet to be proved conclusively.

It is known that Mesolithic man realized the potential of horses as pack and riding animals, as well as herding them, like cattle and sheep, for meat. Familiarity with the animals bred a greater understanding of them, which in turn led to humans eventually training them to carry and pull weights and then to carry people. In doing this, it was a natural progression through evolution—people found that they could hunt more effectively, travel faster, and work the land with far more efficiency. Furthermore, those tribes which had horses were better able to defend their homes and land against nonriding invaders. Or, indeed, accrue more land and wealth.

It wasn't until the arrival of Mesolithic man that the horse began, slowly, to evolve into different breeds—of which there are hundreds today (*see* Chapter 3). Although this evolution was a natural process, people wanted to breed the fastest, hardest-working, and fittest. Because horses provided the means to travel greater distances opportunities were created to swap bloodlines, with each tribe intent on breeding the best horses for their particular purposes.

At this point, the future of the horse was sealed. Over thousands of years, various bloodlines (breeds) were perpetuated, and others became extinct as their usefulness and adaptability dwindled.

left: **A wall painting showing a unicorn in the Lascaux caves in Southern France.**

Domestication around the world

Research points to the vast plains and steppes of Eurasia, from the Black Sea to China, as being the starting point of horse riding and domestication.

At this time, it is known there were two principal types of horse; the Tarpan (northern Europe and Russia) and Przewalski's horse (Mongolian steppes). A third is thought to have existed; a European coldblood heavy horse indigenous to the forests and plains of Europe, therefore referred to as the "Forest horse of Europe." However, it is most likely that this resulted from interbreeding between Tarpans and the Asiatic Wild horse.

Mongolia's Przewalski horse (Asiatic Wild horse) is thought to have been domesticated some 6,000 years ago (around 4,000 BC). It was hunted to extinction in the wild between 1880 and 1969, but 13 survived in zoos and provided the foundation stock for today's Przewalski.

United States

The endless grassland prairies of the Americas, from Mexico to Canada, the plains of Venezuela and Colombia, plus those of Argentina and Uruguay (pampas), provided the ideal habitat for the horse population to expand after their introduction in the sixteenth century. The Plains people of the Americas (Native American tribes including the Apache, Chickasaw, Ute, Blackfeet, Navaho, Pawnee, Comanche, Cheyenne, Sioux, and Nez Percé) soon learned that horses made useful pack and hunting animals, obtaining them from settlers by

above: **A Native American Indian catching wild horses on the plains of America; painted by George Catlin in the 19th century.**

below: **One of an original breed, the Tarpan today roams in protected Polish preserved.**

above: **Native Americans: A brave with a coup lance of the Nez Percé tribe of Idaho and Oregon, photographed around 1900.**

either barter or theft. It was inevitable that some horses escaped captivity to roam free and increase their numbers. For those people who could catch and tame them, these wild horses provided free and plentiful replacements when required. However, these animals were nothing like the Spanish war-horses that the conquistadores brought with them. Without selective breeding, and surviving on what grazing was seasonally available, the feral horses were small (around 13 hh) though incredibly tough.

Training these ponies to be ridden was, as Native Americans grew used to handling them, a fairly simplistic affair. Men would lasso good-looking mustangs from the backs of their own mounts and eventually bring them down exhausted and half-strangled. Hobbles were attached to their feet and a hide loop slipped around the lower jaw. Controlled thus, the lasso was loosened, and the ponies allowed to get up. In the ensuing struggle against people, bridles, and hobbles, the ponies would eventually concede through total weariness. At that point, they would then submit to being led and ridden without much protest. Other means of breaking included the

below: **Native Americans: Nomad turned farmer; a Blackfoot Indian at the plow in Montana, 1914.**

never look a gift horse in the mouth

DON'T LOOK FOR FAULTS IN A FREE GIFT

use of a hackamore that tightened cruelly if the horse fought against its handler. The man would gradually get closer and closer to the animal, talking soothingly to it when it was amenable, and jerking the halter when it was not. The horse soon learned to behave and accept a rider, with the process lasting about an hour or so.

Although legendary for their riding skill and bravery, Native Americans were not so adept when it came to horse husbandry. Because replacements were easily come by, awkward, slow, or infirm horses were eaten or turned loose to fend for themselves. Neither did they breed selectively apart from the Chickasaw, who developed a small, tough breed from Spanish stock, and the Nez Percé—acclaimed for their Appaloosa (Palouse) horses.

Horses changed the Native Americans' way of life. For instance, the Blackfeet were originally forest dwellers,

supporting themselves by agriculture, who did not have horses until the early 1800s. They then turned into buffalo hunters and lived on the plains, their housing being teepees instead of wooden huts, and their transport being the horse instead of dog *travois* (sledge) and canoe.

Probably the most important part the horse played in the lives of the Native American was as a means to catch food— principally the buffalo—more quickly and easily, and to follow animal herds through the seasons ensuring there was always a plentiful supply of fresh meat. Horses became their trading currency, and the more horses a man owned the wealthier he was, with some of the richest families owning up to 100 horses.

Although Native Americans didn't exercise wonderful horse care, they did hold the horse in high regard, with warriors being extremely proud of their favorite mounts; these would be tethered to their owners' teepees for extra security against marauders.

Before hunting or war, warriors would paint their horses, as well as themselves on the face and body, with "magic" colors or pigments to help protect themselves from harm.

below: **The Bronco Buster by Frederic Remington c. 1895.**

My horse be swift in flight
Even like a bird:
My horse be swift in flight.
Bear me now in safety
Far from the enemy's arrows
And you shall be rewarded
With streamers and ribbons red.
(SIOUX WARRIOR SONG)

Horses were very much part of the Native American's traditions and religious beliefs, and even in names—for example, Crazy Horse and Red Horse (both Sioux chiefs). On a Cree warrior's death, one of his horses (usually his favorite) would be killed in order that the warrior could ride into the spirit world, and his widow would receive two others. A dead Apache warrior would be led to his final resting place on his favorite horse, which would then be killed and buried with him and some of his personal possessions.

Native American children were taught to ride at a very young age, becoming daring and competent horsemen by the time they reached seven. Young warriors were passionate about horse racing—pitting their fastest ponies against each other. Gambling on the races was another pastime much enjoyed by the tribes.

The Native American's reign came to an end in the 1800s when hordes of settlers (gold-seekers, homesteaders, ranchers, and hunters) invaded their lands. White hunters slaughtered the great herds of buffalo, mainly for sport, killing the tribes' main food supply, while "white man's diseases" wiped out many tribes. The US Army, brought in to defend the settlers, beat the Native Americans into submission, with many being forced onto reservations (and it wasn't until 1924 that these original Native Americans were given US citizenship). Many of their ponies were captured by US Cavalry troops and sold off. The ponies that were left behind by fleeing tribes, or escaped in the mêlée of battle, ran free to join up with bands of feral horses and swell the numbers of these mustangs.

With the arrival of the settlers and ranchers came herds of cattle—and cowboys to muster them, many of whom were Mexican *vaqueros* who passed on their horsemanship skills to

settlers. Transportation was the horse—for farming and travel. Horses could be bought for $10 and "bronco-busting" was the means of breaking and training them quickly. A cruel and brutal process, little or no effort was made to win horses' trust. Basically a saddle and bridle would be forced onto a bound horse, and then the bronco-buster would mount. When the horse finally, exhausted, stopped trying to dislodge its rider, it was considered broken.

As time went by and people began to breed horses selectively to produce better and, therefore, more valuable stock, their methods of breaking and training improved. Cowboys became proud of their horsemanship and training skills and began to compete—annual rodeos (from the Spanish word *rodear*, meaning round-up) became established and much anticipated events were cattle-cutting, bull-dogging (bringing a steer to the ground), steer-roping, racing horses and chuck-wagons—and rodeo riding unbroken horses. Events were

horsing around /
horseplay

LETTING OFF STEAM

above: **A working horse and cowboy rounding up cattle in United States.**

hotly contested. Prized were the horses that could turn on a dime, anticipate a steer's movements, and race to win. And many a cowboy found fame and fortune from showing off their talents at these events.

Rodeos continue in the US today, with hundreds of professional shows throughout America and Canada offering millions of dollars in prize money. However, the horse is no longer the chief means of herding, its place superseded by the faster and more manpower efficient helicopter and 4WD vehicles. For many older cowboys and *vaqueros* the only job and way of life they have ever known is dying out. South Americans pride themselves on producing horses for performance and achieving absolute obedience from their mounts.

Asia

Research points to the Steppe people being the first to domesticate the horse on the vast grasslands of Eurasia, first herding it as food (meat and milk) on the hoof, and then using it for transport (riding and war chariots), and to work the land during the Copper Age (3,500 to 1,500 BC). Warlike nomads, the "Aryans," as they are referred to because of their language, these people were the forefathers of the Scythians, Mongols, Huns, and Tartars—all famed for their exceptional skills and talents in horsemanship.

For Steppe people, the advantages of domesticating horses were many, not least in enabling them to manage their staple herds of sheep, goats, and cattle far better throughout the seasons. Horses meant that people could travel greater distances quicker, so moving from pasture to pasture became easier. In doing this, friendships among other tribes were forged, integration occurred, and trading links established. The Steppe people soon learned to become expert horsemen, almost living entirely on horseback, with their children taught to ride from a very early age—being put on horseback almost as soon as they could walk.

Homes were portable and were moved along the grazing trails, while sustenance, fuel for fires (dried dung), and footwear and clothing were derived almost entirely from these people's livestock. Fermented mare's milk became a favorite beverage, and still is today among these peoples' descendants. Tools, such as scoops, were crafted from equine shoulder blades, while musical instruments were fashioned from tying hooves together, somewhat like Spanish castanets.

Inhabitants of the steppes of Mongolia still keep their herds of horses in a semiferal state, much the same as was the case thousands of years ago. Indeed, horses are vital for their continued existence. A family's wealth is determined by the number of livestock they own—and the more horses they have, the further they can travel to sustain their herds on the best grazing grounds. Horsemeat and fermented milk (*koumiss*), which varies in alcohol content depending on its preparation, is still a large part of the Steppe peoples' daily diet, with the milk being prepared in skin bags or wooden barrels. Autumn sees the slaughter of specially fattened animals, including young male horses unsuitable for riding or breeding, and their meat stored (either smoked or preserved in brine) for use throughout the winter months. Horse fat is prized during winter for the calories it provides for warmth and energy. Skins are

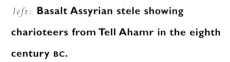

left: **Basalt Assyrian stele showing charioteers from Tell Ahamr in the eighth century BC.**

above: **A drawing of a Mongol: Mongols were famed for their great horsemanship.**

used for curing and carrying *koumiss*, as well as for clothing, while mane and tail hair (from both dead and live animals) is used in ropemaking.

In a tradition not unlike that practiced by the Plains people of America hundreds of years ago, when a man dies today his favorite horse plays a central part in the funeral ceremony. After that, it joins the rest of the herd for a year before being killed at a feast to mark the man's passing.

India yields prehistoric remains of early horses, and from around 1,500 BC, records show their widespread use for hunting, war, and sport. Originating from the Asiatic Wild horse, they gradually became finer and larger through interbreeding with Arabian animals.

Middle East

The Sumerians and Assyrians, the principal tribes of Mesopotamia (now Iraq), were especially diligent in recording their involvement with horses from 3,000 BC. Archeological

horse sense

GOOD INSTINCTS

remains (carved friezes, stone writing tablets, sculptures, and equipment) indicate the importance of work and riding horses as far back as the third millennium BC when the Sumerians first used wild asses—harnessing horsepower came later, in the second millennium, when it is thought that horses were introduced from Turkey.

It was with the Assyrians (whose empire lasted from 2,000 to 600 BC) that horses really came to the forefront in this part of the world. These people soon learned how to use the horse to their best advantage when it came to hunting food and defending their lands.

The Scythians—infamous in war because they were particularly ferocious in defending their territories as well as accruing more—played an important role in equestrian history from the early times of horse domestication.

below: **Tiglath-Pileser III, King of Assyria in his chariot.**

Hailing from lands north of the Black Sea, the Scythians lived a nomadic life—their homes consisted of portable tents (*yurts*) enabling them to travel alongside their herds of cattle, sheep, and horses to find the best seasonal grazing. This horse-riding race were first documented by the Assyrians in 670 BC because of their forays into Persia (Iran), but earlier archeological evidence of their equestrian culture, found in central Asia (Kazakstan and the Altay-Sayan Mountains), dates back 200 years before this. Although not the earliest horsemen, the Scythians were responsible for opening up a whole new world of horse riding. Their adversaries, who included the Assyrians as well as the Steppe people, were forced to improve their own horsemanship in order to compete on equal terms.

Since the horse, hunting, and warfare went hand in hand, ideas developed on how to ensure that horsemen could defeat the enemy. Equipment for horse and rider, especially war trappings (saddle cloths, head masks, and headdresses) to make both look more impressive and therefore fearsome, developed rapidly. Horses' manes were trimmed within inches of the crests so that they stood up to make the animal look bigger and more terrifying; saddlery developed to include rich

above: **Ancient warriors developed chariot warfare into an art, with accomplished tribes vanquishing their opponents by sheer force and practised horsemanship.**

decoration —to impress superiority upon enemies—and grain feeding (among those people who could spare it for animals) was introduced in order to improve their war horses' stamina and appearance.

As equipment developed, it can be assumed that horses were groomed, so that their fine looks reflected their richly crafted saddlery and similarly dressed riders. Chariots became more and more streamlined, embellished with symbols and decorations—the bigger the better, therefore commanding more respect from their foes. Weapons, such as short bows and swords, were developed that could be used effectively from horseback.

Only stallions were ridden by the majority of ancient horsemen, with mares kept primarily for breeding and milk. It was the Scythians who adopted the practice of gelding male horses, and preferred them to noisy, aggressive stallions.

Equine fossils dating from around two and a half million years ago have been found in Africa, but none dating after the Pleistocene Ice Age period (around 12,000 years ago), indicating that horses were not ridden there until relatively recently. They are thought to have been reintroduced by the Hyksos (Shepherd Kings)—Asian nomads who infiltrated the Nile valley around 1,700 BC. It was from them that the ancient Egyptians learned the art of horse riding, driving, and selectively breeding bigger and more finely built animals. Israel in turn procured horses from Egypt in order to help defend itself from Syrian and Assyrian invaders. The horse flourished in most regions of Africa, apart from the equatorial center, where it cannot survive the hot climate and tsetse fly.

Egyptian Arabian horses have been prized for centuries and their bloodlines carefully recorded by their mainly Bedouin owners—with some pedigrees dating right back to the sixth century AD. However, by 1961, the ancient and pure bloodlines were in danger of dying out due to less-than-careful breeding, and King Hussein of Jordan set up a Royal stud at Shuna, near Jericho on the west bank of Jordan. By a painstaking selection process, stallions and mares with substantiated pedigrees were tracked down and procured to ensure their lines endured.

Today the sport of racing, both Arabian and Thoroughbred, are popular in the Middle East—with huge financial rewards for victors.

In contrast though, the humble working horse of the Middle East has a harder lot, although charities such as the Brooke Hospital for Animals and the International League for the Protection of Horses have done great work in improving equine care and health, and are continuing to do so. For many

backing the wrong horse

MAKING AN UNWISE DECISION

working people of these countries the horse represents their livelihood and is looked after as well as any other member of the family—no more, no less; in often abject poverty, with finds from refuse tips sometimes being a main source of food.

Far East

Archeological evidence points to equine domestication in China at least 3,000 years ago on the fertile plains, although horsepower did not really take off until the Bronze Age, when they first became crucial for transport, and then in later years in warfare to repel invading tribes from the north—particularly the ferocious Huns. So heavily under attack were the Chinese that they eventually built the 4,000-mile-long Great Wall of China.

As the Chinese people and their horses derived from the Steppe people, their lifestyle and methods of keeping their horses were virtually the same. Horses were of the small and stocky Mongolian type, around 14 hh, and didn't become larger or finer until after 106 BC when 50 "heavenly horses of Ferghana" were stolen from the Ferghana Mountains in the Persian Empire (now Uzbekistan) and interbred with native Chinese stock. These horses were said to sweat blood, but modern research suggests that this characteristic was due to a parasitic skin ailment.

When Kublai Khan (grandson of Genghis, known as the greatest nomadic horseman of all time) continued his grandfather's conquest of China and became Khan there around 1,259 AD, founding a Mongol dynasty, the traveler Marco Polo recorded that the Great Khan owned a stud of

above: **Part of Trajan's column showing Roman cavalry.**

snow-white horses—stallions and more than 10,000 mares.

Today, horses in China, and neighboring Japan, live hugely contrasting lifestyles. Native ponies are still kept in the traditional nomadic way in northwestern China by Kazaks (descendants of predominantly Mongols); while imported Thoroughbred racehorses, who live in luxury, provide a multi-million dollar sporting and breeding industry, especially in Hong Kong's Happy Valley—hugely popular among the population who love to bet on it. Riding for pleasure at equestrian centers in big cities is becoming increasingly popular among those who can afford it, with British instructors being held in high regard.

Europe

The Greeks and Romans come to mind when one thinks of ancient horsemen, thanks to such notables as Alexander the Great and his legendary black stallion Bucephalus; Xenophon, and Roman emperor Julius Caesar for his cavalry writings. It was the Greeks though who were at the forefront of equine use from around 700 BC, according to archeological evidence; the Romans were not as horse-oriented. For both countries, the principal use of the horse was in battle.

While the Romans are thought to have invented the first horseshoe in the shape of the slip-on *hipposandal* and were the originators of clipping (for smartness), it was the Greeks who are credited with exercising good horse care and improving the quality of horsemanship. Originators of the Olympic Games, first held in 776 BC, the Greeks are most famous for their adeptness in harnessing horsepower to the chariot.

left: **Shigisan scroll from the Kamakura period (12th–13th centuries) depicting the lives of ordinary people; agriculture, represented by the horse and bullock is never far away.**

111

above: **The Mongols: Genghis Khan in battle, 1201.**

Miniature from Persian history completed in 1596.

The Greeks liked their horses to look splendid and be spirited to ride—to impress their foes. From small ponies living on natural forage, Greek horses developed into larger and more finely built animals thanks to the development of supplementary feeding (grain and legume, clover and lucerne, and good hay) and what must have been selective breeding.

Xenophon's ideas on horse care all those years ago were extraordinary when considered today; regarding foot care in the domestic horse (Greek horses were unshod in his time), he recommended that they be stabled for a period daily on a floor of small stones in order to keep the feet worn to the correct shape and level. France, Spain, and Germany are particularly rich in archeological remains relating to early horses and people's relationship with them; one horse-kill site at Solutré in France dates from 32,000 years ago, and it is estimated to contain the remains of some 100,000 horses. Paleolithic cave art and sculpture in Europe tells us that horses in that era bore a striking resemblance to Przewalski's horse.

Research suggests that proper equine domestication (with the Tarpan) began in central Europe around 1,700 BC, but it was in the Ukraine that fascinating evidence has come to light that horses were being ridden with bits as long ago as 4,000 BC, and even as early as around 6,000 BC.

Australia and New Zealand

The Australians and the New Zealanders, have made a great impact on the world of horsemanship, especially in three-day eventing. Australian heroes include Wayne Roycroft (son of

below: **Stockhorse working sheep in Australia.**

above: **Racing at Happy Valley race course in Hong Kong.**

Olympiad Bill Roycroft and Olympic gold medalist at Atlanta 1996), Matt Ryan (Olympic gold medalist at Barcelona, 1992, with Kibah Tic Toc). The New Zealanders include Mark Todd (individual Olympic gold medalist, 1984, with Charisma), three-time Badminton Horse Trials winner and three-time Burghley-winner), Andrew Nicholson, Blyth Tate (individual Olympic gold medalist at Atlanta 1996, with Ready Teddy), and Vaughn Jefferis (1994 World three-day event champion with Bounce).

Yet it wasn't until recently that horses appeared in Australia, introduced by European explorers in the eighteenth century. Horses imported by sea from Britain, Spain, and Holland were essential to early settlers (notably British convicts) in the opening up of Australia's vast area in order to herd the huge population of sheep and later cattle—Australia's staple diet and trade commodity.

Australian Walers (so named because they were first bred in New South Wales) were derived from the hardy Australian Stockhorse—a crossbreed resulting from the various imported breeds which included Arabians, Basutos, and Barbs as well as

113

saddled with a problem

HAVING A LOAD TO BEAR

Thoroughbreds. Walers became famous as tough mounts for the Indian Army during World War I when more than 100,000 were provided for allied forces in the Middle East.

Life in the outback was hard for man and horse. It could take months to round up sheep and cattle that roamed a vast area. Horses were unshod, since the dry conditions and ground were ideal for keeping the feet in good shape. They lived wholly on grass in the summer with supplementary hay given as necessary in the winter. Only the fittest survived, maintaining the toughness and stamina for which these horses gained a considerable reputation.

Australia's feral horses, Brumbies, resulted from domestic stock escaping or being set free. They multiplied rapidly, soon becoming a nuisance because they devoured acres of grazing essential for cattle and sheep. In the 1960s, thousands of Brumbies were shot in a large cull; an event for which Australia received worldwide condemnation.

Understanding and working with the horse

In earlier times horses were the main means of transport—and were also used to work the land. People grew up with horses, and looking after them was a way of life, with the horse-care knowledge passed down from generation to generation. As mechanization was introduced and improved, horses have been gradually phased out for transport and work use —their only real use in many parts of the world is now for pleasure and sport. Because of this, much of the naturally ingrained traditions and knowledge have been lost. Today, the majority of people interested in working with or riding horses have to learn how to handle and care for them when they have the time or inclination, which is not as satisfactory as growing up with horses and learning about them being a natural everyday process.

Horses thrive on a constant routine and kind, yet firm, handling. Providing they receive enough to eat, have plenty of exercise, and time for themselves in the field to let off steam and graze, enjoy other equine company, and do not suffer extreme heat or cold, horses tend to be happy. It is necessary to communicate with them in order for them to learn to carry out tasks. A horse has to be taught to carry loads or a rider, to jump obstacles safely, to pull a carriage, to lead quietly in hand, and so on.

By learning to understand equine behavior and body

language, using the voice and a series of body aids (squeezing the horse's sides with his legs, altering the weight in the saddle, applying pressure on the reins), the handler teaches the horse what is required of it by constant repetition and reward.

Recognizing equine body language is essential if a person is to communicate effectively with horses. Facial expressions, ear movement, muscle tension, and stance all express how the horse is feeling or responding. For example, ears flat back indicates fear or aggression, ears forward means alertness, curiosity, or amenability, while floppy ears means relaxation. In addition to these signs, the horse will be communicating through other body language such as chewing, snorting, tensing muscles, pawing, licking its lips, drooping its lower lip; the combination of body language used indicates the horse's frame of mind.

Equine body language tells the handler who listens a great deal: Biting, bucking, kicking, rearing, refusing to do something, nuzzling, sniffing, and so on are all signs that the horse is trying to tell us something. For example, when a horse bucks with the rider, it can mean high spirits (the horse is feeling

below: **A rodeo performer working at the Frontier Days, Cheyenne, Wyoming.**

above: **Cleveland Bay horses with their liveried riders at the Royal Mews, London.**

eats like a horse
NEVER STOPS EATING

well and is exuberant), discomfort or pain (maybe the saddle is pinching, or it is suffering from an injury), or it can mean that the animal does not want to do what is asked of it and is trying to rid itself of its rider (like you or me saying "No!")

Horses communicate with humans effectively—it is up to us to learn to interpret what they are saying and reply accordingly in order to maintain a happy, working relationship with them. Horses are not machines, but living animals with their own individual likes, dislikes, foibles, and personalities. For a human and horse to work together agreeably for mutual benefit and a rewarding partnership, they have to bond and it is advisable for a person to take great care in choosing an equine partner that will be able to carry out what is required of it both mentally and physically to avoid problems later on.

Whilst a common bond of respect and affection can be forged from the outset of a new partnership, it is more usual for this bond to grow over time as horse and human get to know one another and discover how each other acts and thinks.

Horses and ponies come in all shapes and sizes and have individual temperaments; and there are those more suited to particular tasks than others. For a person to choose the right

mount, it is important to take all these considerations into account, as well as his or her own capabilities and aspirations.

It is unsettling for a horse to move to new surroundings, be tended by strange people and be stabled with other horses who are unfamiliar. For this reason allowances must be made by a new owner until the horse becomes accustomed to its new home. This settling-down period can take many months, and it is a good idea for the new owner to quiz the previous owner about the animal's particular likes and dislikes: what food it is used to and what times is it usually fed; does it usually live in or out; is it used to being rugged up; what bedding has it been bedded on; does it like being patted, stroked or scratched in a certain place, or does it not like being petted at all (some horses don't); is there anything it is frightened of or has a particular aversion to; is it ticklish when groomed; how does it prefer to travel, facing forward or back, in a box (lorry) or float (trailer); what vocal commands/requests is it accustomed to (there are many variations on these); how is it with other horses, a bully, coward or a good mixer; is it allergic to anything; how does it like to be ridden and what aids does it respond to (people often have their own variations of aids which work for them and their horses).

Once a bond between man and horse has been established, there is no greater reward for a horse-lover and rider to feel a fit, willing, obedient horse beneath him, happy to go where and do what is directed of him.

Working horses in modern times

In this age of mechanization, the horse still has an important working role to play in many countries around the world. Despite the increasing use of 4WD vehicles on large ranches in the United States, Australia, and New Zealand, many ranch workers still prefer the horse for working cattle, and indeed cannot manage without them in inaccessible areas, so the cowboy tradition lives on.

Growing in popularity are dude ranches, where tourists can enjoy a holiday living and working as a cowboy, so horses play an important part in encouraging this type of financially lucrative tourism for ranchers. Tourists keen to see and experience renowned areas of great beauty in the world, such as the Welsh mountains, England's Lake District, the Scottish glens, America's Rocky Mountains, and Africa's plains, ensure

below: **Monty Roberts, a well known modern horse whisperer.**

getting the bit between one's teeth

UNSTOPPABLE

there is a constant demand for pony trekking and horse-drawn carriage rides.

The role of riding school horse and ponies cannot be overlooked; their patience, willingness, and good temper enabling millions of horse-lovers to learn to ride each year and carry on enjoying the wonderful sport of riding.

Although many people associate tractors with working farmland, it is surprising just how many horses, usually heavy breeds which are better suited to this task, are still employed around the world for this purpose, especially in underdeveloped countries—and particularly in remote, hilly areas such as Bosnia—where they are used to plow, drill, and harrow the fields as well as cart crops, hay, and straw back to farms or to market.

In the Scottish Highlands, Highland ponies are still employed in one of their traditional roles of carrying shot deer (weighing up to 15 stones/120 lbs) on specially designed "deer saddles" down the steep, rugged hillsides. During the stalking season "deer ponies" may work up to six days a week on Scottish estates.

As countries are becoming more environmentally-aware, forestry commissions are turning back to using horses to help manage conservation areas which are easily damaged by heavy machinery. Indeed, employing horses again has proved more labor-saving and economical than using vehicles. In England, a team of two Percherons pulling a specially designed waste cart is used by the Bath and North East Somerset Council to collect household rubbish (comprising glass, tins, paper, rags, oil, aluminum foil, and batteries) destined for recycling. Other public service duties horses are used for around the world include police and army work, the latter only for ceremonial duties today rather than war. However, police horses still face front line trouble, helping to control rioting crowds at demonstrations and soccer matches. They are invaluable too in patroling areas where vehicles cannot gain access, not least for the value in allowing mounted police officers better vision than afforded behind a steering wheel!

above: **Dr. Reiner Klimke on Ahlerich at the Los Angeles Olympics, 1984.**

In underdeveloped countries horses, as well as donkeys and mules, provide transport on a daily basis, delivering food and other essential goods as well as providing their owners with a means to earn a living. One job involves scavenging items from rubbish tips for resale.

Horses are used for public relations and advertising work too. Many breweries still use heavy horses today to deliver beer—and few watchers can fail to be awed by the impressive sight of long-feathered Shires, groomed and turned out to perfection in their show ribbons and harness, drawing massive brewery drays along busy city strees. A popular sight in London is Harrod's traditional green horse-drawn delivery vehicle—still in use today.

Talking to horses

Ask horsemen worldwide whom they consider noteworthy teachers now, and they state names such as Dr. Reiner Klimke (German dressage rider, trainer, and Olympic gold medalist in 1984), Arthur Kottas (chief rider at the Spanish Riding School of

Vienna), Mark Phillips (former British Olympic three-day event rider who now trains the American event team), Jennie Loriston-Clarke (British Olympic dressage rider), David Hunt (British dressage rider and trainer), and Jack le Goff (former trainer of the US Equestrian Team alongside the showjumping great Bertalan de Nemethy). There are too many other well-known names to list, in addition to the thousands of instructors each doing their own little bit to promote thoughtful riding and excellent horse care all over the world.

Ask many of the general public if they can name a horse trainer, and Monty Roberts is invariably their reply. Although well known in his native America, Monty achieved fame in Great Britain in the 1980s, when he came to the notice of Queen Elizabeth II with his "Join Up" technique—a method of training unbroken, as well as difficult or unmanageable, horses. Join Up consists of communicating with horses through body language—principally by an advance and retreat method (some techniques are similar to those practiced by some Native Americans). The trainer stands with the horse in a small enclosed area and follows it around. Usually the horse's instinctive reaction is to have nothing to do with this "predator" and flees from him. When this happens, the trainer stops and turns away from the horse, ignoring it. When the horse itself stops to turn and look curiously at its pursuer, wondering why it is no longer being chased, the trainer again moves toward it. This goes on until the horse no longer flees, realizing that it is not going to be harmed. At this point, it will either come and investigate the trainer by sniffing and touching him with its nose or will stand warily awaiting the next move. In the case of the former, the first bond of trust between trainer and horse has been established, and the trainer will go on to touch and handle the horse; in the latter, the trainer will stand quietly facing away from the animal and await its next move, which usually consists of it coming closer and closer until it overcomes its mistrust and, anxious for intimacy and reassurance, reaches out to touch the trainer.

It has proven to be a highly efficient and humane way of starting horses as well as re-training awkward ones (usually made so by the ignorance of their handlers in the first place).

It is through all of these dedicated teachers and their like-minded students that the great horse trainers of tomorrow will continue to flourish. There's no truer saying than the old one of, "It takes a lifetime to learn about horses and you're dead before the knowledge is any use to you!"

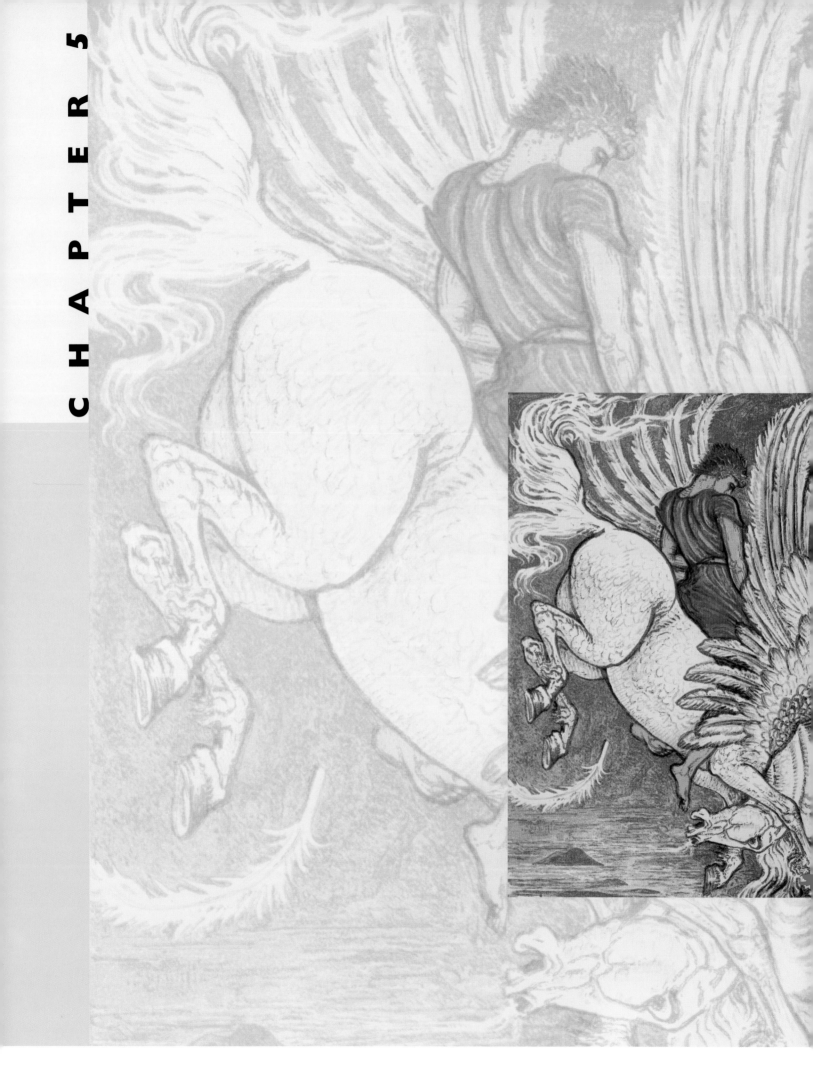

above: **The winged horse Pegasus, mount of Bellerophon, was taken up by the Gods and placed in the heavens as a constellation of stars.**

the horse in myth and legend

Horses are woven so closely into our lives that they have become a powerful source of myth, legend, and superstition. Over the centuries, people have hunted them, relied on them for transport and to work the land, and even worshipped them. Add to that our admiration for their power and beauty, and you have a potent mix of fascination and fantasy.

The origins of the horse are told in stories that span the world. According to the ancient Greeks, the horse was created by Poseidon, god of the sea, and came out of the waves. Even today, the foaming crests of waves that are whipped up by the wind are often nicknamed "white horses." The Arabian horse, one of the oldest of all the breeds, has long been prized by Bedouin tribesmen since about 3,000 BC and, according to ancient tribal legends, was created by Allah from handfuls of the north and south winds.

In American Indian tribal legends, horses were gifts from the gods. The Sioux believed that their arrival had been prophesied by tribal elders and that they were therefore sacred animals; they called the horse *sunkawakan*, which means "sacred, or holy dog."

Dreams had special significance to the Native Americans, and they would often decorate themselves and their horses according to their content. Crazy Horse (1840–77) was a warrior and political leader who took his final and most famous name in his late teens after a dream of prophecy. As a boy, he was called Light Hair and Curly, and in his mid-teens was known as His Horse Stands in Sight. A vision showed him his future and his adult identity; he dreamed of a warrior riding a horse that constantly changed color through thunder and lightning, arrows, and bullets.

In legend, the man or woman with the best horse has

below: **The ancient Greeks believed that the horse was created by Poseidon, god of the sea, and came out of the sea.**

above: **A mosaic from Pompeii showing Alexander the Great and his cavalry in battle against the Persians.**

always been the one with the power. Give him or her a winged horse and he or she becomes more powerful, as long as the horse can be controlled. Pegasus is the most famous, the winged horse of Greek mythology who was tamed by Bellerophon with the help of a golden bridle given to him by Athene, the goddess of wisdom. They defeated a monster with a lion's head, a dragon's tail, and a goat's body called the Chimera, but Bellerophon's arrogance proved to be his downfall.

He tried to fly Pegasus to the heights of Mount Olympus, the home of the Gods, but Zeus, the ruler of heaven and earth, was so angry that he sent the winged horse hurtling to earth. Pegasus was lamed, but the Gods relented and took him up to Mount Olympus, where he was given a permanent place in the heavens as a constellation.

A combination of winged horses and arrogance also sealed the fate of Phaeton, son of the Greek sun god, Helios. In Greek mythology, the passage of the sun across the sky marked the journey of Helios' chariot, drawn by fiery winged horses. Phaeton tricked his father into letting him take the reins, only to lose control and fall to earth. The importance of gaining power over horses runs through many myths and legends.

Some are based in fact: Bucephalus, whose name means "ox-head," was bought for Alexander the Great (356–323 BC) by his father, Philip of Macedonia, in admiration for his son's prowess. Legend says that the magnificent horse, whose concave profile gave him his name, threw everyone who tried to ride him until Alexander realized that he was frightened of his own shadow. By turning him so he could not see it, Alexander gained his confidence. When the horse died, Alexander built a city that he called Bucephala.

Horses have their place in Christian as well as pagan religions. The most frightening are the Four Horsemen of the Apocalypse (in Rev. 6:1–8.) The first horseman wears a crown and goes out to conquer. The second is a swordsman on a red horse—the symbol of war. The third is mounted on a black horse and carries a set of scales—representing famine. Finally, and most frighteningly of all, there is death: "And I looked, and behold a pale horse, and his name that sat on him was Death, and Hell followed with him."

St. Hippolytus and St. Aldhelm both have links with horses. St. Hippolytus was a Roman who was put to death in AD 235 by having his limbs tied to four horses, who were then put to flight so that he was ripped apart. It was said that sick horses could be healed if they were brought to his shrine, which must be the ultimate in forgiveness!

St. Aldhelm (AD 639–709), who was Abbot of Malmesbury and Bishop of Sherborne, Dorset, England, was a magician as well as a monk—roles that seem to sit uneasily together. He made a silver bell that could calm storms and was summoned to the Vatican to demonstrate. According to legend, St. Aldhelm got there by creating a flame that he turned into a winged horse; the horse took him to Rome and had to be fed hot coals as fuel for the return journey.

Unicorns and centaurs

The unicorn, romantically depicted as a beautiful white horse with a single horn in the center of his forehead, is a fabulous beast who grew out of stories of commonplace horned animals, including the rhinoceros. Wild and free, he sadly became the victim of unscrupulous hunters who killed him so that they could take his horn, which had magical and medicinal properties; drinking wine from a cup made from a unicorn's horn was said to be an antidote to any poison, while ground unicorn horn was prized as an aphrodisiac.

It was said that the unicorn could only be caught by a virgin, who sat down beneath a tree until the unicorn laid down beside her, put his head in her lap, and was lulled to sleep by her beauty and purity. This was the cue for the hunters to move in, kill the poor beast, and cut off his horn.

The unicorn appears on coats of arms and is often paired with the lion; the favorite explanation for this is that both beasts represent strength and wildness. A traditional English nursery rhyme is linked to the amalgamation of the Royal Arms of Scotland to those of England when James VI of Scotland also became James I of England in 1603:

> The lion and the unicorn
> Were fighting for the crown,
> The lion beat the unicorn
> All around the town.
> Some gave them white bread,
> Some gave them brown,
> Some gave them plum cake
> And drummed them out of town.

Centaurs, half man and half horse, are less attractive—wild, lustful, drunken beings from ancient Greece who shared the hills of Thessaly with the Lapiths, a much gentler and more refined tribe of people. The Elgin Marbles from the Parthenon

above: **A centaur treading down a Lapith from the Parthenon sculpture, South Metope.**

show a centaur fighting with a Lapith, a war which started when the centaurs got drunk at the Lapith king's wedding and tried to carry off all the women! The same battle is portrayed in Michelangelo's sculpture, The Battle of the Centaurs (1491).

Chiron is perhaps the only centaur who does not have image problems, though he learned his lessons the hard way. Originally one of the Titans—12 huge offspring of Uranus, personification of heaven, and Gaia, the Earth—he rebelled against the gods of Olympus and was turned into a half-man, half-horse by Apollo, the god of music, poetry, archery, and healing.

In his new form, he mastered arts ranging from medicine to archery and many Greek heroes, including Achilles and Jason, were sent into the wilderness to learn from him. Achilles' mother, the sea goddess Thetis, dipped him in the river Styx to make him invulnerable; she held him by the heel, which stayed dry and was pierced by the arrow that caused his death, giving us the "Achilles' heel" or weak spot.

Jason was the son of Aeson, king of Iolcus. Chiron brought him up, and when Aeson died, Jason went to his uncle, Pelias, to demand the kingdom. Pelias set him a series of tasks, including bringing back the golden fleece, and Jason gathered a team of Greek heroes, the Argonauts, to help him.

When Chiron was wounded by a poisoned arrow, he

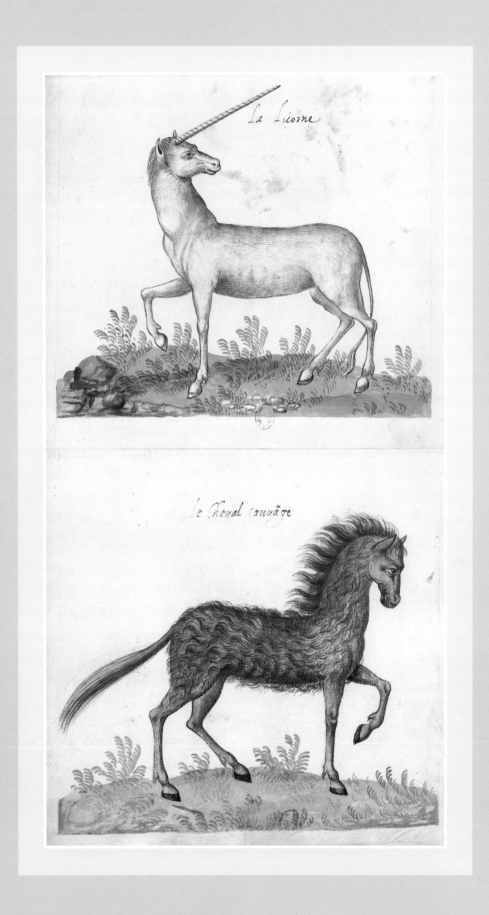

above: **A watercolor of a unicorn (top) and a wild horse (bottom). The unicorn is a fabulous beast with his origins stemming from horned animals.**

above: **According to Homer, the ten-year siege of Troy was ended by the use of the wooden horse. Greek soldiers hid inside until it was taken into the city, after which the soldiers surprised and overcame the inhabitants.**

offered to give up his immortality to save another Titan, Prometheus. Zeus was apparently so impressed by his unselfishness that he put him in the sky, where he can be seen as the constellation Sagittarius.

The Amazons, female warriors of ancient Greek myth, fought on horseback. The tribe had no men and any sons born of unisons with neighboring tribes were either killed or sent back to their fathers. Amazons supposedly burned off their right breasts so that they could draw a bow more effectively!

Celtic horses

Horses have always been highly prized as symbols of wealth among tribes who relied on them both for their livelihood and as a means of conquering others. The Celtic warrior queen Boudicca, or Boadicea, became ruler of the tribe of the Iceni, which means "people of the horse," in AD 60 when her husband, Prasutagus, died. The Romans seized her territory and Boudicca raised a revolt in England. She was routed by the Roman governor Suetonia after she had burned Colchester, London, and St. Albans. She then committed suicide by taking poison rather than being taken alive.

Historians Janet Farrar and Virginia Russell recount that the Iceni horses were about 13 hh, no bigger than a modern child's pony, and were used in pairs or teams of four to pull chariots. Legend has it that scythes were attached to the chariot wheels to cut down the enemy, but historians say this is a colorful but unlikely theory.

Celts believed that the dead rode into the next life on horses. Red horses, often with red-haired riders, were omens of forthcoming disaster. Irish legend tells how King Conaire, the son of the king of Ulster at the beginning of the Christian era, met three red-haired warriors, dressed in red clothing and mounted on red horses. He sent his son after them, but they told him that he would never overtake them because they were both dead and alive.

Celtic water horses are legendary nasties. The Isle of Man is said to be haunted by one who looks just like an ordinary horse—but if anyone tries to mount him, he will carry them out to sea and never return. The Scottish kelpie, or water horse, plays similar tricks, though the Irish version is kinder. The Irish water horse likes to leave the sea to gallop over dry land, and if you can catch him, he will make you a wonderful mount. The only problem is that you have to keep him away from water: If he sees a river or the sea, he will take you into it.

above: **Farriers had their own superstitions, including a reluctance to shoe horses on Good Friday because of the nails used to crucify Christ.**

So how do you spot a water horse? Traditionally they are always gray or black, and their hooves are the wrong way round. Sometimes they will mate with an ordinary horse, but although the foal will be safe to ride, you will still have problems—every time you ask it to go through water, it will lie down in it.

The farrier's magic

Ask most people to name a lucky symbol, and they will think of the horseshoe. Nailed over a door, it is said to bring luck and happiness to a house, while the bride who carries one down the aisle is asking for a happy marriage.

Blacksmiths and farriers—the first being one who forges metal for a variety of uses; the second a specialist in shoeing horses—were once among the most powerful men in the community. Their skills were so essential that they were often

credited with having magical powers, such as being able to stop blood flowing from a wound.

The Irish have many beliefs about blacksmiths' powers. If a 'smith turned his anvil upside down and cursed you, there was no escape. And if you heard the clang of metal coming from the forge at night, you should keep away for the sake of your sanity. The sounds would be made by fairy folk, who would steal the wits of anyone who tried to watch them work.

Nowadays, farriers in many parts of the world travel to shoe horses with portable forges in the backs of their vehicles, but a century ago, the village forge would have been at the hub of the community. The farrier would have a trough of water in which he plunged the red hot iron to cool once it had been shaped, and many people believed that drinking this water would cure all sorts of illnesses.

Blacksmiths had their own superstitions, though few modern ones would admit to any. Right up to the nineteenth century, you would find it difficult in England and Ireland to find a farrier who would shoe horses on Good Friday, because of the nails that were used to crucify Christ.

The horseshoe itself is a powerful symbol, representing fertility. The crescent, or U-shape, is believed to give protection and is seen in the arched windows of churches and temples. It is traditionally nailed on with seven nails, and seven has always been regarded as a special number; the ancient Egyptians and Babylonians gave it particular significance, as did followers of both Christian and Jewish faiths. Think of "lucky seven," seventh heaven, the world being created in seven days, and the reputed seven years' bad luck if you break a mirror.

Iron also has special qualities, perhaps because it can withstand fire. Superstition says that it has healing qualities; if you touch an afflicted part with a piece of iron and nail it to a tree, the illness will be trapped in the tree.

The best horseshoes, according to tradition, are ones that have been found by accident or have been cast by a gray mare! Most people nail the shoes above their doors with the points upward, to stop the luck running out, but farriers prefer to set them with the points downward so that the luck runs into the forge rather than out of it.

Another superstition says that if you nail your shoe above the door with the points facing downward, the devil will not

left: **A horseshoe nailed to a door pointing upward is supposed to keep luck with the house.**

above: **A woodcut of the four Horsemen of the Apocalypse.**

be able to sit in it! Lord Horatio Nelson had a horseshoe nailed to the mast of the H.M.S. Victory, but still died in the Battle of Trafalgar in 1805. The points were facing downward, so perhaps his luck did run out.

The devil has traditionally tried to trick blacksmiths, because cold iron is said to be a talisman against him. St. Dunstan, who became Archbishop of Canterbury in the tenth century, was asked by a mysterious figure in a cloak to shoe him instead of his horse. Realizing that this must be the devil, who had cloven hooves, Dunstan nailed him to the wall until the devil was forced to agree never to enter a house protected by a horseshoe.

Another legend tells of two apprentice farriers in Scotland, who joined forces to defeat a witch who followed the black arts. The younger apprentice became so exhausted that he fell asleep at his work during the day, and when his older brother kept watch at night, he discovered that the witch was turning him into a horse at night with the help of a magic bridle and riding him to her coven.

One night the older brother managed to catch hold of the reins, take the bridle off the horse, and put it on the witch instead. She turned into a black mare, that he galloped through the night and then took back to the forge to shoe. Next day the witch was found with horseshoes nailed to her hands and feet.

Horses and witches

The above story is one of many which tells how witches have the power to turn human beings into horses, but horses themselves traditionally fall victim to witchcraft. Even today, someone who looks particularly tired may be described as "hag-ridden," and this derives from the belief that if a horse is found sweating in his stable first thing in the morning, it is because a witch has taken him during the night, ridden him through the sky, and returned him before daybreak.

It was said that the best way to protect a horse from witches was to hang a hag stone or holey stone on his stable door. This is a stone or pebble in which a natural hole has formed. In the north of England, dobbie stones have a similar purpose; they too have a hole in the center, but are reputed to ward off "dobbies," black, shaggy ghost horses, as well as black magic and evil curses.

Horses are particularly sensitive animals, and their senses of sight, smell, and hearing are far superior to humans. It is often this sensibility which makes them shy or spook at things their riders cannot comprehend; unless, of course, you believe that a horse who shies at something invisible to human eyes has had a spell cast upon him.

Many witches have been credited with the ability to make a horse obey them despite its rider's or driver's instructions. Biddy Early, who lived in County Clare, Ireland, in the nineteenth century, was said to have foiled the local priest by making his horse stand stock still until she allowed it to move on.

Between the fifteenth and seventeenth centuries, innocent women in England, Scotland, and America were tortured, burned at the stake in England, and hung in America, because they were believed to be witches. In 1563, witchcraft meant the death penalty in England and Scotland, while in 1692, 19 supposed witches were executed and hundreds of suspected ones imprisoned during the famous witch hunts in Salem, Massachusetts.

Suspected witches were often accused of bewitching horses to ride to their coven meetings or of worshipping the devil in the form of a black horse. According to historians and practicing white witches Janet Farrar and Virginia Russell,

A selection of playing cards *(above)* **and tarot cards** *(right)* featuring a unicorn and horses. Horses were a recognized symbol for royalty and wealth.

ROY D'ESPEE

ROYNE DESPEE

CHEVALIER D'ESPEE

VARLET D'ESPEE

AR DESPEE

ROY·DE·DENIERS

coven rituals would often be intended to promote fertility of people, livestock, and crops, and would include a man dressed as an animal to represent the potent male. They say that trial references talk about the devil attending on "a great horse"—but point out that as the coven leader would probably be further up the social ladder than the ordinary members, this was hardly surprising!

Horses and fortune

Horses also appear in the Tarot pack, Italian playing cards first used in the fourteenth century, which are still used by believers as aids to prediction or interpretation. The Tarot, which comes from an old Italian word *taroco*, whose original meaning is unknown, comprises 78 cards. They are divided into groups known as major and minor arcana; arcana is the plural of arcanum, or secret.

below: **Sorcery in the Forest, an oil painting by Serge Ivanoff c.1970.**

Our ordinary playing cards derived from the minor arcana, but only the fool has crossed over from the major arcana—to become known as the joker. The major arcana symbolize the development of the person for whom the cards are being read, and horses usually figure in three cards: the chariot, death, and the sun.

The chariot is drawn by two horses, and this card symbolizes the ability or need to balance forces. The sun stands for fulfillment and success, while death is not as ominous as you might imagine; it can stand for regeneration, with the death of the old and the birth of the new.

The horse plays a prominent role in Chinese astrology, where each year is symbolized by an animal in 12-year cycles. In this century, the years of the horse were these:

January 25, 1906—February 12, 1907
February 11, 1918—January 31, 1919
January 30, 1930—February 16, 1931
February 15, 1942—February 4, 1943
February 3, 1954—January 23, 1955
January 21, 1966—February 8, 1967
February 7, 1978—January 27, 1979
January 27, 1990—February 14, 1991.

Horse people are said to be clever but with a tendency to arrogance. They work hard but lose interest quickly, are ambitious, and fall in love easily. There are two particularly important years—1906 and 1966—known as the years of the fire horse, where the above characteristics are said to be exaggerated. The horse is the only animal of the Chinese astrological cycle to have fire years.

Superstitions and dreams

There is an old saying that a good horse is never a bad color, which like many pieces of traditional wisdom can be interpreted in two ways. The first is that if you buy a horse that is a good, strong color, you should not have any problems. Even today, some people believe that a pale chestnut or bay will be sicklier than a horse whose coat is of a deep, strong hue. The second interpretation, which is actually far more sensible, is that if you find a good horse his color will be of no importance to you and buying horses is so risky, even for the knowledgeable, that color ought to be a minor consideration.

Many people believe that color can be linked to certain

below: **A Roman altar depicting the Goddess Epona with two horses from Schwarzenacker, Germany. Horses were so important that they merited their own goddess.**

characteristics. A popular belief is that chestnut horses, particularly mares, are temperamental. Mares can certainly be sensitive, but there are mares with wonderful natures just as there are geldings with doubtful temperaments. The linking of the color chestnut with unpredictability runs along parallel lines with the belief that people with red hair also have hot tempers and unpredictable natures.

Black horses make many people feel uneasy, perhaps because of their association with funerals. In the Western world, black is the color of mourning, and funeral hearses were traditionally drawn by black horses, often with black plumes mounted on their bridles. Another tradition which carried over to military funerals is that the dead man's horse follows his coffin, with the rider's boots reversed on each side of the saddle. The grim forerunner of this mark of respect was that when a king died, his horse would be killed and either buried with him or burned on his funeral pyre, so that he had a fitting mount in the afterlife.

In the days when horse-drawn hearses were the norm, those who attended would keep an uneasy eye on the animals' behavior. If they were reluctant to set off when the coffin was in place, it was said to be an omen that someone else in the family was about to die.

Changes in fashion alter our perception of color. Skewbald and piebald (brown and white and black and white) horses were once looked down on as being of common ancestry,

though they have always been highly prized by the true gypsies. Now the wheel has come full circle and they have their own enthusiasts and societies.

One of the most puzzling superstitions surrounds piebalds, who are less common than skewbalds. It is said that if you see a piebald horse, you should spit, cross your fingers, and make a wish. If you keep your fingers crossed until you see a dog, your wish should supposedly come true. Another belief is that the hair of a piebald horse has the power to cure illness if carried in your pocket, and there are still people who swear that the best way to get rid of a wart is to tie a hair from a horse's tail around it. The most likely explanation is that restricting the blood supply has the desired effect.

White leg markings, known as socks or stockings depending on how far up the leg they extend, have inspired a range of superstitions. One old rhyme illustrates this well:

> One white foot, buy a horse,
> Two white feet, try a horse.
> Three white feet, look well about him,
> Four white feet, do well without him.

Alternatively, you may prefer this one.
> One white foot, keep him not a day,
> Two white feet, send him far away.
> Three white feet, sell him to a friend,
> Four white feet, keep him to the end.

The Irish have a more succinct version.
> One, buy it.
> Two, try it.
> Three, look it over.
> Four, turn it out to clover.

Dreams of horses are said to hold special significance. Tony Crisp, who has written a dictionary of definitions, says that in general, dreaming of a horse denotes pleasurable energy and exuberance or sexual drive. Dreams of controlling a horse, or worrying that you cannot control it, are linked to sexuality, while dreaming of a winged horse symbolizes rising above everyday concerns. A black horse apparently represents unaccepted passions, while a white one can either represent changing sexual drive into love or coming to terms with feelings about death.

131

above: **A hobby horse at a summer festival with Morris dancers in the West Country, England.**

Festivals and customs

Horses have always played an important role in rituals, especially those concerned with fertility and harvest. The legacy remains through the hobby horse—an old fashioned child's toy with a distinctly pagan pedigree. There are hobby-horse traditions throughout the world, including France, Austria, India, and Poland.

Padstow in Cornwall, England, has its "'obby 'osses," who parade through the town on May Day. Each "horse" is a man wearing a covered frame to represent the horse's body with a tail at one end and a snapping wooden head at the other. His aim is to capture girls and young women under his skirts, a boisterous romp which brings (hopefully) good luck to any victims: If the girl is single, she will soon be married, while if she is already married, she will conceive.

Christmas is another time for festivals. Although we now associate Santa Claus with reindeer, the original stories of St. Nicholas had him driving a horse. There is still a Scandinavian tradition where a "Christmas sheaf" is put on the roof of a house; this is called Santa Claus's horse.

The Hodening, or Hoodening, horse made his appearance in England at Christmas or Halloween. Again, the star player was a man disguised as a horse, carrying either a wooden horse's head or a horse's skull. Sometimes he accompanies Morris dancers and handbell ringers and is probably much better behaved than his predecessors of a century ago.

Wales' version is the Mari Llwyd, or gray mare, who is accompanied on her rounds of the houses by Punch and Judy. Some people believe that she represents a mare who was turned out of the stable at Bethlehem to make room for Mary and Joseph.

Ghosts and white horses

Ghostly horses thunder all over the world, their supernatural masters hunting down any mortal unlucky or unwise enough to watch their progress. The wild huntsman is a spectral hunter of medieval legend who appears in England, France, and Germany, often associated with heroes of national legend.

In England, there is the wild hunt—a pack of ghostly hounds with red eyes whose horned huntsman is either Herne, the god of nature, or the devil himself. Legend says that Herne and the wild hunt can still be seen and heard in Windsor Great Park, Berkshire and that anyone who sees him is foreseeing his

right: **The White Horse Hill at Uffington, is a site of great beauty as well as historical importance. Wayland's Smithy, one mile away, is a neolithic chambered tomb. In local legend a horse left overnight would be shod by Wayland the Anglo-Saxon smith god.**

or her own death! This is how Shakespeare tells the legend in *The Merry Wives of Windsor*, Act IV, Scene IV:

> There is an old tale goes that Herne the Hunter,
> Sometime a keeper here in Windsor Forest,
> Doth all the winter-time, at still midnight,
> Walk round about an oak, with great ragg'd horns;
> And there he blasts the tree, and takes the cattle,
> And makes milch-kine yield blood, and shakes a chain
> In a most hideous and dreadful manner.

In Germany, a huntsman and his hounds are said to roam the Black Forest, while France's version is reputedly St. Hubert, the patron saint of huntsmen. He was apparently hunting a stag on Good Friday when he saw a vision of Christ and became an immediate convert.

Again in England, legend has it that the devil also drives a team of headless horses across Dartmoor, though one version of the legend has the driver as Sir Francis Drake rather than Satan. In Somerset, King Arthur and his knights are supposed to ride out on Midsummer Night's Eve.

White horses, huge figures cut into chalk downs, are said to have supernatural powers. The oldest and most famous of the British chalk figures is the White Horse of Uffington, on England's Berkshire Downs; if you stand in his eye and close your own, turn around three times and make a wish, the horse will reputedly make it come true. During World War II, the horse was camouflaged so that enemy bombers could not use it as a landmark. At one time, a special festival was held every seven years to clean or "scour" him, but this has now died out.

Archeologists using laser techniques have recently proved that the Uffington Horse dates back almost 3,000 years to the Late Bronze Age or Early Iron Age, and the favorite theory is that it was held sacred to the Celtic goddess Epona. Epona was a deity who was "imported" to Britain during the Roman occupation around the year AD 55. Her name means "divine mare," and the horse was her symbol or totem. Another English hill figure, the Westbury Horse in Wiltshire, is variously credited to King Arthur and to an eighteenth-century landscaper.

Wherever you look, the horse has a history steeped in myth and legend, superstition, and the supernatural. Perhaps that is why the legends live on and its magic is so enduring.

left: **A sculptured head of the goddess Epona.**

133

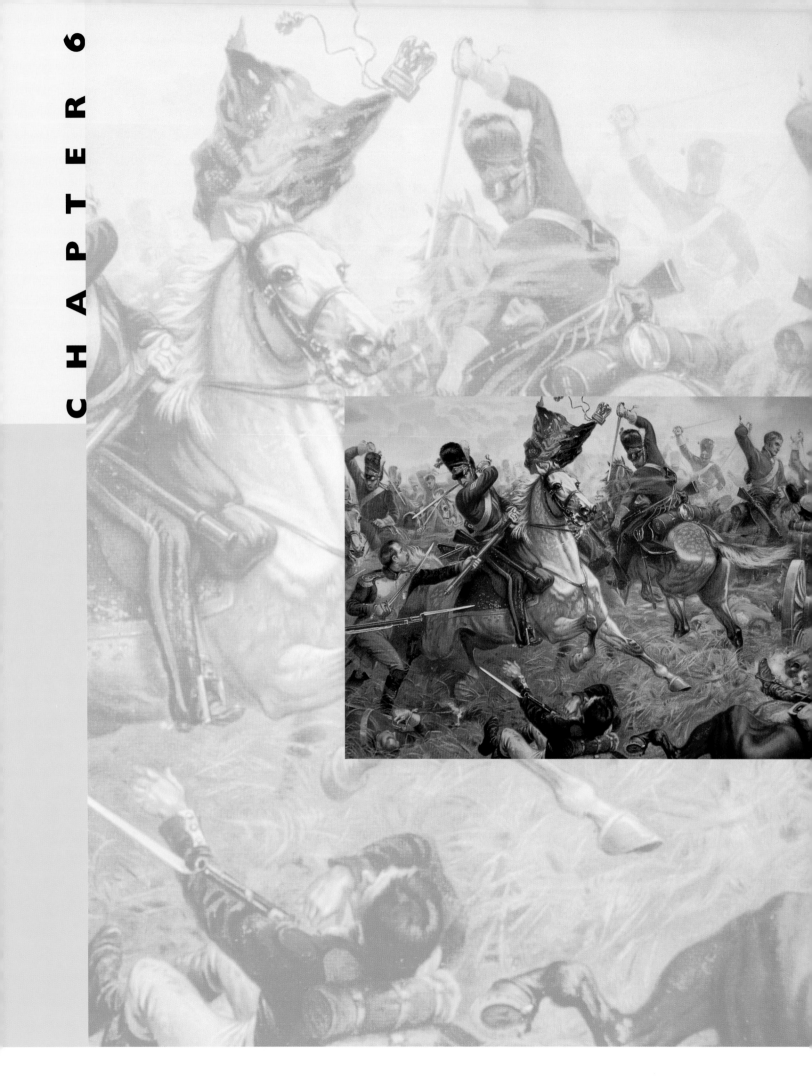

above: **Battle of Waterloo, 1815.** Sergeant Ewart of the Scots Greys captures the eagle standard

of French 45th Regiment. Painted by **W. H. Sullivan, 1898.**

the
horse
in war

the
the
the
horse
horse in w
in war
in
in war the
horse
in war

Hast thou given the horse strength? Hast thou clothed his neck in thunder? Canst thou make him afraid as a grasshopper? The glory of his nostrils is terrible. He paweth the ground and rejoiceth in his strength, he goeth on to meet the armed men. He mocketh at fear, and is not affrighted; neither turneth he back from the sword. The quiver rattleth against him, the glittering spear and shield. He swalloweth the ground with fierceness and rage; neither believeth he that it is the sound of the trumpets. He saith among the trumpets, Ha ha, and he smelleth the battle afar off, the thunder of the captains and the shouting.

Job 39:19–25

Then Allah took a handful of the South Wind and He breathed thereon, creating the horse and saying: Thy name shall be Arabian, and virtue bound into the hair of thy forelock, and plunder on thy back. I have preferred thee above all beasts of burden, inasmuch as I have made thy master thy friend. I have given thee the power of flight without wings, be it in onslaught or retreat.

The Koran

below: **Taiping Rebellion, contemporary painting of Imperial Chinese Troops putting the rebels to flight at Tai and showing a planned military action using cavalry.**

Psychology

The horse has a lot to offer to the military tactician. It is a big, powerful creature that endows a mounted soldier with unparalleled maneuverability and the advantage of extra height. A cavalry charge had so much physical and psychological power, that it was almost unstoppable.

It is hard to imagine what it must feel like to be a foot soldier who has been ordered to stand and face a thundering wall of armored equine and human flesh, as it closes with the enemy at 30 miles per hour. The raw power of the onslaught is enough to guarantee a breech in the enemy line.

above: **Fresco from a tomb at Paestum, Italy, dating to 4th century BC showing a mounted warrior with no saddle.**

However, the cavalry charge needs to be followed by infantry as the unstoppable rush of equine adrenalin and raw momentum can carry a cavalry charge on past the enemy. The gains can be lost without a proper follow-through.

As any soldier knows, there is more to warfare than charging at the enemy. A soldier in the right place is worth any number in the wrong location. The ability to move mounted units to cover your own weaknesses and capitalize on those of the enemy means that each mounted soldier can be worth five on the ground.

Once the main events on the battlefield have finished, the cavalry really comes into its own in preventing the vanquished army from regrouping. For the victors, it is the cavalry alone that can turn a strategic victory into a rout—unless the retreating army has enough mounted units available to allow an ordered withdrawal from the field of conflict.

In a more drawn out conflict, cavalry units could be used for aggressive patrolling along the borders of enemy territory —seeking out weak points and then forcing the enemy to keep ground troops in a constant state of alert. In some cases, the cavalry was used for hit-and-run raids deep behind enemy lines. Mounted troops were the ears and the eyes of the military tactician.

Unfortunately for the military, the horse has a psyche completely unsuited to the rigors and pressures of battle. There are few creatures on earth more timorous than the horse. Equines have two simple rules hard-wired into their brains at birth:

Rule 1. If in doubt, run away.

Rule 2. If you see someone else running, then join in; they might have spotted something you missed.

This survival strategy, combined with a gift for running fast over rough terrain, has served horses well for several million years. When threatened, they can slip into an adrenalin high that creates a blind, rampaging panic attack. Muscles are forced into overdrive, and the naturally conservative mind of the horse is converted into that of a high-rolling gambler, prepared to attempt impossible leaps over ravines, gallop full tilt across rock-strewn mountainsides, and plunge through swiftly flowing rivers.

A terrified horse is running for its life. The pursuing predator is only after its next meal. For the horse, it's all or nothing. So how can the idea of the fear-riddled mind of a horse be squared with its demonstrated ability to face danger in battle?

What horses fear above all is novelty. A familiar but repainted gate post can send them into snorting, side-stepping stupidity. They need to convince themselves that any particular change is not a threat.

A cavalry charge might be made straight into the teeth of enemy fire, and yet the horses keep going. Some of that can be explained by practice and training. If a horse can be taught to ignore threats such as buses or heavy machinery, then it can also be taught not to fear gunshots. But the horse in battle is well aware of the dangers which lie ahead. Rule one is telling it to turn around and run away. Rule two is telling it that all these other horses running in the same direction must mean that there is something really frightening behind. After all, it has always paid to stay with the herd. Now is not the time to form a breakaway party of one. The herd, as far as the mind-set of the horse is concerned, is always right. Try making a one-horse cavalry charge and see how far you get.

A cavalry charge, once underway, has been described as a poorly controlled bolt, which is almost certainly impossible to stop. From the moment that Lord Raglan's orders had been issued to the Light Brigade, no amount of tugging by 600 cavalry troopers on 600 cavalry bits was ever going to stop the charge halfway through.

The other problem with the cavalry charge is that it leaves a vacuum behind. The horses, once underway, have a tendency to continue in the direction they started—often leaving the enemy to pick themselves up off the ground and start firing weapons into the backs of the cavalry as it sweeps on to who knows where. Throughout history there have been military commanders who have been deeply cynical about the cavalry.

The Chariot

Horses have certainly become embroiled in human conflicts ever since they were first domesticated. Their ability to deliver a strong fighting force where it can do the most harm would have been recognized and utilized right away. For hit-and-run guerrilla activity against rival tribes, horses would have proved invaluable. However, as a fighting platform or for classic cavalry charges, early domesticated

Biga - Museo Vaticano - Roma

above: **Ancient Roman chariot and horses in marble, the Vatican Museum.**

horses would have been completely unsuitable. Most were no more than ponies—capable of carrying a man over long distances but too small to be used as an effective fighting platform for a fully armed and armored soldier. In addition, the early saddles were terribly crude—nothing more than felt or leather pads. Mounted archers were used by the Assyrians in 1000 BC but their main role was probably for harrying the enemy rather than as a frontal assault force.

It was in harness, pulling war chariots, that horses first entered the mêlée of conventional battle. The chariot, as an instrument of war, has many advantages: the wheeled platform provides an ideal position from which to launch arrows or javelins; quivers can easily be fitted to ensure that the javelin arm is exhausted long before the supply of ammunition; the provision of a driver separates the functions of navigation and fighting; and finally, the chariot itself is a wonderfully maneuverable vehicle—on the right terrain.

It was on the table-flat plains of what is now Syria that chariot warfare reached its zenith in a series of encounters between the Egyptians and the Hittites 1,500 years before Christ was born.

In the Bronze Age, as in the whole of history, the aristocracy was averse to walking into battle. Cynics might

left: **King Rameses II of Egypt 1300–1230 BC, standing in his war chariot shooting an arrow, from a print published in Cairo, 1944.**

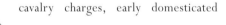

suggest that horses are also extremely useful in escaping from a lost cause should things go wrong. The chariot divisions became the natural home of the upper crust on both sides of the conflict between the Egyptians and the Hittites.

The Egyptian chariots were lightweight affairs made of wood and wickerwork. The axle was placed at the rear of the platform which helped in maneuverability and stability but placed half the weight of the two-man crew on the backs of the horses. It was probably used as a skirmishing vehicle to harry and disrupt rather than destroy infantry. The chosen weapon was a heavy composite bow that allowed the chariot to attack without closing with the enemy. The chariot divisions were deployed in squads of 10, squadrons of 50, and larger units of 250 called *pedjets*. It is believed that the Egyptians had in excess of 2,000 chariots available to them at the battle of Qadesh in 1286 BC—the Hittites might well have had double that number of chariots .

The Hittites used much heavier, all-wood chariots with a centrally placed axle, heavily armored horses, and three-man crews—driver, spear man, and shield bearer. These heavy chariots were the main offensive weapon used in mass frontal charges—taking the battle to the place where the enemy was at its weakest. Javelins were used while closing with the enemy and long lances for close quarters.

Mopping-up operations would have been carried out by the infantry in close support. At their peak, the Hittites could muster nearly 4,000 chariots and 40,000 infantry. At Qadesh, the Egyptian army had split into four units to travel to the prearranged battle site. The pharaoh, Rameses II, was the first to arrive with one division. As the second section was marching across the Plain of Qadesh to join their leader, they were suddenly attacked by a Hittite chariot assault which swept through the center of the two-mile-long column of infantry and Egyptian chariots.

A combination of surprise and raw assault power split the column in half and created a rout. Flushed with success, the Hittite chariots then swept on for a second attack on the pharaoh's main camp. The heavily armored Hittite horses must

below: **Roman sculpture of battle scene on a mausoleum at St. Remy, France. This is the earliest known depiction of a horse with a saddle in Europe.**

above: **Roman soldiers testing the "tortoise," in which soldiers protect themselves under an umbrella of shields.**

have been traveling at top speed for four or more miles and were almost played out by the time they arrived at the pharaoh's camp. The vigor of the charge had been lost. Leaving the infantry to do their best to defend themselves, the pharaoh and his own chariotry fled the camp and rallied out on the plains around Qadesh.

They, in turn, made a fresh assault on the disrupted, spent, and largely unsupported Hittite chariots, which were now under attack from infantry archers in the camp and chariot archers on the plain.

A further Hittite force forded the river Orontes to make a second assault on the pharaoh's camp, but was, in turn, attacked by fresh Egyptian chariot divisions arriving from the north.

Qadesh was the classic chariot battle where the maneuverability and impact of the chariot determined the course of the conflict. It demonstrated both the strengths and weaknesses of the chariot and cavalry; that it could be used to surprise and destroy infantry. However, like the tanks in the First World War, any gains were quickly lost unless infantry were close enough for the follow through operations.

The Roman cavalry

The Romans used chariots for transport, ceremony, and racing but hardly at all in war. Although the Roman military strategy was originally built around the foot soldier, a series of humiliating defeats by rival civilizations equipped with cavalry meant that the tacticians had to deal with integrating cavalry into the Roman army.

The Roman's military machine used equine bloodlines imported from all over the empire and had access to horses up to 15.2 hh, a respectable size even by today's standards.

It is known that Roman cavalry units were issued with spears and swords and managed to use both of these weapons in war without the aid of stirrups—which did not appear until the fourth or fifth centuries AD. Why it took so long to develop such a useful aid to horsemanship says a great deal about 20/20 hindsight. How could people have missed such an obvious and simple idea?

The lack of stirrups was solved with the help of some vicious-looking protuberances from the saddle which all but clamped the rider into position. This would have given the mounted soldier enough stability to use a striking or thrusting weapon but would have held him so securely in the saddle that any chance of rolling clear in the event of a fall would be remote.

above: **Alexander the Great, one of the greatest known warriors in history on Bucephalus, his steed for 30 years, fighting Darius's son-in-law during the Battle of Granicus, 334 BC. From a Persian manuscript.**

above: **Mongolian lariat thrower—sculpture by Mongolian artist M. Mizhir.**

As with all things military, the Romans codified and regulated their cavalry. Initial breaking was carried out in high-walled circular pens—which were adopted by the Spanish and eventually found their way to North America, where identical breaking pens can be found across the West.

Relatively little is known of the way horses were used by the Roman military. The descriptions of cavalry actions tend to be rather sketchy. One of the major sources of information is a training manual called the *Ars Tactica* written in the second century AD by a Roman proconsul of Greek extraction named Flavius Arrianus Xenophon. He saw service in Spain and Turkey—both strong horse cultures.

The manual details an extraordinary range of cavalry maneuvers and covers the use of weapons including bows, javelins, swords, lances, maces, and the axe. Many of the circles, stops, and rollbacks used in training the Roman cavalry would be completely familiar to the modern well-schooled American Quarter horse. Like the Spanish and Western riders of today, the combination of a vicious bit and a gentle hand was the favored mechanism of control. Neck reining left a hand free for the javelin, sword, and spear.

The cavalry units were drilled on specially built parade grounds—patches of pool-table-flat land which were carefully drained and cultivated to a depth of three to four inches to give a perfect surface on which to train—a surface similar to that found on a modern rodeo arena or manège.

Judging by the training procedures outlined in the *Ars Tactica*, great emphasis was placed on the ability of the cavalry to ride close to the enemy, discharge arrows or javelins, and retreat in preparation for a further assault.

Cavalry tactics evolved as the Roman Empire came into contact and conflict with other civilizations, but the frontal cavalry charge was not something that figures strongly in the contemporary Roman military archive. If the classical cavalry charge was a significant part of Roman military strategy, then it would have been mentioned with all the other maneuvers.

The Romans first arrived in Britain in 55 BC—but without cavalry support. The Britons made extensive use of both cavalry and chariots to harry and demoralize the Roman infantry to the point where Julius Caesar pulled his men back across the English Channel.

The Romans always learned more from their defeats than their victories, and when they returned for the second successful invasion they brought cavalry with them.

Mongols

The Mongols were just one of several waves of horsemen to come sweeping out of the East and across Europe. They came from quintessential horse cultures—they drank mares' milk, ate horse-milk cheese, drank horse blood, ate horse flesh, and even cooked over horse-dung fires. Many of their tools and clothes were made from horse bone and skin.

Invading Mongol armies might bring as many as 12 hardy ponies for each rider. Each group was trained to follow a lead mare which was fitted with a bell. The ponies traveled at a frame-jarring jog trot. Forced marches of 120 miles in a single 24-hour period have been recorded—80 miles in a day was far from exceptional. When on the march, the men would swap horses without stopping, and frequently sleep and eat in the saddle. They had even developed techniques for passing water without dismounting. The explorer Marco Polo wrote this about the Mongols on his travels:

> Their horses are fed upon grass alone and do not require barley or other grain. The men are habituated to remain on horseback for two days and two nights without dismounting, sleeping in that position while their horses graze. Their mounts are so well broken-in to quick changes of movement that upon the signal being given, they instantly turn in every direction; and

below: **Genghis Khan captures a Chinese town in 1205; miniature from Persian history completed in 1596.**

by these rapid maneuvers many victories have been obtained.

The Europeans, with their relatively immobile armies, found the hit-and-run tactics followed by mass attacks impossible to counter. Military conventions were being broken at every encounter.

Normans

The horse in battle appears to have fallen out of favor in Britain during the centuries following the Roman occupation. It was used for transport and skirmishing, but the infantry reigned supreme in the densely wooded regions of Britain.

When William the Conqueror invaded Britain in 1066, he brought 1,000 armored cavalry. His chain-mail-clad knights had the benefit of stirrups and good tack and were mounted on stocky type horses ranging in height from 14.2 to 15 hh. For Harold, the horse was such an irrelevance that he oversaw the whole battle on foot.

At the Battle of Hastings, William tried using his cavalry again and again against the English ranks but with no success until Harold's men moved forward off the high ground. William spotted his moment and, using cavalry to take the battle to the enemy at Harold's weakest point, threw the whole weight of his cavalry against what had now become an advancing rabble. Once it had broken rank and come out into the open the bulk of the English army was cut to pieces and the battle turned in favor of the Norman invaders. Britain would never be the same again.

The Normans were successful riders who used their horses for travel, battle, and pleasure. Great store was placed in prowess in the hunt, which has always been regarded as good training for battle.

However, improved technology in the form of plate armor was due to bring irrevocable changes for both horse and rider. Chain mail, where rings of steel are sewn onto a leather garment, offers good lightweight protection to a glancing sword blow but does little to turn a lance or steel-tipped arrow. Plate armor conferred virtual invulnerability on its wearer, but there was a heavy price to pay.

A complete set of body armor plus shield and sword or lance might double the bodyweight of its wearer. The top-heavy knight required an extremely secure saddle if he were to stay put. In addition, there was little point in putting an invulnerable knight into the field on an unprotected horse which could be downed by a single arrow. At the peak of this technological insanity, during the fourteenth century, the battle charger might have to carry almost 500 pounds of man, weaponry, and armor. The small 15 hh horse had to be upgraded to the classic lumbering Destrier or heavy horse.

As the technology improved through the following centuries, the armor and the horses got heavier and heavier— as did the capital cost of keeping such an expensive piece of military equipment in the field. It has been estimated that up to five support staff would have been needed to keep a single mounted knight in battle-ready condition.

The lumbering gait of the Destrier would have been uncomfortable to ride, so each knight would require a palfrey, or riding horse, on which to travel while on campaign. Two or three pack horses or an ox cart would be neeeded to carry the armor and related equipment. The cost of all this was so crippling that it helped to create a social system where lands and titles were allocated according to the number of knights the aristocracy could offer to the King. Some estates became little more than military academies.

The role of the infantry was reduced to that of pawns on

above: **The Crusades: French knight Godfrey of Bouillon (1060–1100) on his way to the Holy Land.**

the chess board—being used to force the hand of the opposition and draw him out into the open.

The historical chronicler Oman wrote about this in his treatise *The Art of War:*

Foot soldiers accompanied the army for no better purpose than to perform the menial duties of camp or to assist in the numerous sieges of the period. Occasionally they were employed as light troops to open battle by their ineffective demonstrations.

There was, however, no important part for them to play. Indeed their Lords were sometimes affronted if they presumed to delay too long the opening of the cavalry charges and ended the skirmishing by riding into and over their wretched followers.

The power that a cavalry charge could deliver to an infantry line was unstoppable—unless archers were given time to take their toll—as happened at Crécy and Agincourt.

At Crécy in 1346, 16 cavalry charges by the 2,500 knights of the French forces were met by hails of arrows from the English and Welsh longbows. More than 1,500 noblemen died. The knights were equipped with the best technology money could buy in the fourteenth century, while the English and the Welsh were using technology developed before man ever planted his first crop. The playing field between cavalry and infantry had been leveled—it was a lesson the aristocracy seriously took to heart.

Reivers

Scotland has always been a strong horse culture, not only for warfare but also for cattle droving. Since 1200 AD it had been the law in Scotland that any owner of land, no matter how small the holding, must own a horse. By 1327, Scotland could put 20,000 cavalry in the field.

In the sixteenth century, the horse really came into its own in the sort of guerrilla activity and raiding seen in the strip of

above: **Two knights jousting in full military attire.**

fertile lands which constitute the borderlands, or marches, between England and Scotland.

Four hundred years ago the Scottish marches were the center of an ongoing power struggle between rival border families. Family names now familar on both sides of the Atlantic—Scotts, Humes, Grahams, Johnstons, Maxwells, and Forsters—all held large swaths of territory. They felt free to make raids and steal cattle and plate silver from rival families. The legal governments on both sides of the border turned a blind eye and sometimes actively encouraged such raiding. Between them, they created the sort of horseback lawlessness not seen again until the American and Mexican regimes came into conflict during the opening up of the western United States in the first half of the nineteenth century.

In Scotland, reiving became so well established in the annual calendar that the raiding season was as much a part of border life as hay-making or planting potatoes. Women folk were reputed to have placed a dish of spurs in front of their menfolk when the time came for raiding.

The traditional reiving season was from September to Christmas when the horses would be in peak condition and the ground still fairly dry. The lengthening nights would have been a tremendous advantage to the raiders. The idea was to ride deep into rival territory under cover of darkness. After traveling all night and covering upward of 60 miles, the raiding parties would rest in some hidden valley through the day and make their raid just as night was falling. The men would steal what they could carry and capture as much stock

145

left: **William of Normandy, also known as William the Conqueror, from the Bayeux Tapestry.**

above: **Battle of Crécy, 1346. Edward III defeated the French as depicted in *Froissart's Chronicles*, 14th century.**

as they could drive. There would then follow a mad cross-country dash to return home with the booty before the locals could organize a hot pursuit and catch the culprits red-handed.

Revenge attacks and hot pursuits were given semi-official sanction—both the English and Scottish National governments appointed March wardens whose job it was to keep the peace. The March wardens were chosen from the most powerful families in the area. They were powerful, because they were rich and had strong armies of reivers at their disposal—thereby blurring the boundary between illegal raids and legal recriminations.

The raiders were mounted on the same tough ponies or hobblers that can still be seen today in the borders and highlands. Most were bordering on 15 hh and able to carry their fully armed riders upward of 50 miles during a long, cold November night. Raids involving as many as 2,000 mounted reivers were not uncommon.

The only armor plate the men wore were their steel bonnets—their main protection was their thick leather jackets, nimble horses, strong sword arms, and their lances. Their aim was to cut and run. The borders were the last European bastion of the war bow—its cheapness, rapid fire capability, and silence were much prized.

Raiding and pursuit were a dangerous business. One night in 1528, a small raiding party made up of some 30 Nixons and Crosers crossed the border into Bewcastle and lifted a herd of cattle from Thirlwall. They also kidnapped a tenant of the March warden, Lord William Dacre.

The warden raised a party and set off in "hot trod" hoping to catch the raiders. A mile before the border, they overhauled the raiders and were about to exact their revenge, when a host of mounted Elliots, Armstrongs, and Nixons appeared on the hills all around them and swept down upon the hapless pursuers. Forty of the wardens' men were taken prisoner and 10 dispatched on the spot. The rest were kept as hostages against further cross-border reprisals.

Firearms

The gradual introduction of firearms eventually toppled the horse from its position as the premier weapon of war— the infantryman could now with the mere squeeze of a trigger, could bring all that investment in metal and flesh crashing to its knees.

left: **French cavalry in the 16th century armed with firearms at the time of Henry IV, 1595.**

147

By 1520 Machiavelli wrote this about the cavalry.

> It is right to have some cavalry to support and assist infantry, but not to look upon them as the main force of an army for they are highly necessary to reconnoiter and to lay waste an enemy's country and to cut off their convoys; but in the field battles which commonly decide the fate of nations, they are fitter to pursue an enemy that is routed and flying than anything else.

Few could contest that the world had changed, but another 500 years would pass before the horse completely disappeared from the battlefield. It was the repeating rifle which finally put an end to the conventional cavalry charge.

The horse remained indispensable for its ability to move men and equipment to the place where it was most needed. No enemy could be completely vanquished without the cavalry to prevent a rally, and neither could a retreat be well ordered and disciplined, and function properly without the cavalry to cover the rear.

The cavalry unit remained the premier means of reconnaissance and the best way of maintaining control of vast areas of newly conquered lands.

The Napoleonic Era

It was during the Napoleonic wars (1803–13) and those in Crimea that the cavalry charge underwent something of a resurgence in popularity—if such a term can be used where so much destruction of human and equine flesh is involved.

Battle tactics had evolved to the point where well-disciplined and armed ground troops in classic square formations with musketeers ranged three or four deep could withstand and repulse almost any cavalry attack. However,

developments in field artillery that could rapidly be brought to bear on troop formations shifted the balance of power away from the infantry. The field pieces needed to be highly mobile —hence the teams of six light draft horses which allowed the artillery to keep pace with the cavalry.

Batteries could be established out of range of musket shot, but within range of their own grapeshot and exploding ordnance. These could be used to disrupt the infantry formations and the cavalry could be brought in to finish off the job.

Unfortunately, the gun batteries were extremely vulnerable to being attacked themselves. Infantry was not such a threat—the artillery could fire off a couple of rounds of grape and then pack up and move to safety before they arrived.

Cavalry was much more mobile and could be in among the guns within a minute or two. Suddenly the cavalry came back into favor, and the deadly alliance with the artillery proved to be the most potent military development of the nineteenth century. The artillery went from being one of the grubbiest arms of the military to being one of the smartest.

However, any cavalry charge can result in horrendous destruction. The most famous was the Charge of the Light Brigade in 1854, where some 673 mounted men participated in the charge. The aim was to silence an enemy gun battery— a perfectly achievable mission and one which might be expected to cause five to 10 percent losses in the cavalry. Unfortunately, the whole length of the charge was open to fire from a number of other units—hence the loss of 234 dead or injured men and the loss of 470 horses.

Battle casualties among horses were generally reckoned to be about a third higher than those for the men. Grape and gunshot wounds were common, but saber cuts around the head and neck from enemy horsemen or even their own riders were a major cause of death. However, it was poor management which accounted for the majority of equine losses throughout all the major European campaigns of the nineteenth century.

Obtaining good-quality forage was the perpetual problem. Most European cavalry and artillery mounts lived on protein and energy-rich diets of oats and hay. When forced to live off local herbage, they suffered terribly.

left: **French Cuirassiers (heavy cavalry) of the Napoleonic period, *Carrying the Standard at Austerlitz, 1805*, painted by Edouard Detaille.**

For example, the 14th Light Dragoons were involved in the Peninsula campaign for the whole of its six-year duration (1808–14). They arrived in Lisbon with a full complement of 720 chargers and over the following six years of the campaign were issued with 1,120 replacements. When they returned to their barracks back in Weymouth, they had a mere 278 mounts. Wellington himself lost 12 horses during the first three years of the Peninsula campaign.

The American West

When the first feral horses appeared in the Great Plains, they no doubt caused almost as much disruption to the life of Native Americans as would the arrival of the White man some 200 years later.

The nomadic tribes which adopted the horse suddenly became supercharged societies. Before the horse arrived, they could only own as much equipment as they and their dogs could carry as they followed the seasons and the game around the Great Plains. Suddenly they could build and move large buffalo-hide lodges, they could hunt and kill as much game as they required, food could be preserved and moved to winter quarters, but most importantly of all, they could mount raiding parties on rival tribes. The Sioux, Apache, and Comanche expanded dramatically at the cost of their more sedentary and peaceful neighbors. The horse-equipped Plains' warriors became supreme hit-and-run guerrilla raiders.

above: **English Civil War: a re-enactment of the Battle of Langport, 1645.**

One time Philadelphia lawyer George Catlin spent many years in the West with his beloved Native Americans. In one of hundreds of letters home written all through the 1830s, he described the horsemanship of the Plains' people.

The Comanches, like the Northern tribes, have many games, and in pleasant weather seem to be continually practicing. In their ball plays, and in some other games, they are far behind the Sioux and other Northern tribes: but in racing horses and riding they are not equalled by any other Indians on the continent.

Among their feats of riding, there is one that has astonished me more than anything of the kind I have ever seen, or expect to see in my life: a stratagem of war, learned and practiced by every young man in the tribe; by which he is able to drop his body upon the side of his horse and the instant he is passing, effectually screened from his enemy's weapons as he lays in a horizontal position behind the body of his horse, with his heel hanging over the horse's back; by which he has the power of throwing himself up again, and changing to the other side if necessary.

In this wonderful condition, he will hang while his

above: **Crimean War 1854–56: The Charge of the Light Brigade, 25 October 1854, painted by R. Caton Woodville.**

horse is at fullest speed, carrying with him his bow and his shield, and also his long lance of 14 feet in length, all or either of which he will wield upon his enemy as he passes; rising and throwing his arrows over his horse's back, or with equal ease and equal success under the horse's neck.

This astonishing feat, which the young men have been repeatedly playing off to our surprise as well as amusement, whilst they have been galloping about in front of the tents, completely puzzled the whole of us; and appeared as the result of magic rather than of skill acquired with practice.

I had several times great curiosity to approach them, to ascertain by what means their bodies could be suspended in this manner where nothing could be seen but the heel hanging over the horse's back. In these endeavours I was continually frustrated, until one day I coaxed a young fellow up within a little distance of me by offering a few plugs of tobacco, and he in a moment solved the difficulty, so far as to render it apparently more feasible then before yet leaving it one of the most extraordinary results of practice and persevering

endeavours. I found on examination, that a short hair halter was passed around under the neck of the horse, and both ends tightly braided into the mane on the withers, leaving a loop to hang under the neck and against the breast, which being caught up in the hand makes a sling into which the elbow falls, taking the weight of the body on the middle of the upper arm. Into this loop the rider drops suddenly and fearlessly, leaving his heel to hang over the back of the horse to steady him and also to restore him, when he wishes to regain his upright position on the horse's back.

I am ready without hesitation to pronounce the Comanches the most extraordinary horsemen that I have yet seen in all my travels, and I doubt very much whether any people in the World can surpass them.

It was the Comanche Indian who prevented the Spanish conquistadors from expanding north from Mexico—their repeated raids made frontier life too unbearable for Spanish military and settlers alike.

Neighboring tribes that were slow to take advantage of the horse for the hunt and for war. They were quickly swept aside in the face of such consummate skill.

The ponies used by the Native Americans were hardy creatures—able to withstand the incredibly cold winters and disgustingly hot fly-ridden summers that afflict the Great Plains. The centuries of running wild was one of the finest breeding policies yet seen—resulting in ponies with incredibly tough constitutions, tough feet, fleet and sure-footed.

It is hardly surprising that so many people lost their lives during the Native American wars which were to sweep the plains in the years after the American Civil War (1861–65.) Catlin also wrote of the buffalo hunt:

> Such is the training of men and horses in this country that the work of death and slaughter is simple and easy. The horse is trained to approach the animals on the right side, enabling its rider to fire his arrows to the left: it runs and approaches without the use of the halter, which is hanging loose upon its neck, bringing the rider within three or four paces of the animal.
>
> An Indian, therefore mounted on a fleet and well-

trained horse with his bow in his hand, and his quiver slung on his back containing an hundred arrows, of which he can fire fifteen or twenty in a minute, is a formidable and dangerous enemy.

Many of them also ride with a lance of twelve or fourteen feet in length with a blade of polished steel; and all of them with a shield made of the skin of a buffalo's neck which has been smoked and hardened with glue extracted from the hoofs. These shields are arrow proof and will glance off a rifle shot with perfect effect by being turned obliquely, which they do with great skill.

The American Civil War

Military tactics in Europe ossified during the second half of the century with 40 years of peace. There was some rewriting of the history books, and the cavalry charge was held to be more effective than it had really proved itself to be. At the same time, weapons technology continued to improve with the appearance of breech-loading and repeating rifles. The

below: **Comanche feats of horsemanship painted by George Catlin in 1834, demonstrating the skills that would have been used by Native Americans in battle.**

left: **American Civil War: Captain of US cavalry, showing saddle equipment and saber.**

its toes and forced the commanders to commit huge forces to guard duty on a whole range of vulnerable facilities. Almost nothing within 150 miles of the front could be left unguarded.

Many northern generals were disparaging of the cavalry and relegated them to picket duty and the job of messenger boys. It was two or three years into the conflict before the northern states accepted the advantages that mobility could confer on an army and started pouring resources into its cavalry and artillery just as the South was starting to run out of steam and the years of conflict were exacting a toll on the mounted units.

The American Civil War was primarily an infantry and artillery war. In most of the major set-piece battles mounted action by cavalry was all but irrelevant. Even at the battle of Brandy Station on June 9, 1863, when there were some 10,000 mounted combatants on either side, most of the action took place between dismounted cavalry troopers and their accompanying field artillery.

The horse-drawn artillery played a crucial role in almost every set-piece conflict. In many cases, the life expectancy of an artillery horse was even less than that of the cavalry mount. The secret of success with artillery was its ability to move rapidly from one location to another as priorities changed. This meant that the artillery teams had to stand near to the batteries while they were firing. When gun batteries came under fire, then so did the horses.

John D. Billings, who was part of the Army of the Potomac, was an artillery man who took equine carnage to heart. Writing in August, 1864, of an action that took place at Ream's Station on the Weldon Railroad he said this:

In this battle, the 57 horses belonging to my company stood out in bold relief, a sightly target for the Rebel sharpshooters who, from a wood and cornfield in our front, improved their opportunity to the full. Their object was to kill off our horses, and then by charging, take the guns if possible.

It was painfully interesting to note the manner in which our brave limber horses—those which drew the guns—succumbed to the bullets of the enemy.

A peculiar dull thud indicated that the bullet had

effective range of small arms increased to 800 yards, allowing a hail of lead to be poured into a charging line of cavalry long before it could close with the infantry. Commanders also started coming to terms with the idea that it was no disgrace for an infantry unit to actually duck down behind a wall or ridge while reloading their weapons.

Despite the use of trains for the first time in moving troops around the field of operations, the horse retained its tactical benefits of greatly improved troop mobility. The southern states in particular were a horse culture par excellence—and an affluent one at that. Hunting on horseback with rifle and hounds was a major pastime for many southern landowners and farmers. The Confederacy was able to raise some of the best mounted, manned, and armed cavalry units the world had ever seen, and they had the advantage of fighting on familiar territory, so the quality of the horseflesh could often be well maintained through the campaigning season.

It is reckoned that at the start of the war, there were over six million saddle and light draft horses available—Quarter Horses, Saddlebreds, Morgans, as well as the humble Mustangs. All are suitable breeds for mounted operations.

The southern cavalry with light artillery support ran rings around the northern forces by mounting spectacular hit-and-run raids in considerable force deep behind enemy lines. Unexpected appearances and raids by brilliant southern commanders such as J. E. B. Stuart kept the northern army on

above: **American Civil War: Portrait of
General J. E. B. Stuart of the Confederate Army.**

penetrated some fleshy part of the animal, sounding much as a pebble does when thrown into mud. The result of such wounds was to make the horse start for a moment or so but would finally settle down as if it was something to be endured without making a fuss, and thus would remain until struck again. I remember having my eye on one horse at the very moment when a bullet entered his neck, but the wound had no more effect on him than to make him shake his head as if pestered by a fly. Some of the horses would go down when hit by the first bullet, and after lying quiet a while would struggle to their feet only to receive additional wounds. When the bullet struck the bone of a horse's leg it made a hollow snapping sound and took him off his feet.

I saw one pole horse shot thus, fracturing the bone. Down he went at once, but all encumbered as he was with harness and limber, he soon scrambled up and stood on three legs until a bullet hit him vitally.

It was sad to see a single horse left standing with his five companions all lying dead or dying around him, himself the object of a concentrated fire until the fatal shot laid him low.

I saw one such brute struck by the seventh bullet before he fell for the last time. Several received as many as five before succumbing.

We took but four of our fifty seven horses from that ill-starred fray.

Gettysburg was the pivotal battle of the Civil War (June 9–14, 1863). There were some 70,000 horses present at the battle—8,000 of them were attached to artillery units, and it was these that took the worst of the 5,000 equine casualties during the three-day conflict.

The artillery teams obviously became completely at ease with the sound and fury of gunfire. The 9th Massachusetts battery arrived at Gettysburg field with a full complement of 88 horses—by the end of day three, 60 had been killed and 20 disabled.

Lieutenant John H. Calef of Battery A 2nd US Artillery wrote about the battle:

Illustrating how indifferent horses become to the noise and turmoil of battle and care of trooper from his

below: **The American Civil War:** *Bringing up the Guns* **chromolithograph by Judge Publishing Company, 1889, after a picture by Gilbert Gaul.**

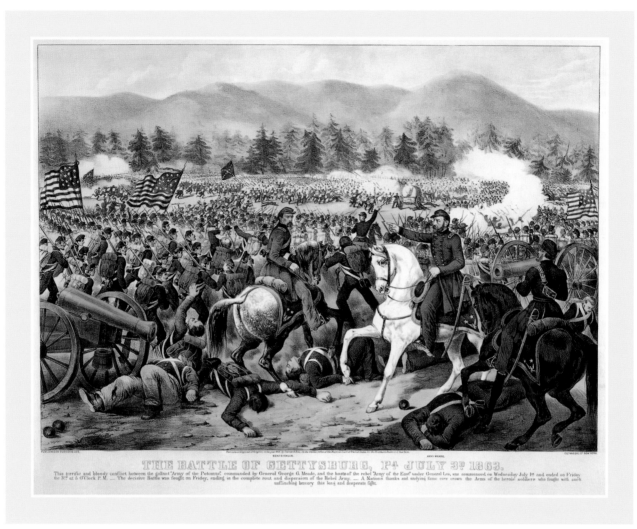

beast, I recall that in the midst of all this firing my drivers secured a lot of oats and fed them to their horses who ate them with as much relish and as little concern as though they were at the picket rope, merely raising their heads if a shell burst near, some of them being killed while munching grain.

One federal gunner, Frank Haskell wrote, "The shells swoop down among the battery horses standing there apart. Half a dozen horses start, they tumble, their legs stiffen, their vitals and blood smear the ground."

Brigadier General John Gibbon wrote, "One thing which forcibly occurred to me was the perfect quiet with which horses stood in their places. Even when a shell, striking in the midst of a team, would knock over one or two of them or hurl one struggling in his death agonies to the ground, the rest would make no effort to struggle or escape but would stand

above: **The Battle of Gettysburg, June 9–14, 1863.**

stolidly by as if saying to themselves, "It is fate, it is useless to try to avoid it."

In nearly every case, the best thing to do to the injured horse was to put it out of its misery with a bullet in the ear. General Meade, the federal commanding officer, set up his headquarters in a small farmhouse on the far side of a ridge. Although hidden from the direct-line sight of the Confederate artillery, it was repeatedly hit by stray shells. Orderlies and messengers would arrive at the farmhouse and be left standing outside. By the end of the battle, the farmhouse was surrounded by the corpses of the best messenger horses the army had available.

One staff officer saw his horse wounded by a piece of shrapnel. He ran back into the headquarters to retrieve his pistol and came out to put two bullets into a similar colored but completely uninjured horse belonging to a fellow officer.

CUSTER'S LAST FIGHT.
The Original Painting has been Presented to the Seventh Regiment U.S. Cavalry
BY **ANHEUSER BUSCH BREWING ASSOCIATION,**
ST. LOUIS. MO. U.S.A.

The Native American wars

In the two decades following the American Civil War, the United States Cavalry with its host of Civil War veterans took on the might of the Native American nation—and got their fingers burned again and again.

The cavalry units would be out on campaign right through the summer months. One trooper, George Howard of the 2nd Cavalry, covered 2,600 miles in eight months of campaigning sometimes covering 60 miles in one day.

Again and again it was the maneuverability and flexibility of the Native American tribes that created problems for the US military forces.

There was an overriding belief in the US Army that once troops closed with the enemy, no matter how large the numerical disparity, then their military triumph was assured. This would account for Custer's arrogance at the battle of the Little Big Horn.

Custer and most of his fellow officers were convinced of their own military superiority. The Little Big Horn was a lesson the US cavalry never forgot after the total decimation of Custer and his troops.

above: **Custer's Last Stand at Little Big Horn.**

The First World War

By the coming of the First World War, the role of the horse in combat was all but ended—the machine gun, gattling guns, the long-range rifle, and the massive artillery piece had seen to that. However, it took a while for the military top brass to learn their lessons, and there were around one million horses on both sides of the front line.

Although the horse did not see much action at the front in the early phoney war stages of the conflict, there was a lot of aggressive patrolling along the rest of the front lines. Horse-mounted patrols were in use extensively by both sides all through France.

Even at this time, most mounted units, upon encountering the enemy, would dismount and move the horses to the rear. The soldiers would then fight as normal infantry and even took machine guns carried on pack animals out on patrol.

Corporal Percy Snelling of the 12th Royal Lancers kept a diary all through his service career. His unit saw action during the early stages of the First World War. On August 22, 1914, he wrote, "We have patrols out, and I expect mine will be the next and we are standing to. Moved off about 4 PM and patrolled the village and reported no enemy. The town of Binch is burning in the distance. Dismounted several times for action, but the enemy did not appear. The Grey's Maxim [mobile machine gun unit from the Scots Greys] did good work and they had an Officer and a man hit.

"Had a gallop of about four miles across country at dusk to dodge shells and had to ride hard. A patrol of the 20th Hussars captured by enemy."

These mounted patrols could cover an extraordinary distance in an extremely short time, turn up ready for action and well supplied with ammunition, and then withdraw with equal alacrity. Once the combatants dug themselves in, and trench warfare came to dominate the conflict, then the horse became an irrelevance for almost everything but transport.

On the August 23, Percy wrote, "Our infantry division has arrived and is entrenched from Givry to Merbes St. Marie. Our brigade stood at Ruveroy trying to draw the enemy on to our line of trenches when we will get round their flanks if possible." This showed again that the mounted divisions were to use their ability to move rapidly to new positions to outflank the enemy.

But, technology was chipping away at the chief advantage of the mounted divisions. Again from Percy's diary on August 27, 1914, "Heard news of victory for English and French all along the line and stood to in reserve. We are watching a German aeroplane, they are our worst enemy, they sail over us out of range and report our position and their artillery promptly shell us out."

However, there was still a strong desire among some of the officers, and probably the men, to make use of the cold steel they carried.

On August 28, 1914, a contingent of the 12th Lancers was resting on the grounds of a chateau near the river Oise at Moy in northern France. They had been out on patrol since first light and had not seen any sign of the enemy. At four o'clock in the afternoon, they heard the sound of distant gunfire. They quickly saddled up and soon spotted a German cavalry unit, the 2nd Prussian Dragoons, heading toward the town of Moy. The first Lancers to engage the enemy were from C squadron.

The Lancers dismounted, removed their horses to the rear, and at once opened fire on the advance party of German mounted troops, who also dismounted before returning fire. The Germans were now pinned down and fresh squadrons of Lancers and a field battery were brought into position.

157

top: **Native American warrior with feathered coup stick.**
below: **Forward the Guns by Lucy Kemp Welch.**

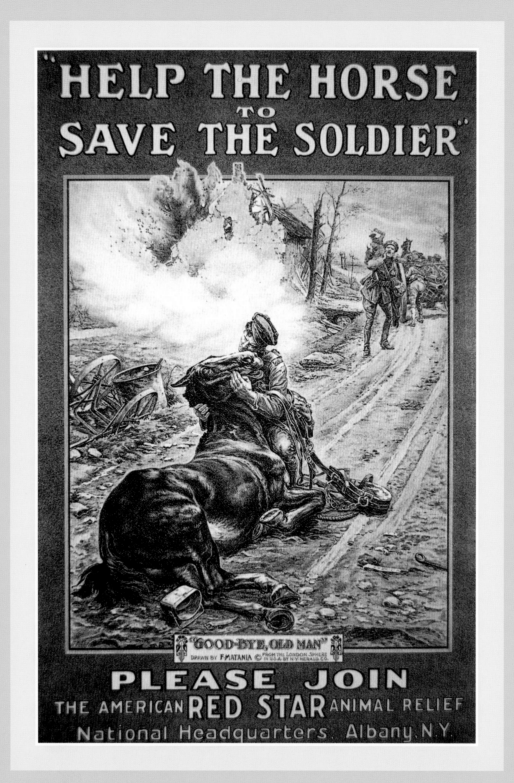

above: **World War One American recruiting poster.**

C squadron was ordered to mount to move across to another position under cover of their colleagues and the field battery. The intention was to move to a forward position and dismount, however, the ground was so favorable that the commanders soon realized that they could get within 50 yards of the Germans without being seen.

The order to charge was given, and with the aid of complete surprise, an incredibly short charge, and cold steel, the German unit was overrun and all but annihilated.

In his diary, Percy gave his own version of the events. "Saddled up quickly and galloped out through the streets and found the enemy holding a ridge. The country was fairly open and the enemy kept well out of sight, although their bullets were dropping thickly around us. We galloped over a couple of ridges and then we got it, so we retired and dismounted, crawled to the top of the ridge, and opened fire.

They kept up a hot fire but their aim was too high and they sang over our heads. At last we quietened them and the other two squadrons attacked their left flank, our Maxims were playing on their right and a couple of J Battery's guns. The Knut [Percy Snelling's horse] was shot through the leg when I went to mount, so I had to walk while most of the squadron galloped on and charged them, most of them threw down their arms but some of them picked them up again and fired them after our chaps had spared them. About 90 were lanced and lots surrendered. I walked on and caught the regiment up when they halted for a roll call."

Strip the glory from this encounter, and it becomes clearly apparent that even the cavalry officers at the time recognized that the classic charge had been reduced to the point where it could only work over the shortest distances and with the aid of complete surprise. However, the ability of mounted soldiers to move rapidly from one position to another and to control large swaths of territory was well recognized. And, as the Snelling diaries reveal, even units such as the 12th Lancers soon found themselves involved in trench warfare and the mobility of cavalry became almost as irrelevant as the full-blown mounted charge.

top right: **World War One American recruiting poster for The American Red Star Animal Relief: "Help the Horse to Save the Soldier."**

right: **World War One American recruiting poster with cavalry theme, painted by H. Devitt Welsh, 1917.**

159

НА КОНЯ, ПРОЛЕТАРИЙ!

Рабочая революция должна создать
могущественную красную конницу.

above: **Bolshevik poster of 1919: Main caption reads: "To horse, Workers!" Bottom caption: "The workers revolution must create a powerful Red cavalry. The Communist must become a soldier on horseback."**

However, the horse still had a crucial role to play—probably the worst job it had ever been asked to do. It gave rise to the classic First World War image of a horse mired down in the mud of the Somme. Although mechanized transport could bring munitions and supplies to within a couple of miles of the trenches, it was the horses, mules, and even donkeys that were used for the final part of the journey—wheeled transport was as good as useless in the clinging mud of France.

In previous conflicts from the Crusades onward, it had been poor fodder that had been the cause of most equine casualties. The First World War was the best organized conflict Britain had ever undertaken. Now that horses were generally out of the areas of actual conflict, the bullet and the shell were no longer taking such a terrible toll. A primary cause of injury and death among the horses in the First World War was the

nails used in the packing cases in which the food and munitions were taken to the front. The remains of these cases were to be found everywhere and were even used to create temporary walkways. The nails started the damage—disease and septicemia did the rest.

The First World War generals continued to take their chargers to war—not for combat but for an entirely different reason. Major General J. E. B. Seely wrote, "If you are to be seen by a number of soldiers, you must ride a horse. If you go on your feet, you are lost in the crowd; if you go in a motorcar, you either block the traffic on the road to which you are confined or pass so swiftly no one knows you are there."

The First World War was also the first war in which Britain paid serious attention to the veterinary needs of horses. The British Expeditionary Force that went to France in 1914 was accompanied by a veterinary corps of 122 officers and 797 ranks.

At first, farm buildings were used for the equine hospitals, but eventually the veterinary corps started using circus tents and marquees—but made in regulation green or brown.

As the war picked up pace and the pressure on the

transport horses increased, so did the casualty rate—still mostly foot injuries. March, 1917, in the Somme, when the mud and the transport problems were at their worst, produced some 16,000 equine hospital cases—this rose to 20,000 in April. The army veterinary corps dealt with two and a half million hospitalized cases during the four years of conflict—78 percent were returned as fit for service.

The level of horse injuries and fatalities during the First World War meant that large numbers had to be purchased in North America. Some 800,000 horses and mules were bought in Canada and the US. Most of the imports were the light draft horses used on US farms. They were 15.2–16 hh and weighed in at around 1,200 pounds apiece. They proved ideal for the artillery teams and for pulling light wagons.

Some were sent as cavalry remounts, but they were not popular—too straight in the shoulder—but the occasional Quarter Horse that came over was much admired by the officers who found the mile-eating lope much to their taste.

Horses and mules continued in military service right through the Second World War—but their role was diminishingly small. A few pack animals were used by patrols in mountain and jungle, but beyond that they were irrelevant in the age of the tank and airplane.

The First World War should have seen the end of horses on the battle field. Unfortunately some armies took longer to accept change than others. During the two week Blitzkrieg which heralded the start of the Second World War, Polish cavalry units were thrown into action against the might of the German armored divisions as they swept across Eastern Europe. In the developed world the horse has left the battle field forever—and no real horse lover can have any regrets about that.

below: **World War One: German Red Cross unit under bombardment on the Western Front, showing the sad fate of many horses during the war.**

above: **Preparing to Start for the Doncaster Gold Cup, 1825, with Mr. Whittaker's "Lottery," the race winner in the foreground, Mr. Craven's "Longwaist," Sir John Shelley's "Cedric," and Mr Farquharson's "Figaro," by John Frederick Herring Senior.**

the horse in art

More than 20,000 years ago, artists first depicted the horse. In the caves of Lascaux in France and Altamira in Spain, the rock surfaces are covered with paintings of animals which paleolithic artists created, for art was a powerful talisman. These vigorous representations of animals hunted for food, including the horse, contained something of the spirit of the original, and so a power was transferred to the image. In this way, stone-age man possibly sought to influence the future and ensure success through his art.

These same people made carvings which, being tactile and portable, were even more powerful totems. A small horse carved in mammoth ivory from the Haute Pyrénées, is such an object. The magic of the image acted as an obscure reassurance to early man in a world dependent on unknown forces.

Cut into the chalk downs of southern England is the Uffington White Horse, certainly one of the earliest and largest artistic representations of the horse. It probably dates from the Iron Age, and may well have had some spiritual significance for the tribes who inhabited the hill fort close by.

From the Middle East, the cradle of the early civilizations, there are numerous examples of the horse in art. In Egyptian tombs and temples, conceptual portrayals of the life of the

Pharaohs are carved in relief or painted, and inscriptions in hieroglyphs tell the story. Their elegant horses are usually depicted harnessed to light chariots in which the Egyptians went to battle. A painted wooden casket from Tutankhamun's tomb shows him drawing his bow while his pair of horses prance along, and an even more beautiful pair is harnessed to the war chariot of Seti I.

King Ashurbanipal of Assyria is depicted riding his stallion on a lion hunt in the series carved about 645 BC which decorated his palace at Nineveh. The animals and the people are beautifully observed and very detailed, and the horses, like those in Egyptian art, clearly show many characteristics—the dish face, short back, and high-set tail—which we associate with the Arabian breed.

The Greek ideal of beauty, which even today dominates western culture, is idealized perfection and probably best expressed in sculpture. The horse figures prominently in Greek works of art, and the marble frieze of horsemen from the Parthenon in Athens shows the wonderful realism of the carving. Although the procession retains the controlled design of earlier civilizations, the flowing garments of the riders and the restrained vigor of the horses give the work enormous vitality. The sculptor (or sculptors) of the frieze are not known, but during the Greek civilization the arts attained such importance that painters and sculptors became famous, and books were written about their lives and works.

Greek ideals in art influenced Imperial Rome, yet Roman sculpture and paintings expressed more realism. The large equestrian statue of Marcus Aurelius, cast in gilded bronze, is one of the earliest portraits that makes use of the horse to add

left: **Assyrian relief from Palace at Nineveh, 650 BC, King Ashurbanipal on his chariot, British Museum.**

above: **Marcus Aurelius, Caesar Marcus Aurelius Antonius
Augustus 121–180** AD, **Roman equestrian statue.**

above: **Page from a Persian manuscript of Nizami's Khamsa showing a game of polo, middle of 16th century.**

monumentality and authority to the figure. Aurelius sits easily astride a powerful stallion, making a triumphant entrance. The Roman Empire was in turn to influence Byzantium and even India. A relief from Gandhara in India of Buddha riding his horse Kanthaka is quite western in style.

Further east, Chinese artists have a tradition which dates back to the mythical Yellow Emperor of 2,900 years ago. More recently in the eighth century, Han Kan achieved fame for his portraits of the horses of the royal stables. In China in 1974, the spectacular terracotta army of the Emperor Chin Shih Huang Ti was unearthed. In his mausoleum dating from the third century BC, there were over 8,000 sculptures of warriors and horses, a remarkable find. *The Sacred White Horse* by the Japanese Ukiyo-ye artist, Suzuki Harunobu, shows a beautifully caparisoned horse being led out by two grooms.

Persian fifteenth and sixteenth century miniatures from the Timund and the Safavi schools of painting, which illustrate

poems including the epic Shah-nama (*Book of Kings*), are full of horses and horsemen out hunting, playing polo, and in battle. In the *Book of Kings*, the Persian hero Rustam rides a chestnut horse in a fight against his grandson whose bay is shown at a canter. In a miniature of a polo match which appears in the *Bustan*, a manuscript by Sa'adi, the horses gallop in a stylized manner and are of unusual colors and markings.

Although of a much earlier date, the horses which appear in the Bayeux Tapestry are treated in a somewhat similar manner. This record of the Normans landing in England in 1066 shows horses colored black, yellow, and blue, but they are altogether of a coarser type with low-set tails and heavy heads. The style of riding is also markedly different, the Persians with short stirrups and snaffle bits, while the Normans ride with long stirrups and curb bits. The recently discovered wall-paintings at Claverley in Shropshire, England, dating from 1200, bear a close resemblance to the Bayeux Tapestry. Here, knights mounted on their horses are depicted in real or perhaps mythological battle.

Not all art during the years following the fall of the Roman

Empire lost its realism. A statue dating from about 1240 of a horse with a royal rider at Madgeburg Cathedral in Germany is exceptionally accurate and perfectly carved.

Many of the world's greatest painters and sculptors come from the period known as the Renaissance, the rebirth of classical learning, and where the horse appears in their work, it is rarely the principal subject. The early Renaissance artists Piero della Francesca (1420–92), and Paolo Uccello (c.1396–1475) whose series of the *Battle of San Romano* show the horse as the mount of heavily armored knights, both depict solid rather wooden horses, though many are shown performing high-school movements such as the levade and croupade. These "airs above ground" were originally for use in battle, but today they are still performed by the Spanish Riding School of Vienna and by the Cadre Noir in France. It is interesting to

below: **Bayeux Tapestry: Battle of Hastings, the Death of Harold; made c.1080, Bayeux Cathedral.**

compare Uccello's *St. George and The Dragon* of 1460 with Jacobo Robusti Tintoretto's composition painted about 100 years later. Uccello's white horse looks rather like a rocking horse, whereas Tintoretto's is much more alive. The subject of St. George and the dragon was taken up again some 500 years after Uccello by the Surrealist artist Salvador Dali (1904–89).

Two great equestrian bronze statues, that of the Condottiere Gattamelata by Donatello (1386–1466) and the Colleoni Monument by Verrocchio (1435–88) owe much to an earlier work, the equestrian statue of the Roman emperor, Marcus Aurelius. In Donatello's work, a very powerful horse is shown in a correct walk, and Verrocchio's horse is a magnificent stallion which appears to be about to stride off its plinth. Leonardo da Vinci (1452–1519) was commissioned in 1489 to make an equestrian statue in honor of Francesco Sforza, and wishing to break with tradition, he chose to represent the horse rearing. The sculpture was to stand 25 feet tall, but in 1490, he abandoned the idea as too difficult and

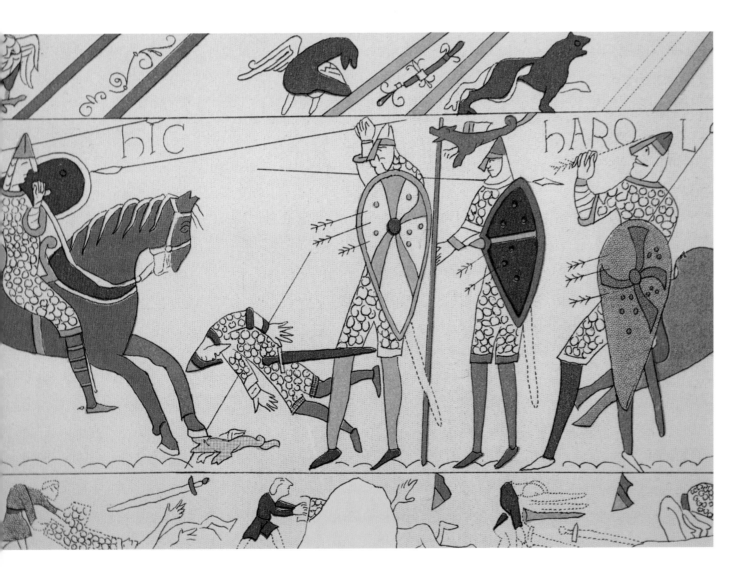

three years later completed a clay model of the statue with the horse walking. Sadly, the planned statue was never cast in bronze, and the clay model was later destroyed by French archers. One small bronze of a rearing horse is, however, attributed to Leonardo da Vinci. It was probably cast from a wax model made by him in Florence in 1508.

The influence of the Renaissance spread across Europe, and portraits of royalty on horseback, the equestrian portrait, gained great popularity. Titian (Tiziano Vecellio) (c.1488–1576) painted a magnificent canvas of the Emperor Charles V riding an elegant brown stallion, while Anthony Van Dyck painted the same rider on a gray stallion. Van Dyck (1599–1641) also produced a number of portraits of King Charles I of England. Most of the horses pictured are majestic, high-stepping stallions that appear to be of the Andalusian breed, though the portrait of Francis I by François Clouet

below: **The Rout of San Romano by Paolo Uccello, c.1456–7. This is one of three huge canvases painted by Uccello for Lorenzo de' Medici's palazzo. It commemorates a recent victory, and demonstrates the "new learning" in the foreshorteningof the fallen soldier and in the perspective implied by the fallen lances.**

(1516–72) shows him on a small dun stallion, albeit in sumptuous trappings and the king in richly engraved armor.

Two post-Renaissance artists who used the horse as a major figure in compositions of religious subjects were El Greco (1541–1614) and Michelangelo de Caravaggio (1571–1610). In *St. Martin and The Beggar,* El Greco fills the picture with a fine gray, the mount of the saint who is in the act of dividing his cloak in order to give it to the beggar; and in the powerful painting *The Conversion of St. Paul,* a skewbald horse modeled in strong chiaroscuro dominates the fallen figure of the disciple, Paul.

Another painting by El Greco, who lived at Toledo in Spain, includes a horse of literary fame—the Wooden Horse of Troy. The subject of the picture is Laocoon, who had warned the Trojans about the horse, and in the background the horse is seen approaching Toledo, not Troy.

Diego Velásquez (1599–1660), court artist to King Philip IV of Spain, painted Philip astride a great bay horse performing a levade. He also painted a portrait of Prince Carlos Baltasar on his fat pony.

The Polish Rider by Rembrandt van Rijn (1606–69) is a large canvas of a leggy gray stallion being trotted fast along a mountain road. Another Polish rider, Count Potocki, was painted by Jacques-Louis David (1748–1825) riding a

above: **The *Emperor Charles V on Horseback* at Mühlberg by Titian, The Prado, Madrid.**

powerful gray Andalusian stallion. Count Potocki's family were renowned horse breeders in their own country, his descendants being famous for their Arabian stud. David, a Neo-Classicist who lived during Napoleon's rise to power, naturally painted Bonaparte, and in one canvas, he is mounted on a white Arabian horse. The Emperor sits somewhat insecurely in the saddle, whereas in paintings of Napoleon's campaigns by Antoine-Jean Gros (1771–1835), and in a wonderful painting by Meissonnier (1815–91), he appears more at home on his horse!

Jacques-Laurent Agasse (1767–1849) left his native Geneva to study art in the studio of David in Paris. He then moved to England in 1800 to establish himself as a sporting artist under the patronage of Lord Rivers. Commissions for portraits of leading racehorses followed, as well as the portrait of the newly imported gray Wellesley Arabian. One of Agasse's finest works is the huge canvas of *Lord Rivers' Stud Farm* at Stratfield Saye, painted in 1806–7. Agasse also painted a number

of pictures of horse fairs, a subject popular with other nineteenth century artists, including J. F. Herring Snr., Rosa Bonheur, and in the twentieth century, Sir Alfred Munnings.

"Mr. Stubbs the Horse Painter" is probably the most celebrated of the many English artists who specialized in painting the horse. His portraits of such famous racehorses as Eclipse and Gimcrack followed in the tradition of earlier artists such as John Wootton (1682–1764) and James Seymour (1702–52), but George Stubbs (1724–1806) was the most original of the animal painters, and in his life-size picture of Hambletonian, he gives us a powerful representation of a racehorse who had just experienced a grueling ordeal. His work obviously owes much to his knowledge of the anatomy of the horse, which he studied by dissecting bodies and making detailed drawings of the muscles and skeleton. In 1766, his studies were published. Despite his accurate anatomical knowledge, Stubbs still painted the galloping horse in the traditional outstretched manner, and it may be that he felt bound by convention; it was not until pioneer photographic work by Eadweard Muybridge that artists were able to appreciate the true four-beat sequence of the gallop. Stubbs' painting

above: **Napoleon Bonaparte crossing the Alps** by Jacques-Louis David, 1801. Musée Malmaison, France.

of mares and foals in a river landscape, one of his best-known works, seems to epitomize the English scene, although its frieze-like quality echoes the work of the Assyrians and Greeks.

J. F. Herring Snr. (1795–1865) was one of the most eminent and popular animal painters of his time. A prolific artist, his paintings of racehorses include 23 of the winners of the Derby between 1827 and 1851, famous stallions, hunting scenes, coaching, and varied agricultural subjects. In many of his paintings there appears a white Arabian stallion named Imaum, which had originally been a gift to Queen Victoria in 1849 from the Imaum of Muscat. The following year, J. F. Herring Snr. bought the horse at Tattersall's Sales for 12½ guineas to serve as an artists' model.

During the nineteenth century, many English artists specialized in painting the horse. Ben Marshall (1768–1835) was one of the better artists after Stubbs. He moved to Newmarket, the home of the British Thoroughbred, in 1812 and is reported to have boasted that in that town there was,

below: **1814 – Campaign of France by Meissonier, The Louvre, Paris.**

"many a man who will pay me 50 guineas for painting his horse, [but] who thinks 10 guineas too much for painting his wife!" Marshall received royal patronage through the Prince of Wales. John Ferneley Snr. (1782–1860), one of the best sporting artists, studied under him.

James Pollard (1792–1867) and Charles Cooper Henderson (1803–77) were both celebrated for their paintings of coaching scenes, a mode of transport then in its heyday. George Morland (1763–1804) and his brother-in-law, James Ward (1769–1859), George Henry Laporte (1799–1873), and numerous others were employed in the business of portraying horses for proud owners.

Sir Edwin Landseer (1802–73) was perhaps the most popular of British animal artists, though his subjects are often endowed with too much sentiment for today's tastes. The paintings of horses by Théodore Géricault (1791–1824) must be regarded as among the most powerful and vital depictions of the equine by a French artist. His paintings of cavalry officers on their rearing chargers and of *The Capture of a Wild Horse* display great skill and knowledge, yet in his canvas of the Derby he, like Stubbs, J. F. Herring Snr., and others, still

above: **Mares and Foals in a River Landscape by George Stubbs, 1763–1768, The Tate Gallery, London.**

persists in painting the horses in the traditional outstretched style. Alfred de Dreux (1810–60), a fashionable painter of horses, was very much influenced by Géricault, and his close friend Horace Vernet (1789–1863), based the horses in his painting, *The Start of the Race for the Riderless Horse*, on studies and drawings done by Géricault.

Eugène Delacroix (1798–1863), one of the great French Romantics, was, like Vernet, fascinated by Orientalist subjects of Moroccans and Arabs and their horses. He also painted a small watercolor of a horse being attacked by a tiger. Such violent and combative subjects were, it seems, a constant source of interest to many artists including Stubbs, whose series of paintings of lions attacking horses are well known. Two other Orientalists who specialized in painting the horse were the German, Adolf Schreyer (1828–99), and John Harrington Bird (1846–1936). Most of Schreyer's oils show bedouins mounted on their little Arabian horses racing across the sands, while Bird's precise watercolors of Arabians concentrate more on the quieter aspects of desert life.

Arabian horses were the great passion of the Polish artist Juliusz Kossak (1824–99). During the nineteenth century, large numbers of horses were imported from Arabia by the Polish princes in order to establish studs, and Kossak recorded in paint many of these now famous stallions and mares. Their descendants graze the pastures of the great state studs of Poland, notably Janow Podlaski and Michalow. The horse has always played a leading role in Poland's history, and other artists including Kossak's son Wojciecjh, Piotr Michalowski, and Chelmonski depicted them in their work. During the Second World War, Ludwik Macaig (1920–) painted many powerful and disturbing canvases, not official communist commissions, but personal expressions of his own experiences. These, like some of the First World War paintings by Munnings, show the patient acceptance of the horse of his lot in war. More recently, Macaig has turned to painting the Arabian horses at Janow and Michalow.

The French Impressionists broke with the classic tradition in painting. Not that *plein-air* was new, for horse artists had painted their subjects outdoors for years. Still, the lighter palette, broken brush strokes, and the juxtaposition of analagous colours were an overture to a new age in art.

top: **From a series of engravings by George Stubbs showing horses devoured by lions, 1763.**

above: ***The Horsefair, Southborough,*** **1871, by Ben Herring and J. F. Herring Snr.**

above: **Light Cavalry Officer,** an unfinished painting by
Théodore Géricault (1791–1824).

above: **Racecourse Scene with Jockeys in front of the Stands, 1869–72 by Edgar Degas, Musée de l'Impressionisme, Paris.**

Edouard Manet (1832–83) drew horses racing at Longchamp. Edgar Degas (1834–1917), whose compositions show the influence of Eastern art, worked on a series of pastels and paintings of racehorses and jockeys. In his latter years, Degas turned to sculpture and produced numerous waxes of horses at rest and in action, including a rearing horse which in its boldness of form and simplicity reminds one of da Vinci's bronze. Henri de Toulouse-Lautrec (1864–1901), probably better known for his incisive portraits of Jane Avril and Yvette Guilbert, also painted some fine pictures of horses, and Georges Seurat (1859–91) included horses in his circus pictures. Paul Gauguin (1848–1903), in self-exile in his island paradise, depicted the Tahitians riding along the beach on small ponies, each painting an exotic medley of bright color.

The Animaliers were a broad group of sculptors who worked in France during the nineteenth century. Bronzes of horses, dogs, and other animals by the best of them such as Antoine-Louis Barye (1796–1875) and Pierre Jules Mene (1810–1877) are remarkable in their truth to nature. A number of Russian sculptors came under the influence of the French Animaliers. Prince Paul Petrovich Troubetzkoy's work includes an equestrian portrait of Tsar Nicholas II and a bust of Tolstoy. An oil of Leo Tolstoy plowing with a white horse was painted by Ilya Repin (1844–1930), one of the leading realist artists of a group known as The Itinerants. One of his pupils, Valentin Serov (1865–1911) who also joined the group, painted horses in many of his compositions, including *Foals at a Watering Place*.

The Polo Match by Max Liebermann (1847–1935) seems to have little in common with Persian miniatures of the same subject, other than the game, whereas *Horses in a Landscape* by Giorgio de Chirico (1888–1978) returns to the monumentality of Roman sculpture.

*left: **Sketch of the Haute Ecole** by Henri de Toulouse-Lautrec, 1899.*

of Egyptian sculptures in the Louvre. His series of British champion animals all have a harmonious monumentality which makes his work unique among horse sculptors.

In England, the art world had been somewhat taken aback when an army captain with no training in sculpture produced outstanding models of horses. What is more, Adrian Jones (1835–1948) could work with equal skill and facility on small commissions or with bigger than life-size monuments such as *The Peace Quadriga,* which stands on top of the archway at Hyde Park Corner in London. Not too far away in Kensington Gardens, there stands another monumental sculpture, *Physical Energy.* G. F. Watts (1817–1904) saw this work of man and horse as symbolizing creative activity which impels man to undertake new enterprises.

During the latter half of the nineteenth century, the horse in art gained its freedom. Painters and sculptors still employed the horse as mans's servant in sport, work, and war in a supporting role, but artists also began to see the horse as a symbol in its own right, of power, strength, courage, and dignity, free from servitude.

Lucy Kemp-Welch (1869–1958), best known for the massive canvases *Timber Hauling in the New Forest* and *Forward the*

Across the Atlantic, the cowboy and his horse provided artists with an image to paint even before Western films had given the world some of its greatest stars and heroes, from Roy Rogers to John Wayne. Foremost of the cowboy painters was Frederic Remington (1861–1909). His pictures tell the story of the way of life out West—Native Americans, range-riding, cattle drovers, rustlers, and shoot-outs at high noon.

Charles Russell, another of the finest painters of Western subjects, often concentrated on the harsh and tough reality of the daily life of the cowboy. The sculptures which Remington modeled focus on the violent activity of bronco busting (see page 106) or the chase, whereas the horses of Herbert Heseltine (1877–1962), which had first been in the animalier tradition of realism, were later influenced strongly by his study

*right: **The Tower of Blue Horses**, by Franz Marc, 1913–4.*
Marc's sympathy with horses lasted until his death. One of his diary entries before he was killed at Verdun in 1916 expressed sympathy for the sufferings of the artillery horses.

above: **Start at Epsom Races, a sketch by Sir Alfred Munnings, 1929.**

Guns (see page 157), also painted intimate scenes of horses at rest, mares with their foals, and pictures entitled *The Joy of Life* and *Foam Horses*. Joaquin Sorolla (1863–1923), the Spanish painter of sunlight and shadow, paints the nude boy and horse bathing together.

Munnings (1878–1959), one of the last great horse painters, provoked controversy. He used his position as President of the Royal Academy to vilify the art of moderns such as Pablo Picasso (1881–1973) and saw himself as working in the tradition of the great horse painters of the past. Yet his best work, of ponies in Norfolk and on Exmoor and of gypsies

with their horses in the Hampshire hop fields, have a colorful vitality akin to Impressionism, but with less sugar. Lionel Edwards (1878–1966) was a master in depicting the hunting field. Gilbert Holiday (1879–1937) made wonderful pictures in charcoal, and Charles Wellington Furse (1868–1904), had he lived longer, may well have rivaled Munnings.

Among the moderns, we can include Franz Marc (1880–1916), one of the group called the *Blaue Reiter*. His *Blue Horse* paintings may be better understood when we note his aphorism "Nowadays we are shattering the undefiled and every illusory phenomena of nature, and putting them together again

according to our own will." The bronzes of horses by Marino Marini (1901–80), although twentieth century images, have a certain affinity with early Greek horse sculptures made during the Geometric period 750 to 700 BC.

The horse is used in pictures of war by Le Douanier Rousseau (1844–1910), where a woman rider gallops a black horse over the bodies of fallen men, a vision of *The Night Mare*. In *Der Goldene Ritter* by Gustav Klimt (1862–1918), the canvas is filled by a great black horse that is ridden by a puny knight in shining armor. The huge painting *Guernica,* by Picasso is an allegory of the bombing of a Basque town by the Nazis in the Spanish Civil War, 1936–9. Picasso uses the horse in agony and injured, much as a picador's horse may be gored by the bull, as part of the image of destruction. The horse is a symbol of suffering, no longer a source of power and majesty.

below: **Guernica by Pablo Picasso, 1937. Centro Arte Reina Sofia, Madrid. This was the outcome of a commission from the Republican government of Spain for a mural at the World's Fair in 1937. At the end of that year, the Basque town of Guernica was bombed. Picasso paid tribute to the victims both in its historical and stylistic content.**

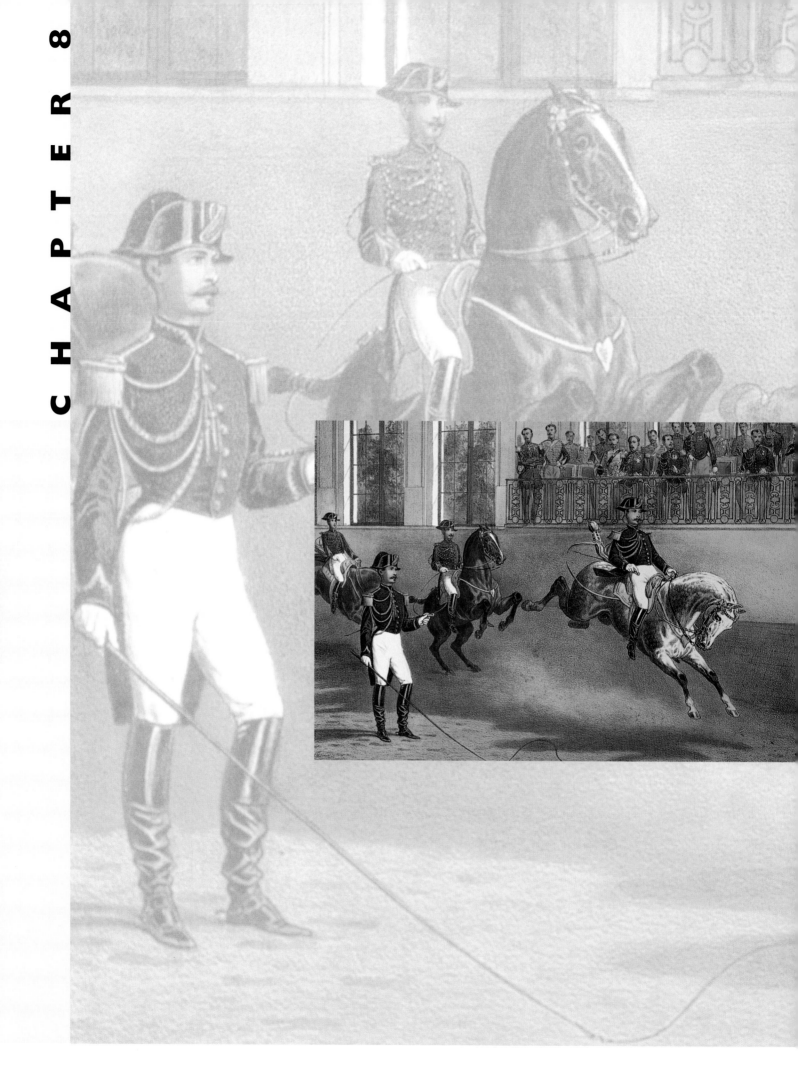

above: **The riders of the Cadre Noir School at Saumur, France in action during the reign of Napoleon III.**

horse
manship

horse
horse
horsemansh
manship
manship
horse
manship

Ever since man first sat on a horse, which American anthropologist David Anthony suggests may have been about 6,000 years ago, he has been trying to find effective and comfortable styles of riding. Some theories and methods have been more effective than others, but different approaches have evolved for different disciplines. The development of horsemanship has been a gradual process with highs and lows; occasionally, brilliant individuals have revolutionized general thinking, as at the end of the nineteenth century, when American jockey Tod Sloan developed the crouch seat with short stirrups used by modern Flat-race jockeys throughout the world.

The first influences

Xenophon (430–356 BC) wrote the first known book on horsemanship. An army officer and a member of ancient Greece's wealthy equestrian class, an elite corps which had to provide its own horses and equipment, he stressed that persuasion was better than force and said that "riders who force their horses by the use of the whip only increase their fear, for they then associate the pain with the thing that frightens them."

Xenophon and his pupils had neither saddle nor stirrups: the first saddle built on a tree (framework) was probably invented about a century after his death by the herdsmen of the Ukraine. Bits of Xenophon's time were potentially very severe, with long cheekpieces and smooth or rough rollers (called *echini*, or "seahorses") on the mouthpiece. But Xenophon urged a light hand and fair treatment, sentiments which have earned him recognition as the founder of classical horsemanship.

He stressed the importance of teaching a horse to canter on the correct leading leg to remain balanced: that is, with the

below: **Greek horsemen attendants riding bareback with no saddle or stirrups, from the west frieze of the Parthenon.**

above: **The Levade, a movement admired by Xenophon, is still carried out at the great Classical schools.**

left leg taking the longer stride on a circle to the left and the right leg on a right-hand circle. Horses had to learn the "career," turning sharply at the end of a straight line like a modern polo pony. Parade animals were taught a measured, high-stepping trot that was the equivalent of the *passage* of the modern advanced dressage horse—and Xenophon also admired the Levade, a demanding movement where the horse "sits down" on his quarters and performs a half-rear, which is today carried out at the Spanish Riding School of Vienna and the Cadre Noir of Saumur.

Riders as well as horses had to be athletic. They usually mounted by vaulting, sometimes using a javelin as a vaulting pole. Historian Elwyn Hartley Edwards says that Greek horsemen often rode naked—which is why Xenophon warned young men to take care when mounting, lest they provide an

unseemly spectacle to spectators standing behind them!

Today's teachers emphasize the importance of a balanced, secure seat that is independent of the reins. British-based Mary Wanless, whose "ride with your mind" approach has devotees in Europe and America, says that if the horse were suddenly taken out from underneath the rider, he should land on his feet —not fall flat on his backside as would happen from a "chair seat." All those centuries ago, Xenophon wrote: "I do not approve of a seat which is as though a man were on a chair, but rather as though he were standing with his legs apart."

Apart from Xenophon's work, no complete book on riding survived, though horsemanship remained bound up with commerce and war. Medieval warhorses had to be controllable in battle, and in the reign of Charlemagne (742–814), whose domain stretched from the Pyrenees to Naples, horsemen were given land and titles in return for serving the king.

"Tourneys," mock jousts between teams of knights, were held to provide training as well as entertainment. Knights rode

above: **The Capriole (the leap of the goat), as performed by the Cadre Noir, originated as a battle movement.**

right: **An old woodcut depicting the famous Federico Grisone, who wrote *Ecole de Cavalerie*, 1751.**

with their reins in one hand and relied on their mounts to be maneuverable and cooperative. Many of the High School movements originated in battle: the Capriole, where the horse leaps in the air and kicks out his hind feet, was designed to kick out the enemy's brains.

The Saumur region of France, home to the Cadre Noir, one of the great schools of horsemanship, was a center for tournaments and riding contests. As warfare changed and speed and mobility became more important, horses were bred to be lighter and more spirited—which in many ways put greater demand on their riders. Original warhorses, or destriers, were necessarily heavy animals bred to carry the weight of a knight and his armor. The emergence of a lighter, more hot-blooded cavalry mount called for greater sensitivity on the rider's part, and more innovation and development.

The Renaissance

It was not until the sixteenth century that the art of riding really advanced, though the twelfth century onward saw a tradition of circus horsemanship based in Naples. The Renaissance, with its huge upsurge of interest in the classics, led to new interest in Xenophon's teachings and in 1559, Count Fiaschi wrote a book emphasizing the importance of suppleness and obedience in the horse. By this time, the horseman had the advantage of saddle and stirrups, the saddle padded in front and behind to help the rider maintain a central position. Fiaschi was the first teacher to describe a system of combined aids—communicating with the horse with legs, hands, and voice.

Fiaschi's star pupil, Federico Grisone, spread his teacher's methods throughout Europe and started his own influential academy, the School of Naples, in 1532. He detailed schooling and suppling movements used by modern riders, such as the Volte, a six-metre diameter circle, and the Serpentine, a series of equally proportioned loops across the arena. Not all sixteenth-century training methods were humane: one instructor, Vincentio Respini, advised that the best way to quickly cure a nappy, recalcitrant horse was to fasten a hedgehog between its hindlegs.

Grisone's work was carried on and taken further by his pupil Giovan Pignatelli, who was open-minded enough to employ circus riders from Constantinople to stay with him and teach him their training methods—methods which achieved obedience and grace without harsh riding or severe bits. Pignatelli introduced lateral work, where the horse moves forward and sideways at the same time, and work "on the pillars." Pillar work, where the horse stands between two pillars with "pillar reins" going from each one to the bit, is still used today in the modern Spanish Riding School to work the horse in hand.

In France, Antoine de Pluvinel was tutor to Louis XIII, and in 1623 wrote *Manège Royal*, an explanation of riding technique in the form of a conversation between a teacher and a royal pupil that follows a similar philosophy. Some 50 years later, William Cavendish, Duke of Newcastle (1592–1676)—Master of Horses to Charles I and governor of his son Charles II— brought a more dominant approach to horsemanship in *A General System of Horsemanship*. He believed that rather than the rider following the ways of the horse, the horse should obey the rider and even fear him, a way of thinking that many have

followed since but which is definitely out of favor with the many modern trainers who believe that cooperation is far preferable to submission. Cavendish fought on the side of the Royalists during the Civil War and was banished in 1645. He was exiled in Antwerp, Belgium for many years and gained a great deal of knowledge of equestrian art.

De la Guérinière and the great schools

If one name stands out in this "age of enlightenment," it is that of Francois Robichon de la Guérinière, who wrote *Ecole de Cavalerie* in 1751, equerry and royal riding master to Louis XIV from 1730 to 1751. He taught his pupils to sit upright, with a longer, straighter leg and for the first time to draw the lower leg slightly behind the vertical so that an imaginary straight line could be drawn through the rider's ear, hip and heel.

De la Guérinière took the schooling and suppling exercises

below: **De la Guérinière founded l'Academie des Tuileries, Paris in 1730 and its fame soon extended abroad. He became known as the father of French horse riding and his work became the bible to the Spanish Riding School in Vienna.**

185

already in use one step further by developing the shoulder-in movement and counter canter—both vital in the training repertoire of the modern rider. The shoulder-in is a lateral movement, with the forelegs following one track and the hind legs another; it has been described by one leading dressage trainer as "the aspirin of riding" in that it can be used to rebalance a horse as soon as he falls out of balance. The counter canter, where the horse is deliberately asked to lead with the "wrong" leg while maintaining flexion to the leading leg, is also used to achieve greater suppleness.

De la Guérinière's influence showed in the establishment of the two great schools of classical equitation, the Spanish Riding School in Vienna and France's Cadre Noir in Saumur. The Spanish Riding School was founded in the second half of the sixteenth century and its present home—the *Hofreitschule* forms part of the Imperial Palace. It is famous for its dancing white horses, the Lipizzaners, and for its preservation of the

above: **Antoine de Pluvinel—one of the most famous French equerries and under-governor to the future Louis XIII, he gave the prince lessons in horse riding and continued to do so until the early years of his reign. His royal involvement gave him fame and kick started the growth of horsemanship in France.**

below: **The Spanish Riding School of Vienna, which upholds the great traditions of classical riding, uses only Lippizaners.**

FIGURE EQUESTRE DE LOUIS XIV
que la Ville de Paris a elevée dans la Place de Louis le Grand en 1699
Avec Privilege du Roy

classical tradition of horsemanship. A plaque above the baroque building that houses the school is inscribed "This Imperial Riding School was built in 1735 by order of the Emperor Charles VI to be used for the education and instruction of young nobles and for the training of horses for Haute Ecole and combat."

The French school is a cavalry school, founded in 1593. It has a wider base than Vienna, educating riders in all disciplines, but is firmly rooted in the same principles.

Hunting, jumping, and racing

Although riders have been exhorted by masters of horsemanship from Xenophon onward to ride their horses across different terrains, it was the growth of foxhunting in England from the eighteenth century onward that placed emphasis on riding cross-country and jumping natural obstacles. But what those hard men and women to hounds had

above left: **William Cavendish, Duke of Newcastle, believed that the rider should dominate the horse.**

above: **An engraving of Louis XIV on horseback.**

in courage, they lacked in technique—at least by modern standards. The "English hunting seat" required a gentleman to lean back in the saddle and push his legs forward; this was thought to give stability and security, but in fact meant that the rider was interfering with the horse's center of gravity and impeding rather than helping his effort over fences.

It was Federico Caprilli, a captain in the Italian Cavalry, who between 1896 and 1898 revolutionized equitation over fences with a system that came to be known as the "forward seat." In Italy, it was called "natural equitation;" a contemporary officer of Caprilli wrote that "one of its fundamental principles required the rider to allow the horse to use his limbs, balance himself, and so forth as nature prompted him, without interference direct or indirect from the man on his back."

The keynotes of Caprilli's system were that when riding at speed or over fences, a shorter stirrup is needed to allow the rider to keep slightly out of the saddle and to fold the upper body forward, with the rider's knee as his base of support. The old English hunting seat placed great reliance on grip; Caprilli showed that balance was far more important and proved it with overwhelming victories at the Turin show in 1901 and at the Olympia Show in London.

Caprilli's system has been the basis of jumping technique ever since. In the 1960s, showjumpers such as Britain's Alan Oliver—now a leading course designer—tried to take all their weight off the horse's back when it was in mid-air, but this technique proved short-lived. Today the emphasis is on balance, security, and giving the horse sufficient freedom of head and neck; American coach George Morris is the great stylist of our time and a great influence on top riders.

While Caprilli was revolutionizing jumping techniques, American jockey Tod Sloan was employing the same principles on the racetrack with amazing effect. He proved that riding with long stirrup leathers and a fairly upright body, which until then was the conventional racing style, was inefficient.

right: **The sliding stop is an advanced move in Western riding and is mainly used in shows. It requires the horse to wear special protective shoes to prevent injury. The horse learns to halt from a gallop, tucking its hind legs well beneath it, with its back rounded and neck arched, as it slides, perhaps up to 30 feet to a stop.**

left: **The Texas style of Western riding evolved from that of the working cowboys.**

Sloan adopted exaggerated short stirrup leathers and crouched over the horse's withers and center of gravity. When he first rode in England in 1897, jockeys regarded him with curiosity and then as he left them standing quickly followed suit by changing stirrup leathers. Frankie Dettori and other modern heroes of the racetrack owe a great debt to Sloan, who sadly died in obscurity in 1933.

Western riding

Western riding, where the rider adopts a straight leg position and directs the horse by shifts in bodyweight rather than direct pressure on the bit, is enjoying increased popularity. At one time, this style was looked down on as "cowboy riding" by many riders outside its home country, but at last the message is getting through that a trained horse and skillful rider can operate as skillfully as those in any other discipline.

The original Western riders were indeed cowboys, sixteenth-century Spanish settlers who herded cattle. Their horses had to be able to cut a single cow from the herd, gallop in short bursts, and turn sharply. The horse worked in three gaits: a ground-covering walk, a comfortable, two-beat jog, and a three-beat lope that were comfortable for a rider spending long hours in the saddle.

above: **One of the most difficult leaps of the "Schools above the Ground" is the Courbette. The horse raises its forefeet, as for the Levade, then takes several leaps forward on its hind legs without lowering its forefeet.**

Today there are still working ranch horses, but Western riding also has its own competitions. There are two main styles of riding: the Texas style, which developed from that of the working cowboys, and the flashier California style. The Texas rider wants his horse to carry his head in a natural way, while the California style calls for him to work with an arched neck, behind the bit rather than on the bit like the dressage horse.

Side saddle

Side saddle equitation, one of the most graceful and elegant forms of riding, is currently enjoying a boom in popularity. The British Side Saddle Association, the discipline's

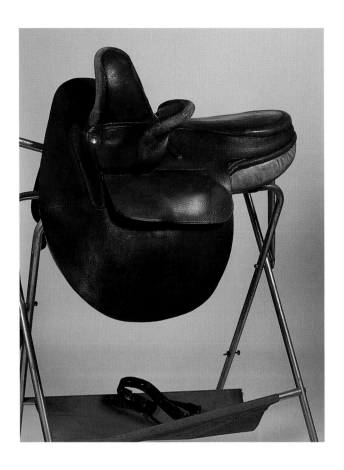

right: **A side saddle made by Champion and Wilton— modern side saddle riders still prefer side saddles made in the early twentieth century. The hunting head supports the rider's leg and the leaping head below, usually has a screw fitting so its position can be adjusted to suit the leg.** *below:* **Side saddle riders, jumping fences; riders also hunt side saddle.**

stronghold, has 10 overseas organizations affiliated to it, and instructors throughout the world, including North America and Japan.

Up to and including the Middle Ages, women either rode pillion behind a man or wore divided skirts and rode astride. The side saddle originated in the royal courts of fourteenth-century Europe, and Anne of Bohemia, wife of Richard II (who came to the throne in 1377), introduced it to the English court. At first it was simply a stuffed "seat" with a wooden platform on which the rider rested her feet, but it gave little security and not all women adopted it.

Its design was revolutionized in the sixteenth century by Catherine de Medici, wife of Henri II of France (who reigned from 1547–59). She added an extra "horn" to the top left-hand side so that she could adopt a more forward seat and wedge her leg between the pommel of the saddle and the horn. This meant that women could ride at speed, especially in the hunting field, on much more equal terms with men.

In 1830, French riding master Jules Pellier developed the design further by adding the leaping head, a pommel which curves over the rider's left thigh. The rider was now able to jump with security—a feat that had formerly taken a great deal of courage. The basic design of the side saddle has remained virtually the same ever since, and leading riders today believe that the best side saddles were those made in the early twentieth century by manufacturers such as Owen, Mayhew, and Champion and Wilton.

Some new designs are now being manufactured with the revival of interest in side saddle riding, in the majority, the rider's legs will lie on the horse's near side—this is purely a matter of preference, as previously most side saddles were custom made. The chief item of dress it the habit, which can be quite expensive and is usually made-to-measure, and is made of heavyweight fabric to weigh it down. The skirt should hang correctly and cover the right boot.

Anyone can learn to ride side saddle, and it can be more comfortable and secure than riding astride for some riders with minor disabilities, back problems or arthritic hips. Most side-saddle riding is now centered on the show ring, though some women still follow hounds. In 1995, British rider Carolyn Wofford set the world side-saddle high-jump record

below: **Jo Thompson riding side saddle on March Wind at the Concours d'Elegance, Royal International Horse Show, 1997.**

by clearing a 5 feet 7 inches fence. No special allowances need be made for jumping side saddle.

In the show ring the rider has only one leg, mainly the left leg, to give the commands or aids to the horse, and has to rely on using the cane on the off-side, which compensates for the lack of the right leg. Side saddle horses at this level are generally very well-schooled and responsible to the rider.

Etiquette demands that if you talk to or ride past a lady riding side saddle, you do so on her offside (right-hand side), because she is more secure than if she has to twist to her left.

above: **Start of the race by Sir Alfred Munnings, (1878–1959).**

the
horse in
sport

the
the
horse in
horse in sport
sport

Horses have been raced since time immemorial, but the origins of today's racing of Thoroughbreds lie in the Middle East. There they bred and developed the beautiful Arabian horse and were reputed to have deliberately kept their steeds thirsty, training them to race to the nearest water. These Arabian horses were the foundation stock for the Thoroughbred, and James I of England imported some to upgrade the local stock. It was during his reign, too, that the Suffolk village of Newmarket was turned into the center of British racing and remains so today.

Flat Racing

It was Charles II who was responsible for taking the sport forward. He actually rode in races at Newmarket and founded the Town Plate, which he decreed had to be run on the second Thursday in October forever.

It was during his reign, too, that the first of the three

below: **Flat racing at the Kentucky Derby, 1995.**

stallions to which all Thoroughbred racehorse stock can be traced—the Byerley Turk—was imported. His progeny, together with that of the Darley Arabian and the Godolphin Barb, became faster and taller through the eighteenth century as a result of selective breeding. Alongside this development of the horses, the Jockey Club, founded in 1752, gradually took more and more control over the way races were run. Their secretariat Weatherbys was started in 1778 when they

left: **The Byerley Turk brought to England c.1688 by Robert Byerley. Painted by J. Wootten.**

below: **The Darley Arabian brought to England by Richard Darley in 1704. Painted by J. Wootten.**

above: **Eclipse, (1764–89) one of the greatest British racehorses, descendent of the Darley Arabian and the Godolphin Barb. He never lost a race and was a remarkable stud.**

right: **The Godolphin Barb brought to England c.1729 and came into the possession of the second Earl of Godolphin. Painted by George Stubbs.**

published the first racing calendar and 13 years after this the General Stud Book was published.

The Classic races for three-year-olds started with the St. Leger in 1776, followed by the Oaks in 1779, and the Derby in 1780. The two other English Classics, the Two Thousand Guineas, and the One Thousand Guineas were first run in 1814 and 1819. These five races still remain the highlights of the British racing calendar.

In the US, there is record of a race meeting on Long Island in New York in 1665. The first top class Thoroughbred to go there was Diomed, winner of the inaugural Derby, who lived to 31 and founded a dynasty. The British might have developed the Thoroughbred racehorse, but American-bred stock became

below: **The General Stud Book is the registry for the Thoroughbred racehorse.**

above: **Iroquois, a famous American Thoroughbred was the winner of the Derby of 1881, ridden by his jockey, Fred Archer, from *The Graphic*, June 18, 1881.**

the equal of any country's, a fact first established when the American-bred yearling Iroquois made the long voyage to England, was trained at Newmarket, and won the 1881 Derby. Americans have their own classic races—the Belmont Stakes which was first run in 1867, the Preakness in 1873, and the Kentucky Derby in 1875.

France is the other country with an early history of Thoroughbred flat racing, with their Prix du Jockey Club being run at Chantilly for the first time in 1836, and their greatest race, the Prix de l'Arc de Triomphe, starting in 1920.

Around the world this exciting sport grew in popularity, presenting horse lovers with the challenges of breeding, recognizing, training, and riding winners, and spectators with the thrill of it being such a good betting medium. Today the richest race in the world, the Dubai World Cup, is run in the Middle East at the state of the art racecourse built by the Maktoum family at Nad Al Shiba.

In the early days, the horses ran over long distances, carrying big weights, but today the Thoroughbred is a faster, more refined animal that runs in races that may be between five furlongs and two miles six furlongs.

To make the races more competitive horses are handicapped by carrying weights. Experts award horses a rating based on their past form, and the standard of the races in which they have run. Thus a horse that keeps on winning will be given a higher rating. By comparing the ratings of different horses, they can be allocated their handicap weights—a horse rated 76 will carry six pounds more than a horse rated 70. In some races (conditions' races), the weight awarded will depend on the age of the horse (older horses carrying more weight), sex (the fillies getting five pounds less), and some have penalties of a set weight for winners. The weight the horse carries adds another dimension to racing, and the punters have to take this into account when they are determining which horse is most likely to win.

The first great racehorse was Flying Childers (born 1715), who won matches over four and six miles and was said to have covered 82½ feet in a second—a speed of 56 mph. The next was Eclipse (born 1764), who won 18 races, was never beaten, and went on to breed 344 winners of races.

In more recent times the greats include the American horse Secretariat (born 1970), who won the three classic races

above: **The Brooklyn Jockey Club Race Course in the USA, a poster of 1886.**

(known as the Triple Crown) in 1973. He won the Belmont by an amazing 31 lengths. In Australia, Phar Lap (born 1926) is the most famous, because he won 38 races including one in the US. In Italy, Ribot (born 1952) was bred by the great Italian racehorse owner Federico Tesio. Ribot won races there, in England, and France, including the Prix de l'Arc de Triomphe twice before retiring to stud, unbeaten in 16 races. In Britain,

197

below: **Racing at Longchamp, passing the Windmill at the Prix de l'Arc de Triomphe race.**

above: **The winner, Quirinus, clearing the notorious taxis fence at the Pardubice, Czechoslovakia.**

Nijinksy (born 1967) won Britain's Triple Crown and was only beaten twice, and Mill Reef (born 1968) won most of Britain's top races and France's Prix de l'Arc de Triomphe.

Jump racing

The largest fences to be raced over are those in steeplechasing. Ireland is the home of the steeplechase, because in the mid-eighteenth century, the church steeple was used as the landmark for the finish in a race over natural countryside.

The sport spread to England, where the most famous of all the steeplechases—the Grand National—was first run in 1839 at Aintree on the outskirts of Liverpool. One of the participants was Captain Becher who, when in the lead, fell at the obstacle with the big drop over the brook. Becher's Brook was named after him and remains, along with the five-foot, two-inch Chair, one of the most formidable obstacles on this, the biggest steeplechase course in Britain.

The Grand National is Britain's most famous race, but it requires a certain amount of luck to avoid fallers and a very special type of horse to take on its fences. Many horses are not capable of jumping so high or of racing so far, and some owners are unwilling to risk their horses over such a unique course. There are, however, plenty of other options for racing over fences.

All over Britain and Ireland, there are National Hunt courses where the fences are uniform brush fences with the occasional ditch in front of them, or a water jump with a low brush fence and an expanse of water that has to be cleared on the landing side. The most prestigious course is Cheltenham, and the meeting that lovers of jump-racing flock to is the National Hunt Festival, where the Gold Cup is run over 3¼ miles. The greatest steeplechasers in England, Ireland, and France have won this race. Cheltenham is the Mecca of steeplechasing, and there are also races over hurdles, smaller

top: **Lester Piggott on Nijinksky in the Derby, June 3, 1977.**
below: **Jumping a fence a the Grand National at Aintree racecourse, Liverpool.**

above: **Red Rum, next to a statue of himself at the Grand National, Aintree racecourse, with Philip Blacker in 1989.**

timber obstacles that will fall down if hit. With these lower obstacles, the races are faster and participants are often ex-flat-race horses or younger horses that will eventually become steeplechasers. The most famous of Britain's hurdle races is the Champion Hurdle.

While National Hunt steeplechasing developed as the official (and mainly professional) branch of jump racing, point-to-pointing developed as the amateur branch. Point-to-points are race meetings for amateurs, on horses that have been regularly hunted, and each hunt runs one each year for the enjoyment of their members and to raise funds. Nowadays, the courses have much in common with the minor National Hunt tracks, but for many years—almost up to the Second World War—many had strong echoes of their steeple-to-steeple origins, being run largely over the national hunting country of the local area.

right: **Desert Orchid ridden by Richard Dunwoody.**

America's version of steeplechasing started at the end of the nineteenth century with the National Steeplechase Association's formation in 1895. Most of the obstacles raced over in the US are movable fences which can be brushed through: they are smaller and softer than British fences, but are larger and more solid in appearance than hurdles. The US

became best known internationally for timber races over fixed timber obstacles. In some cases, these were quite small, around three feet, six inches, but in the Maryland Hunt Cup, started in 1895, there are huge upright timber obstacles. This course remains today one of the most testing races over obstacles in the world.

The other racecourse with massive obstacles is the Pardubice in Czechoslovakia. This is more like a cross country course with a huge variety of obstacles over its 4¼ miles, the largest being the Taxis. This fence has been modified recently, but for a long time, the fence was five feet high, and the ditch behind it six feet, six inches deep and 16 feet, five inches wide. To jump it was an immense achievement, and many of the winners of this extraordinary race fell and were remounted before galloping on to success.

In Europe much of the steeplechasing is over fences, which vary like those on the Pardubice course, but the fences are of a more uniform height and smaller than the Taxis.

Around the world, there are many variations of jump racing with the obstacles used often being determined by the type of fences hunted over in that area. They vary from cross-country courses, to timber races, to four to five feet birch fences, to plastic movable fences, and hurdles. As in flat racing, the majority of these races are handicaps, with horses carrying a weight determined by varying circumstances, but there are also some conditions' races.

Probably the greatest achievement of any steeplechaser was that of Golden Miller in 1936, when he won the Cheltenham Gold Cup, and then 17 days later, carrying 12 st 2 lb (170 pounds) he won the Grand National in record time. Many, however, argue that Arkle, winner of the Gold Cup in 1964, 1965, and 1966 was the greatest steeplechaser of all time. The most famous Grand National horse was Red Rum, who won it three times, and one of the most popular is Desert Orchid, a spirited eye-catching gray who won the King George VI Cup three times and the Cheltenham Gold Cup once.

Harness racing

An early version of harness racing, chariot racing, was the first Olympic equestrian sport. The modern form developed during the eighteenth and nineteenth centuries all over the world. In Russia, Count Orlov (1737–1808) developed the Orlov Trotter, in France, the first trotting track was established in 1836, and in the US, it began seriously in 1788 when

above: **Harness racing is one of the most profitable types of horse racing.**

201

Messenger, an English Thoroughbred, was imported. He became the foundation sire for the American Standardbred—the breed Americans developed for harness racing.

The horses pull a light vehicle called a sulky, or speed car, which has two wheels with wire spokes and pneumatic tires. The horses can trot when the legs move in diagonal pairs, or pace when the legs move in lateral pairs. The latter are the fastest and can go nearly as fast as the Thoroughbred racehorse can gallop. The pacer Cambest completed a mile in one minute 46 seconds, and the world-record-breaking trotter Pine Chip covered the same distance in one minute 51 seconds. The first great pacer was Dan Patch (1896–1916), and he was nicknamed the Immortal. He was so fast that, after 1903, he was not allowed to race because no other horse could match him, so he ran in exhibitions against the stop watch.

Harness racing is big business, and in the US the leading money-winning driver John Campbell has earned around $140 million. In France, the sport is very popular, and they have developed their own breed, the French Trotter, although American Standardbred blood has been introduced to help produce even faster harness horses. All over Europe, there are harness racing tracks, as there are in Australia and New Zealand.

Endurance riding

Endurance riding developed out of distance riding in America, where riding over long distances was part of its history. Organized rides started there in the middle of the twentieth century. The first competitive ride was held in the US in 1913 and was sponsored by the Morgan Horse Club of Vermont. The cavalry took up the idea and ran the United States Mounted Service Cup, but it could hardly be called an organized sport until the 1950s. The turning point was the establishment of the Tevis Cup, a tough ride from Nevada to California that was run by the Western States Trail Ride.

The sport soon became popular, with the first international competition being run by the Federation Equestre Internationale (usually known as FEI) in 1986 in Rome, with 11 countries participating. American rider Cassandra Schuler took the first individual gold medal, and the team gold went to Great Britain. It will be made an Olympic sport in the year 2000. It is one of the six sports at the World Equestrian Games.

Endurance is a tough sport, with the top events being run more than 100 miles through natural countryside over about 12 hours. It is a great achievement just to cross the finishing

above: **Endurance riding—one of the toughest riding disciplines—is soon to become an Olympic sport.**

line, and to win requires skillful tactics.

All the competitors start together and have to complete a number of mandatory stops and rest periods. At every check, the rider and the horse have to rest for a specified time (15, 20, or 40 minutes), and the horse's pulse is taken. If it is too fast, then penalty minutes are given, and if this happens three times, they are eliminated from the competition. The condition of the horses is a very important factor, and there are special prizes for best condition.

The endurance ride used for major championships is a big test of fitness and ability. There are, however, many easier variations and with the goal of completing the ride within a certain time. In Britain, for example, there are the Bronze Buckle Qualifiers that are rides of 20 miles ridden between 6½ and 8 mph and with a vetting only at the start and finish. These are some of the easiest, and then there is a series of Silver and Gold Stirrup rides, when longer distances have to be covered at greater speeds. It is a sport where most riders can find a level in which they can participate.

Vaulting

In vaulting, the emphasis is on gymnastics rather than horsemanship, and the need for suppleness means that it is dominated by young people. It has early origins, as classical Greek and Roman drawings show equestrian acrobatic exhibitions, and carvings and drawings from even earlier times in Scandinavia and Africa show people jumping onto horses from the ground.

As a competitive sport, it started in Germany in the 1930s, where it was used as a way for riders to improve their position and balance on the horse and to develop unity with it. In the mid-1980s, the FEI took control of it as an international discipline. The first world championships were held in 1986, where the individual and team gold went to Germany. This is the country where it is most popular and which produces the largest number of medalists.

Countries around the world have set up organizations to promote and control this sport that is so good for young people and is relatively cheap. An expensive, high-quality horse is unnecessary, since all that is needed is for it to work on a circle with smooth gaits and a willing character. The horse wears a surcingle with two handles that the vaulters can use. It is lunged on the left rein by a person standing in the center of the circle who can control its path and speed. Competitions are held for individuals, *pas de deux,* and teams, and consist of freestyles and compulsory figures.

The key factors are balance, rhythm, and stability; mechanics, form, and consideration of the horse. These are assessed in six main movements, which are performed in the compulsory tests. There is the basic riding seat, the flag (vaulter kneels and then extends the right leg behind and the left arm in front), the mill (from sitting position, the right leg is lifted to adopt side saddle position, then the left leg is lifted to face back and so on until sitting forward again). The exercises become progressively more difficult involving handstands on the horse's back. The remaining three are called the scissors, the stand and the flank.

below: **A vaulting competition at the World Equestrian Games.**

above: **The Prince of Wales playing polo.**

The team consists of eight people, and each must vault individually onto the horses and carry out each of the six positions. In the freestyle competition, there is a time limit of five minutes. All eight team members participate, but there must never be more than three on the horse at one time. They are free to carry out elaborate positions that must be held for three canter strides. In the freestyle, the degree of difficulty is assessed as well as the composition (creativity, artistic merit, variety). In the individual freestyle, the time limit is one minute.

Vaulting is becoming more and more popular. In 1996, it was used as a demonstration sport at the Atlanta Olympics, raising hopes that it might become an Olympic discipline.

Polo

A Persian manuscript dated about 600 BC records a polo match between the Persians and Turkomans on a ground that is about the same size as today's (886 feet × 591 feet maximum). Polo spread to China, Japan, India, and Asia Minor, and it was in India in the nineteenth century that the modern game took off. The British played it and brought it back to England, holding a game in 1871 between the 9th Lancers and the 10th Hussars. The first polo rules were drawn up by the Hurlingham Polo Association, which still runs the game today.

America took up the game, and most successfully of all Argentina, where the Criollo ponies, when crossed with Thoroughbreds, proved to be the ideal type for the game. Today, the largest number of top players in the world come from Argentina, but the US is not far behind with the two major polo centers being Florida and Palm Springs. Australia and New Zealand run very competitive polo, and their best players go all over the world to play.

In Britain, too, the game has enjoyed a big expansion, helped by the participation of HRH the Duke of Edinburgh, the Prince of Wales, and by the Pony Clubs turning it into one of their sports and bringing many young people in.

A team consists of four players numbered one to four with number one playing the forward position and number four the back with the other two in between. A match consists of between four and six chukkas, each of which lasts for seven minutes of playing time.

below: **Playing polo on snow in St. Moritz, Switzerland.**

The rules aim to make this fast, exhilarating sport as safe as possible. The right of way has to be clear to minimize collisions, which, at speeds of about 30 mph, can be very dangerous. The player following the line of the ball has the right of way, and anyone who crosses the line or path of the player who has acquired this right of way will be penalized.

It is permissible to "ride off" an opponent by bumping into him and pushing him off the line of the ball. Riders can also hook an opponent's stick, but they are not allowed to carry their stick in the left hand.

As in racing, there is a handicap system, but with goals, not weights. The very best players in the world are awarded a 10-goal handicap, the beginners to the game a -2. A handicap committee reviews the handicaps of the players in its country each year, awarding goals between -2 and 10. Each team then starts with a handicap arrived at by adding the goals of its four

below: **A rodeo, 101st Cheyenne at Frontier Days, Cheyenne, Wyoming.**

members, and if this is less than their opponents' total, they will start with goals on the scoreboard before the game commences. This helps to make matches more competitive.

Western riding

Western riding has as its special features a large heavy saddle with a deep seat, long stirrups, and a prominent horn on the pommel, all of which gives riders security, comfort, and room for gear. The bridle, with its strong bit, allows for one-handed techniques. Although this equipment is likely to have originated with the Spanish cavalry, it was the cowboys of America who used it most extensively. Today, this equipment is used in a huge range of western riding sports that began in the US but have spread around the world.

The most famous are the rodeos where contestants test their prowess at staying on bucking broncos, and those who are successful can earn big incomes. Some of the major contests are saddle bronc-riding, bareback bronc-riding, and steer-wrestling.

Less dangerous and requiring skillful training are contests run under the regulations of the American Horse Shows Association, with the original aim of keeping alive the spirit of the American frontier.

The classes include one for the rider—the stock seat equitation—which tests the basics of Western horsemanship. The contestants have to show off their ability to maintain the correct position at the walk, jog (slow trot), and lope (slow canter), coming to a halt and backing in a straight line.

Western pleasure tests the horses, who are to remain relaxed and free-moving on a loose rein when at the walk, jog, lope, and hand gallop.

Reining has similarities with dressage, because the horses are assessed on the way they perform various movements and patterns that include circles, figures of eight, spins, stops, and the sliding stop, in which the horses stops in a skidding fashion. In reining, there are compulsory figure classes and freestyles where costumes and props are allowed.

In the working cow-horse division, an additional require-ment is introduced that the horse has a "cow sense"—an ability to anticipate what the cow will do. Contestants have to perform a number of the reining movements and then hold a cow in an area, then direct it into a different area. The horse must show courage, initiative, controlled speed, and quick reaction to the rider's commands. An extension of this is the cutting contest, where the horse separates a cow from the herd and tries to keep it from returning to the herd.

Trail horse competitions test the horse through obstacles that simulate those found when out trail riding. The horse has to show off smooth comfortable gaits as well as the agility and willingness to cope with obstacles that may include gates, water, jumping over logs, going through brush, ditches, and over bridges, and even back through obstacles. Usually there are six to eight obstacles, and there is a 90-second time limit.

below: **Steer wrestling at Frontier Days, Cheyenne, Wyoming.**

Mounted games

Most young people, when they take up riding, practice some form of mounted games or gymkhanas, as they are often called. Gymkhana is derived from *gendhahana*, meaning "racket court." These games on horseback were practiced by the British Army when they were stationed in India during the nineteenth century. Originally they were mostly speed races, but gradually less risky games like bending races and musical chairs grew in popularity.

These gymkhanas were a great way for children to have sport without having to pay big sums for the ponies, and they were taken up by the Pony Club that was started in 1928 for riders under 21. The branches run gymkhana events at camps and their shows, but in Britain a more formal type of gymkhana was started with the Mounted Games competition for the Prince Philip Cup at the Horse of the Year Show.

Pony Clubs put together teams of riders, and the winner is the team of riders that completes the test first. There are sack races, running along flower pots, throwing balls at an object until it is knocked down, and many imaginative fun events for participants and spectators.

Showjumping

Showjumping has a large following, with its easily understandable rules and events which are held in nearly every country in the world. Showjumping, like steeplechasing, started in Ireland, but much later as it was thought that the 1865 Dublin show was the first important one to hold competitions over fences. There were experiments with the rules, with marks being given for style, points being deducted if a fence was touched (not just knocked down), and more penalties being given if it was hit with the horse's front than the hind feet. The authorities in the sport realized that simplification would be a key to making the sport more popular, and for the last fifty years, the penalties for mistakes have been easily understood.

Knockdown or foot in the water	4 faults
First disobedience (refusal)	3 faults
Second disobedience	6 faults
Third disobedience	Elimination
Fall of horse or rider or both	8 faults

The other key factor in show jumping is the time.

above: **Pierre Durand on Jappeloup at the Olympics, 1988.**

Competitions have a certain amount of time allowed and any competitor taking longer than this incurs penalties. Time is also used to determine who wins when there is equality of faults. Those with clear rounds may go forward to a jump off "against the clock," and if there is equality of faults in this, then the fastest round wins.

In speed competitions, the fences are smaller, but the competitors have to jump them as fast as they can. There are many forms of competition, from 10 seconds being added to the time taken to jump the course for any fence knocked down, to relays, to take your own line, to bareback, and fancy dress events. The showjumpers both have and give plenty of fun with this infinite variety of competitions.

For all the really important competitions, however, they have to prove they can jump big fences clear before they are tested against the clock, and in one, the Puissance, there is no time element, with the fences simply getting bigger and bigger, but smaller in number. The big wall, which is often one of only two fences left in the final round, can go as high as seven feet or even more.

Another prestige competition is the Nations Cup, and each country can only stage one of these in a year. It is a team event with three riders' scores counting, although four selected riders from each country can start, with the highest score being discarded. Each team member has to jump the same course twice, and the scores are added together. In 1997, a new team championship was sponsored by Samsung, and those who earn the highest number of points in the Nations Cup qualify for a final.

For any showjumper, the greatest event is the Olympics, and the individual gold is the aim, but this happens just every four years, and there are plenty of other important occasions. Every four years (two years apart from an Olympics), there is the World Championship to aim for, and in the years in between (alternate years), there are the European or Pan American Championships. All these have gold, silver, and bronze medals for teams and individuals.

Each year, too, there is a World Cup, with riders qualifying in their regions (Europe, Pacific League, America) for a final which is staged in April and usually in Europe. World Cup qualifiers are held at major shows around the world during the winter indoor season.

Then there are the famous shows for each nation where there are important individual events. In Germany, it is the Aachen Grand Prix which every competitor wants to win, in Britain, the King George V Gold Cup or Queen Elizabeth Cup and British Derby, all of which are held at Hickstead. These have a long history, but some newer individual events have the added attraction of huge prize money. Foremost among these is the Calgary Grand Prix in Canada.

Top showjumpers are seasoned travelers flying internationally and spending hours and hours in horse boxes on the roads or in ferries to get to the events around the world. The successful horses become great favorites with the crowds and are seen time and time again on television. The greatest star of recent times was Milton—the big gray who, with John Whitaker, won two World Cups (1990 and 1991), practically every major competition, and many medals. The first mare for many years to be a top star is Ratina Z, who was the 1992 Olympic individual silver medalist, 1994 Olympic team gold medalist, 1993 World Cup winner, and 1997 European

Champion. ET is a horse who achieved the great feat of winning the World Cup for two successive years, 1996 and 1997. He is ridden by the very popular Hugo Simon from Austria, who was 55 years of age when he won his second World Cup. Abdullah, the Trakehner stallion, is one of the greats from the 1980s, having been the 1984 Olympic team gold and individual silver medalist and 1985 World Cup winner.

Eventing

This is the ultimate test of all-around horsemanship as horse and rider have to prove their ability in the dressage arena, over a steeplechase course, along roads and tracks, over a cross-country course, and in showjumping. The horse has to be obedient, agile, fast, have stamina, and jumping ability. These

below: **Conrad Holmfeld on Abdullah at the Los Angeles Olympics.**

qualities are tested at different levels from the One Day Event, where there are no speed and endurance tests, and the jumping, cross-country, and dressage are all run on the same day, through to the Three Day Event, which is used for all international competitions, and up to 18½ miles can be covered on the day when the horses go across country.

Eventing started to test the stamina and versatility of the military chargers and is often called the Military to this day. It was part of the Stockholm Olympics in 1912 but it was not

below: **John Whittaker on Milton at Stockholm, 1990.**

until after the Second World War that civilians started participating in large numbers.

Events are judged on the basis of penalty points, which are cumulative over the three phases. Mistakes in the dressage test are converted into penalty points and added to those for refusals, falls, and exceeding the time allowed on the cross-country, and, when they are included, the steeplechase and roads and tracks. Showjumping penalties for fences down and exceeding the time allowed are also added, and at major Three Day Events even more excitement is created by the show-jumping being run in reverse order of merit, with the leader after the dressage and cross-country going last.

The dressage test is not as difficult as for pure dressage, with half-passes, extended trot, and canter being some of the most difficult movements. The horses, however, are extremely fit and tuned up to go across country, so these more modest requests are still a great test of their harmony with their rider, their athletic ability, and good training.

The cross-country is the main feature of the Event and has been as long as five miles over as many as 40 obstacles. In the Three Day Event, this is tackled after completing a two-mile-long steeplechase course at top speed and roads and tracks of three or four times this length. There is a compulsory stop before the cross-country, when the horse can rest and will be looked at by the vets.

The authorities are well aware that in these formidable tests, it would be unfair if a horse were feeling ill or in pain. There are, therefore, veterinary tests that include a trot up before the competition starts and another before the final phase—the showjumping.

As with showjumping, the goal for all ambitious riders is the Olympics, but also very important are the World and European Championships. The major annual event is Badminton run each May in Gloucestershire in England. This is considered to be the most formidable cross-country test, but more and more countries are running Three Day Events. The Eventers' season is shorter than for showjumpers, lasting from March to October, although increasingly more riders fly to New Zealand and Australia to take part in their events in November, December, and January. Another difference from showjumping is that the Three Day Event is a test of endurance, and once completed, the horse needs to rest. Eventers cannot take part in nearly as many competitions as showjumpers.

Probably the greatest star of eventing was the little New

above: **Mark Todd on Charisma at the Seoul Olympics, 1988.**

Zealand horse Charisma, who, with the long-legged Mark Todd in the saddle, won two successive Olympic titles—in 1984 and 1988. Mark Todd remains the great rider of this era, having won practically every event with a huge range of horses and having represented New Zealand in the 1988 Olympic showjumping a few days after winning the individual gold in Eventing. Another New Zealander, Blyth Tate, won the 1996 Olympics on Ready Teddy, and he was adding it to his 1990 World Individual title that he won on Messiah.

Women have also been very successful, and Ginny Leng (now Elliott), had a string of Badminton successes and Olympic, World and European medals with Priceless, Night Cap, and Welton Houdini. The current top female rider is Mary King who, with Star Appeal, won the 1996 Burghley and was runner up at the 1997 Badminton. Bruce Davidson from the US is the rider who has stayed at the top the longest with a team silver medal to his name in 1972, team gold in 1976, the World Championship (individual) in 1974 and 1978, the 1995 Badminton on Eagle Lion, and another team silver at the 1996 Olympic Games.

Dressage

Dressage is the oldest of the Olympic equestrian disciplines—there are horses in dressage movements depicted upon the Parthenon frieze. It was an activity that was taken up in the courts of Europe during the seventeenth, eighteenth and nineteenth centuries as good training for the young noblemen and a great entertainment for spectators when performed to music. Most of the movements actually originated as ways of making the horses in war more agile, controlable, and therefore more likely to save their rider's life. Following the disintegration of court life from the end of the nineteenth century, it was the cavalry who maintained the traditions of dressage and turned it into a competition that could be run at the 1912 Olympics.

At first it was little more than an obedience test with horses having to go past obstacles like balloons, but gradually all of the movements that are now part of the Grand Prix—the ultimate test used in the Olympics and major championships—were included.

It is a sport that holds the status of fastest-growing equestrian sport in many countries like US, Britain, and most of Europe. The great attraction is that it is challenging at any level, so those lacking ability or talented horse power can enjoy the preliminary tests where only transitions, circles, and the basic paces are asked for. Dressage championships have major competitions for the disabled, and the old and very young can enjoy it. At top international levels, however, it requires enormous talent and dedication.

The most difficult movements are the piaffe (a trot on the spot), the passage (a trot that has much more suspension to the steps), and the canter pirouettes (when the horse must keep cantering as it turns 360 degrees without moving forward). There are eye-catching movements when the horse moves forward and sideways as in the half-pass and shoulder-in, and it has to be able to stop dead from a canter without losing its balance, to be able to reverse in rein-back, and to vary the length of its steps in walk, trot, and canter without changing the tempo (speed of the rhythm). The collected steps are short and high, the medium longer, and the extended the longest of all. It is a huge test for any horse and depends on horse and rider building up a great partnership. Nor can the movements be achieved by *demanding* obedience. The spirit and natural athleticism have to be retained and developed so the horse has

to build up the musculature to be able to do the movements with ease, and to learn a language between it and its rider known as the aids (of the leg, hands and seat). This takes years, and, although a preliminary test when the horse simply walks, trots, and canters could be tackled soon after the horse is backed, the Grand Prix takes four or more years of training with a talented horse and rider.

Just as for showjumping and eventing, the supreme goal for any dressage rider is the Olympics, where there are three tests, the Grand Prix, the Grand Prix Special, and the Music Freestyle (Kür). In this the rider can devise his own choreography from the Grand Prix movements and put them together to his own choice of music. It gives the rider more opportunity to be artistic and the crowd a great chance of entertainment.

The greatest horse of modern times is the elegant but mischievous Rembrandt, who won two successive (1988 and 1992) Olympic individual and team gold medals with Nicole Uphoff from Germany. He was eventually beaten by another combination from Germany, Isabell Werth and Gigolo who became the 1996 Olympic champions. The most successful World Cup (Freestyle to Music) winners are Olympic Bonfire and Anky van Grunsven who won it for three successive years —1995, 1996, and 1997.

212

below: **Nicole Uphoff on Rembrandt, Barcelona Olympics, 1992, where they won individual and team gold.**

above: **Multi-medalist Bruce Davidson from the USA on**

Eagle Lion at the famous Three Day Event at Badminton.

Driving

Driving has a long history, but as an international and competitive sport, the rules were only drawn up in 1969 by the international authority, the FEI. The international competition started for teams (four) horses, but it has proved so popular that there are now major championships for pairs and ponies, although the teams are still considered the ultimate test.

There are three sections:
Competition A: dressage
Competition B: marathon
Competition C: obstacle driving

In the dressage test, the horses are judged for the freedom, regularity of paces, harmony, impulsion, suppleness, ease of movement, and correct positioning of the horses on the move. The movements tested are the walk, collected, working, and extended trot, the halt, the rein-back, and the transitions.

In the marathon, the contestants go through phases that are at the trot, the walk, and at the trot when hazards are included. The hazards are extremely demanding tests, including going through water and twisting and turning through the most extraordinarily difficult courses. The contestants have a time allowed of about 25 seconds for each hazard that begins as they enter the penalty zone and ends when they leave it. There is also a time limit and if exceeded, the competitor is eliminated, as he will be for going the wrong side of a flag in a hazard (red flags on the right and white on the left).

The final phase is the obstacle driving when the contestants go their way between bollards with balls on top, which fall off if the bollard is hit. There are about 20 pairs of these bollards, which are laid out in a set on a twisty course with a tight time allowed. The width between a pair of bollards is determined by the width of the vehicle, so they are taken further apart for the wider vehicles. If a competitor dislodges a ball, penalties are incurred, as they are if the time allowed is exceeded so no one can creep around in an attempt to be accurate. The scores for the three sections are added to determine the winner.

The great drivers of teams of horses in recent times include Ijsbrand Chardon from Holland, who won the 1992 World Championship and always figures high in the placings at international events; Michael Freund from Germany, who took the individual and team gold at the 1994 World Equestrian Games; Felix Brasseur from Belgium, who won the individual and team gold at the 1996 World Championships; and George Bowman from Britain, who took the individual silver at these 1996 championships and added it to a host of medals and championships that he has won in the past.

below: **Michael Freund at the World Championships.**

GLOSSARY OF TERMS

Aids: (Natural) aids are signals that the rider employs, via his hands, seat, weight, legs, and voice, to tell the horse what to do. "Thought" aids (i.e. by positive thinking) also play a part. Artificial aids are spurs, whips, and other gadgets such as draw reins and martingales, employed to enhance or reinforce natural aids.

Anvil: An iron stand used for shaping horse shoes.

Astride: The term used when a rider sits on a horse with one leg either side of it.

B

Bareback: Riding without a saddle or saddle pad.

Barrel racing: A sport practiced in rodeos and Western riding competitions where horse and rider race between and around barrels laid out in a standard pattern.

Basic paces: Walk, trot, canter, and gallop.

Bay: A color term, bay describes a horse with a brown (varying shades from light to dark) coat with a black mane and tail.

Behind the bit: A horse which refuses to keep contact with the bit by drawing his head in toward his chest. Also termed as *overbent*.

Bit: A straight or jointed bar (made of stainless steel, iron, rubber or composite material) that fits between the bars of a horse's mouth and is kept in place by a leather or nylon harness called a bridle. A straight bit is considered kinder than a jointed one as it does not employ a "nutcracker" action which affects the roof of the mouth and pinches the tongue. A bit acts upon one or more areas of a horse's head—the corners of the mouth, bars, tongue, curb groove (when a bit is used in conjunction with a curb chain), poll (when a gag bit is used), and the roof of the mouth. A "bitless" bridle (hackamore or bosal) is effective as it acts by exerting pressure upon the nose and curb groove. Bits are used, in conjunction with other body aids, to direct a horse to its rider's wishes.

Blaze: A wide white marking that covers the whole of the forehead and extends down the front of the face down to the muzzle.

"Boc": A colloquial French term for a "market cart"—a two-wheeled horse-drawn vehicle designed for speed and flexibility over rough ground. A country or sporting horse-drawn vehicle, less expensive and ornate than a coach, typical of a trap, and drawn by a cob or pony.

Bolt: Bolting describes a horse galloping out of control.

Brave: A Native American Indian warrior. Termed a brave after his first hunting kill or act of bravery.

Breeding barn: An establishment where horses or ponies are bred, such as a stud.

Bridle: Leather or nylon head harness, the purpose of which is to hold the bit or bits in place. A single (snaffle) bridle holds just one bit in place, whilst a double bridle has two bits—a bridoon snaffle and a curb. A bitless bridle (known as a hackamore) carries no bit—the horse is directed via pressure on the noseband and chin groove. In the case of some hackamores, only the noseband (bosal) exerts pressure.

Bronco (broncho or bronc): A wild horse—a term given to American Mustangs used in rodeos. Used also to describe a hard-to-handle horse. The name is taken from the Spanish meaning for "wild and untamed" or "rough."

Brood mare: A female horse used for breeding foals.

Buck: A movement done in high spirits (or in an attempt to dislodge a rider) when a horse puts his head down between his forelegs, lifts his hindquarters and kicks his hind legs out.

Bug-eyes: Excessively protruding eyes.

C

Canter (or lope): A horse's three-time pace.

Caparison(ed): A cloth covering, usually of richly-decorated material, laid over the saddle.

Castration: An operation, done under local or general anesthetic, whereby a male equine's testicles are removed. This makes the animal more docile, as well as incapable of breeding. Also known as *cutting* or *gelding*.

Cattle cutting: Separating certain cattle from a herd. A skill practiced in modern-day Western riding competitions and rodeos by mounted riders.

Cavalry: Mounted soldiers.

Charger: A warhorse.

Cheekpiece: Part of the bridle. Used in a pair to attach the bit to the headpiece. Also the vertical portion of a bit outside the horse's mouth (*cheek, sidepiece, cannon,* or *shank*). Also part of a horse's face below the eye and just above the lower jaw bone.

Chestnut (Sorrel): An equine color (also spelled *chesnut*) that varies in shade from dark to light red/brown. The color of a horse chestnut tree fruit. Also the name of the horny growths on the inside of equine legs above the knees and below the hock. These may be referred to as *night eyes* or *castors*.

Chromosome: A rod-like portion of the chromatin of a cell nucleus, performing an important part in mitotic cell division and in the transmission of hereditary characteristics.

Chuckwagon: A mobile cookhouse drawn by horses, mules or cattle, used on ranges in the US for both trail rides and roundups. Also called a *growler, camp wagon* or *the wagon*. Modern-day mechanical versions are called *chuck trucks*.

Classic races: Prestigious flat races. English Classics are for three-year-olds and are the Epsom Derby, the Oaks (fillies only), St. Leger (entire colts and fillies only), 1,000 Guineas (fillies only), 2,000 Guineas. US Classics are the Kentucky Derby, Preakness Stakes, Belmont Stakes and the Coaching Club American Oaks.

Clear round: A horse and rider who complete a showjumping or cross-

215

country course round without incurring any faults/penalties. Also known as a *clear, clean,* or *clean round*.

Clipping: Shaving a horse's coat. Usually the thick winter coat is removed to allow horses in work to perform comfortably. Some show horse producers clip summer coats too for a sleeker appearance.

Coldblood: A generic term for any northern European horse breed, originating from colder climes, that are heavy-boned, ie draft horses such as the Shire and Percheron. They are not actually coldblooded. A horse may be termed "hot-blooded" if it is of a frisky nature. See also **Warmblood**.

Colic: Abdominal pain in the gut due to a variety of causes, most commonly changes in diet, lack of water, blockages, poor quality or unsuitable feed, circulatory disturbances, flatulence, and damage to the gut wall by worm larvae or, on rare occasion, ingestion of a foreign body. Sparse grazing on sandy soil can often result in colic due to soil being ingested. Colic is also referred to as *gripes, stomach staggers, spasms of the gastrointestinal tract,* and incorrectly *as bloat or enteric fever*.

Collected (as in steps): Collection means a shortening of a pace (walk, trot or canter) yet still maintaining power (impulsion) from the hindquarters. In this state a horse is ready and able to respond immediately to its rider's aids.

Colt: An uncastrated male horse up to the age of four.

Conformation: A horse's make and shape.

Conquistador(e): The name applied to Spanish conquerors of Mexico and parts of South America in the 1600s.

Cowboy: The term affixed to men of the American West during the 1800s who tended and herded cattle. The term is still used today. Other terms are *buckaroo, cowpoke, cowprodder, cowpuncher, saddle slicker,* and *wrangler. Vaquero* and *gaucho* are South American terms for a cowboy.

Cow-hocked: Said of a horse whose hind legs from the top to hock joint slope inward so that the hocks meet and the lower limbs then splay out again so that the base is wide. So-called as it resembles the hind leg conformation of a cow.

Cow horse: A horse used for herding cattle. Quarter Horses are commonly referred to as cow horses.

Cow sense: A horse is said to have *cow sense* or be *cow smart* when it appears to have an ability to anticipate the movements of a cow.

Croupade: A High School "air above ground" movement in which the horse rears from a standstill and performs a vertical jump forward with its fore and hind legs drawn up toward the belly.

Curb (bit): A bit with straight downward shanks at each end of the mouthpiece, to which the reins are attached. Its name literally means to restrain or curb; its action combined with a curb chain (which is positioned underneath the horse's jaw in the curb groove and attaches to each side of the curb bit), primarily on the poll and bars of the mouth, is to bring the horse's head down and can be extremely severe depending on how sensitively it is employed. The mouthpiece is usually straight with a port in the middle to allow room for the tongue. A curb bit is usually used on a double bridle, or alone in Western riding.

D

Dam: A horse's mother.

Deep-bodied: Describes a horse with a generous depth of body from the chest to back of the rib cage.

Deep chest: A horse with plenty of heart room (deep through the girth with a broad and open chest) is said to be deep-chested.

Deep girth: A well-ribbed-up horse with a generous depth of girth behind the elbows.

Dentine: The bulk of equine teeth consists of dentine—mineralized tissue with a composition similar to bone.

Destrier: A French term for a war horse.

Diagonal: One forefoot moving in unison with its opposite hind leg

Dish face: Concave below the eyes or forehead; a conformation trait common to horses with Arabian blood.

Dorsal stripe: A black, brown, red or gold stripe running down a horse's coat from the withers, along the spine, to the tail. Also known as an *eel stripe, list* or *ray*.

Draft (draught): Any heavy or light breed of horse used to pull a (usually farm or heavy transport) vehicle.

Dragoon: A mounted infantryman armed with a fire-spitting musket of the same name.

Dressage: Training a horse to become supple and obedient to a rider's directions, and capable of performing intricate movements as the training progresses. Ballet on horseback.

Dun: A generic term describing equines with a lighter-colored coat, with or without black points. The mane and tail are black. Various dun colors are yellow (ranging from a pale creamy gold to a dark tan), blue, golden, red, silver, lilac, zebra. A dorsal stripe may or may not be present.

E

Ease of movement: Moves easily without hindrance, encumbrance, or pain.

Equerry: Originally the stable (écurie) of a royal establishment; now refers to an officer of the British Royal Household in occasional attendance on the Sovereign.

Equestrian: Of or relating to horsemanship, or to the Roman order of *equites* (knights). Also a term for a male rider, a female is termed an equestrienne.

Equitation: The art or act of riding on horseback.

Extended: As in paces: a lengthening of the stride at any pace or gait.

F

Family horse: A horse that is suitable for any member of a family to ride, young and old alike.

Feathering: An abundance of hair on the lower legs of an equine. Also a hunting term, said of a hound when he waves or moves his hindquarters and tail side to side whilst on the scent trail of a fox; feathering indicates that the scent is faint and the hound is uncertain whether the trail is positive or not.

Feral: Wild and untamed.

Filly: A female horse up to four years old.

Flat racing: Horse racing without jumps.

Flaxen (as in mane and tail): Blond color.

Flexion: When a horse keeps its head held high, bends at the poll and yields its jaw to the pressure of the bit.

Foal: A young equine under 12 months of age. An ungelded male is known as a colt foal, while a female is a filly foal. A gelded male is known as a gelding foal.

Forage: Food, specifically bulk food for herbivores, such as grass and hay. Also known as *fodder*. To *forage* means to wander in search of food.

Forehand: The front of a horse, including the head, neck, shoulders, and forelegs.

Forge: A furnace in which horse shoes, or other metal, is heated and wrought. If a horse *forges* (or *clicks*) he is striking the underside of a forefoot with the toe of a hind foot when he moves.

G

Gait: The pattern of leg-movements used by a horse in walk, trot, canter (or *lope*), gallop, pacing and tolt. Pacing is a trot where both fore and hind legs on the same side move together, as opposed to the usual diagonal trot where opposite fore and hind legs move together. Tolt (also known as *rack*) is a fast four-beat running walk.

Gaucho: see **Cowboy**.

Gelding: See **Castration**. A *gelding* is a castrated male horse.

Gestation: The term of pregnancy, from conception to birth. In horses gestation lasts for approximately 355 days (11 months).

Girth: A belly band used to keep the saddle in place and secure. Also known as a *cinch*.

Good front: A horse is said to have a good front if it is well-muscled in the front end and has a balanced neck on its body. Also known as *good rein, good outlook*.

Grain: Seed of a food plant or cereal grass suitable for horses, such as oats or barley.

Grand Prix: Literally translated it means the Chief Prize and the term originated from the Grand Prix de Paris, a famous horse race. It denotes the most demanding class in both showjumping (where it is over the biggest course of the show) and dressage (a set test of standard exceeded only by the Grand Prix Special) competitions.

Gray (or Grey): A common horse color, ranging in shade from dark gray to white.

Groom: A person engaged in the general care of a horse. Groom also means to clean a horse.

Grullo: A slate- or mouse-colored horse (dense, dark, gray).

H

Hackamore: A bitless bridle.

Halter: A hemp or cotton headcollar, without fittings, for leading a horse, or tying it up in a stall. American halters are generally of leather with brass fittings.

Hand: A measurement of four inches. Horses are measured in hands.

Hardy: Denotes a horse of tough constitution, able to withstand cold, exposure or fatigue.

Harness: Equipment (bridle, collar, pad, hames, and reins) for a driving horse.

High School: Also known as *Haute École*. The more advanced movements of the classical art of riding, as practiced today by the Spanish Riding School, Vienna, and the French Cadre Noir.

Hindquarters: The area between the rear of the flanks and root of the tail, stretching down to the top of the gaskin.

Hobbles: Straps made of rope or leather to fasten a horse's front legs together at the fetlocks. Usually padded where they come into contact with the horse, hobbles are used to prevent straying.

Hobbler: A person required to keep a horse for military service; also a horseman (mounted soldier in this case) employed to reconnoitre areas.

Hobby-horse: A stick with or without small wheels at the bottom and a horse's head at the top, used as a toy by children.

Horn: The outer surface of hooves. Also the horn-like prolongation of a stock saddle pommel.

Horse: An equine that measures over 14.2 hh. Also a generic term for horses and ponies of all sizes.

Horse fair: A market for the sale of horses and ponies.

Hound: A dog used for hunting.

Hunter: An equine used for hunting.

Hussar: A soldier of a light cavalry regiment (originally a soldier of the national cavalry of Hungary in the fifteenth century).

I

Ice tail: A fan of hair at the top of the tail.

Impulsion: Forward propulsion created by the energetic use of the hindquarters, resulting in the hind legs coming well under the horse's body. Impulsion passes through the horse's body up to the mouth where it is contained and directed by the rider's hands through the reins.

In-hand: Leading a horse.

J

Jousting: Combat between two mounted riders (knights) with lances. Also known as *tilting*.

K

Knight: A man in the Middle Ages who performed mounted military service for his lord in exchange for land. Also, in feudal times, a gentleman bred to arms admitted to a certain honorable military rank.

L

Lasso: Also *lariat, catch rope, lass rope*. A long rope, made of rawhide leather or fiber, with a slipknot loop at the throwing end used for capturing cattle or horses.

Leathers (stirrup leathers): The leather straps used for attaching stirrup irons to the saddle.

Levade: A High School movement where the horse rears itself from the ground then draws the forelegs in under it whilst "sitting" on its hindquarters with the hind legs bearing the entire weight of the body.

Light Brigade (Charge of): The Light Brigade was made up of five units of cavalry—the 11th and 13th Hussars and 17th Lancers (Union Brigade) of the Royals (English), Scots Greys (Scotch), Inniskilling Dragoons (Irish), Scarlett's Heavy Brigade, and 4th and 5th Dragoon Guards. The Brigade's show of bravery was unsurpassable; their self-sacrifice so splendid, their losses so heavy, and their failure in overcoming the enemy (Russian cavalry corps) so strong, that the sound work of their Heavies (supporting units) was overshadowed. Out of some 674 mounted men, 243 died or were injured and 470 horses were killed within minutes of the Charge starting. Lord Raglan was the infamous commander in charge—his orders to charge, allegedly, misinterpreted by Lord Cardigan (commander of the Light Brigade and Lord Lucan (commander of the Cavalry Division).

Limber: A detachable two-wheeled vehicle containing ammunition that precedes the gun carriage and forms part of a field gun unit. Also the shaft of a vehicle.

Loins: Part of the back which extends down either side of the spinal vertebrae and lies immediately behind the saddle.

Lope: See *Canter*.

M

Manège: A schooling arena for horses.

Mare: A female equine aged four years and over.

Measuring stick: A straight shaft of wood calibrated in inches, and centimeters, and hands with a sliding right angle arm (generally incorporating a spirit level for exact measuring) at the top. Used for measuring the height, at the withers, of horses. Also known as a *horse standard*.

Medium (as in steps of pace): A pace between working and extended. Energetic, with impulsion, yet calm and relaxed.

Medium back: A horse's back that is neither too long nor too short.

Mettle: A temperament of sprightliness and spirit. A *mettlesome* horse is one of high spirits. A horse *on its mettle* is ready for best effort.

Mule: The offspring of a donkey stallion and a horse mare.

Mustang: Feral horses of the plains of western American pampas of South America.

Muzzle: Lower end of a horse's neck, including the lips, chin and nostrils. Also a term for a protective covering for the nose to prevent a horse from biting or eating.

N

Nap (nappy): A form of resistance by a horse, including rearing, bucking, shying, running away, and failing to obey the rider's aids.

Neck reining: Guiding a horse by rein pressure on the neck as opposed to bit pressure.

O

On the bit: When a horse takes a light but definite feel on the reins, without resistance and with a relaxed jaw. The head remains steady and slightly in front of the vertical with the neck raised and arched, the poll being the highest part of the neck.

Oxer: A jump comprising of two sets of wings (*standards*) and any combination of poles, angles or spreads. Also known as an *ox fence* or *post and rails*.

P

Pack horse: A horse used to carry and convey burdens of kit or merchandise from one location to another.

Paint: Also called *skewbald*.

Pairs: A team of two horses hitched and driven abreast. Also two horses ridden side by side.

Palfrey: A saddle horse of medieval times, especially, for a rider's comfort, one that could amble, ie a four-beat lateral gait derived from the pace and performed in four-time without a moment of suspension. Leg movement would be left hand, left fore, right hand, and right fore—the same sequence for walk with rhythm and execution making it closer to pacing.

Pas de Deux: A freestyle dressage program ridden by two riders.

Picador: A mounted bullfighter with a lance.

Piebald: A color consisting or large irregular patches of black and white. Also known as *pinto*.

Pillion: A type of saddle attached to the back of an ordinary saddle on which a second person, usually a woman, could ride. *Riding pillion* means a second person sitting on the horse behind its rider.

Pinto: See *Piebald*.

Points: A term elaborating color, e.g. a bay with black points indicates a bay horse with black mane, tail, and lower portions of the legs.

Pole horse: A horse harnessed to the pole of a horse-drawn vehicle.

Polo: "Hockey on horseback."

Pommel: The raised, arched, part of the front of a saddle.

Pony: The name given to an equine not exceeding 14.2 hh. However Arab horses, no matter how small, are always referred to as horses. In designated rules, a Hackney pony measures no more than 14 hh, whilst a Hackney horse must exceed 14 hh. Also a betting term meaning a wager of £25 (approximately $40.00).

Post-chaise: To travel by post chaise. A post chaise, also known as *po'chay, pochay* and *po'chaise*, is a four-wheeled carriage, used in delivering mail, for two or four passengers with a postilion (*postillion*). A *postilion* is a person who guides the carriage horses by riding on one of them.

Presence: A horse is said to have *presence* if it commands admiring and respectful attention—that special *je ne said quoi* (a special unknown ingredient of quality).

Puissance: Literally meaning physical power (of a horse). Specifically a non-timed "knock out" competition where the fences are fewer but higher than usual showjumping competitions and where the victor is ascertained by jumping rounds of increasingly raised fences, until only one combination of horse and rider are successful in completing the course.

R

Rasping: Horses' teeth are rasped in order to remove sharp edges which prevent proper mastication of food. Also known as *floating*. A farrier rasps domesticated horses' hooves in order to keep them level and at a correct length.

Ration(s): The term given for a horse's portion of food.

Rear: A horse's action when it rises up onto its hind feet with its forelegs off the ground. A vice.

Rein-back: A term to describe a horse moving backwards. Specifically a dressage movement where the horse moves backwards in a straight line at an even two-time pace with diagonal feet touching the ground simultaneously. Also known as *backing up* or *back*—a movement in which the horse steps backwards in a diagonal pattern in a four-time beat, each leg setting down independently.

Reining: A Western competition in which the athletic ability of a ranch-type horse is demonstrated, and judged, in any variety of nine specific patterns. Patterns include small circles, large, and fast circles, flying leading leg changes, 360 degree spins and sliding stops.

Reins: Straps of rope, leather or synthetic material attached to the bit and held in a rider's hands to guide the horse. Also known in the driving world as *ribbons*.

Reiving: To plunder/rob. A Scottish term. Also known as *reaving*. Reivers—plunderers/robbers.

Remount: A fresh horse used to replace a tired or lame horse. Also a general term for all horses taken in for military service. Remount also means to get back on a horse after getting off or a fall.

Rollback: A term that describes the action of a galloping horse that stops suddenly, lifts its forelegs, turns around 180 degrees, and starts off again in gallop in the direction from which it came. Also known as *set and turn*.

Roller: A band of leather, synthetic material or jute (usually padded either side of the spine to keep pressure off this vulnerable area) used to secure rugs in position. Also known as a *surcingle* or *body roller*. Also a moveable part of a bit which rotates about the mouthpiece to encourage salivation, as well as (in theory) prevent a strong horse from setting its jaw and pulling.

Roman nose: Denotes a horse with a convex face from poll to muzzle. Also known as a *Roman profile*.

Royal Lancers: Light cavalry soldiers armed with a lance; or soldiers of a regiment formerly so armed.

Rug: Also known as *horse blanket*. A material covering for a horse to protect it from cold and/or wet weather conditions.

Rump: The hind part of a horse's body; usually the buttocks are referred to as the rump.

Rustler: A horse or cattle thief.

S

Saddle: A material or leather seat for a rider on a horse. A part of driving harness which sits on the horse's back is also called a saddle.

Saddleseat: Riding a horse.

Sclera: The outermost membrane of the eyeball adjoining the cornea. A white sclera is characteristic of Appaloosa eyes.

Scots Greys: A regiment of dragoons established in 1683. Famous for their involvement, as part of the Light Brigade, in the Charge of the Light Brigade—"an expensive failure in terms of men and horses"—at Sevastopol (Sebastopol), Balaklava, during the Crimean War (1854).

Seat: The posture of a rider in the saddle. Also part of the saddle upon which a rider sits, between pommel and rear of the saddle (cantle).

Side-saddle: Sitting on a horse with both feet on the near (left) side of the horse.

Sire: The biological father of a horse.

Skewbald: A coat color denoting large irregular patches of white and other colors apart from black. Also known as *skeebald*.

Snaffle: A bit comprising a straight or (more commonly) a jointed mouthpiece with a ring on either end to affix one pair of reins. Also known as *snavel* (Dutch term) or *schnabel* (German term).

Sock: A white leg marking extending from the coronet to the middle of the cannon bone area. Also known as a *half cannon*.

Solid: A color term denoting one color only with no other markings.

Sorrel: A coat color describing a reddish-brown or light chestnut color, without black points.

Sound(ness): Denotes a horse free from illness, disease, physical or conformation defect.

Spavin: A degenerative bone disease affecting the hock, due to wear and tear.

Splint: A bony growth which forms between the splint bone and cannon bone in either the fore or hind limbs. Caused by excessive concussion, or bad conformation, in the limbs of a young horse when the bones are still forming. Seldom causes trouble after the splint is formed unless it interferes with joints.

Springhalt (stringhalt): A nervous condition in which one or both hind legs are lifted in a jerking movement. Non-painful and does not cause lameness, nevertheless constitutes a technical unsoundness. Also due to strain or trauma to the hock resulting in restriction of extensor tendons at the hock. Often gets worse with age.

Spur: A metal instrument, having a sharp or blunt point, attached to a rider's boot heels for decoration or to enhance or reinforce leg aids.

Stallion: An ungelded male horse aged four years and over.

Star: A white marking on the forehead of a horse's face.

Steed: A horse used for riding, especially a spirited one.

Steer: A young, castrated, bovine—especially one raised for beef.

Stirrup (iron): Often referred to as *stirrups*, a stirrup (iron) is a D-shaped fitting, connected to the saddle by stirrup leather, into which a rider places his foot. Made of metal (preferably stainless steel for safety), leather, synthetic material or wood. Also known as a *pedal*.

Straight in the shoulder: A conformation defect where a horse's shoulder lacks sufficient angulation for comfortable and sound riding or driving.

Stock horse: A horse used for herding cattle or sheep.

Stocking: A white leg marking extending from the knee or hock down to the coronet.

Strawberry roan: A color term describing a mixture (flecking) of red hairs mixed with white. Also known as *sorrel roan*.

Strong feet: Tough hooves.

Surcingle: See *Roller*.

Sure-footed: Not liable to stumble. A horse to be depended upon.

T

Three-day event: A three-phase competition testing a horse's obedience, physical prowess, and endurance over two or three days. Comprising a dressage test, a showjumping course, and a speed and endurance test involving completing a steeplechase (Phase B) course of roads and tracks (Phases A and C) within a set time and then jumping a "natural" course of obstacles (Phase D) across country, again within a set time. Also known as *Concours Complete, Concours d'Equitation,* or *Complete Test.*

Toad-eye: Prominent eyes with mealy-colored upper and lower lids, typical of Great Britain's Exmoor pony.

Track: Prints of a horse's hooves on soft ground (going).

Trail: To make a definite mark (*path* or *track*) by treading the ground down, i.e. made by the repeated passage of a route by horses, or men.

Transition: A change of one pace to another, e.g. from walk to trot.

Tree: The internal framework of a saddle (traditionally made of wood, then iron and steel, and recently of synthetic material reinforced with steel plate).

Trekking: Riding through countryside, usually no faster than at trot.

Trot: A two-time gait with the horse using diagonal pairs of legs to propel itself forward, i.e. right fore and left hind and then left fore and right hind simultaneously. Also known as *jog* or *pure trot.*

Trot up: Where a horse is trotted up on level ground to ascertain soundness of limbs. A sound horse does not nod its head in trot whereas an unsound one will.

Twisted gut (twist in the gut): Also known as *torsion colic* or *twisted bowel*. Resulting when part of the digestive tract (gut) twists on itself, causing a blockage of feed through the intestines.

V

Vaulting: Gymnastics performed on horseback. Also known as *voltige*.

W

Walk: A four-time equine gait that is naturally flat-footed. Each diagonal pair of feet is lifted alternately off the ground and strikes the ground separately and independently, e.g. left hind, left fore, right hind, and left fore without a moment of suspension. The term *walking* is used when boarding out fox-hound puppies to be trained in socializing and learning their names.

Warmblood. A race of horse developed from the pedigree bloodlines of various breeds, namely that of the Arabian and English Thoroughbred breeds. A light, as opposed to heavy (which evolved from colder climes), horse. Also refers to horse temperament—a manageable horse used for general riding and driving, not racing or agricultural or industrial work.

Way of going: The way in which a horse moves.

Western film: A movie (film), specifically relating to life among the cowboys, Plains Indians and pioneers, in the western United States during the late 1800s.

Wolf teeth: Shallow-rooted teeth in front of the premolars (bottom and upper jaws), having no purpose save to hinder bit comfort and action. Best-removed by a veterinary surgeon should they cause problems.

Working (as in walk, trot or canter): Also known as a *free* pace. An energetic, forward-going, workmanlike (well-performed) pace, yet remaining calm and relaxed.

Z

Zebra stripes: A color pattern of dark-colored stripes, front to back, from the fetlocks up to the hocks and knees of a horse. Known also as *zebra marks, tiger stripes,* or *leg barring*. Also stripe markings on the withers and neck.

credits

The publisher would like to thank and acknowledge the following photographers and photographic agencies for permission to reproduce material. While every effort has been made to ensure this listing is correct, the publisher apologizes for any omissions.

p.8, 121, 124, 131, 137, 139, 149—Lesley and Roy Adkins; p.6, 194 Simon Bruty, p.114 (b), 197, 205 Pascal Rondeau, p.189 Stephane Kempinaire, p.200 Chris Cole, p.199 (t) Allsport/MSI, p.30, 199 (b) Mike Hewitt, p.204 Julian Herbert, p.206, 207 Brian Bahr—Allsport UK, 3 Greenlea Park, Prince George's Road, London SW19 2JD, England; p.154, 155, 156, 157(b)—Anne S. K. Brown Military Collection; p.184 (br)—Charles Chenevix Trench; p.118, 120, 123, 127, 128, 129, 130—J. Charmot; p.108 (bl), p.133 (bl), 136, 164, 165, 169, 170, 172, 175, 182—E.T. Archive;p. 26, 27, 42, 43—Eugene Fleury; p.162—Richard Green Gallery, 44 Dover Street, London W1X 4JQ; p.132—Will Green; p.16 (bl), 18, 22, 25, 32, 46, 47, 50, 53, 54, 64, 66, 68, 113 (bl), 115, 117, 125 (t, br), 184 (t), p.190, 191, 200, 203, 209, 210, 212, 213—Kit Houghton; p.2, 13, 15, 16 (tl, tr, br), 19, 20, 34, 35, 38, 39, 40, 44, 51, 52, 57, 59, 60, 61, 62, 63 (b), 65, 67, 70, 71, 72, 73 (t), 75, 76, 77, 79, 80, 81, 82, 83, 85, 86, 87, 89, 90, 94, 95, 96, 97, 98, 99, 100, 103 (br), 107, 113 (tr), 116, 126, 186 (b), 188, 201, 202, 208, 211, 214—Bob Langrish; p.103 (t), 104, 105, 106, 108 (tr), 109, 112, 134, 138 (t, b), 140, 141, 142, 143, 144, 145 (bl), 146, 147, 148, 150, 151, 152, 153, 157 (tr), 158, 159, 160, 161, 166, 167, 171, 183 (tl, br), 195 (cr, cl), 196 (t), 197 (tr)—Peter Newark's Pictures; p.180, 185, 186 (tl) A. Laurioux—School of the Cadre Noir, Saumur, France; p.133 (tr)—Graham Fletcher, Vale of White Horse Council; p.14, 102, 111 (tr), 122, 173 (b), 174, 176 (t, b), 177, 178, 192—Visual Arts Library.

index

221